Full Praise for Gwyneth Olofsson and
When in Rome or Rio or Riyadh . . .

"At last! A truly practical guide for the international business executive on how to survive and prosper in different cultures. This book should be in the 'essentials' kit of all who travel for work—or for pleasure."

—Michael Pitfield, Director of International Business,
Henley Management College

"*When in Rome or Rio or Riyadh. . .* is a winning combination of very useful practical advice and extremely valuable cultural insights. The letters format is very engaging. And Ms. Olofsson turns out to be a fine, amusing writer; you end up reading more than you meant to just to linger in her company."

—Craig Storti, cross-cultural consultant and
author of *Americans at Work* and *The Art of Crossing Cultures*

"In what is a fascinating and highly readable review of intercultural differences, possible misunderstandings and helpful solutions, Gwyneth Olofsson has produced a book that I could have done with fifteen years ago when first elected to the European Parliament.

Ms Olofsson's experience as a language and intercultural consultant shines through the pages. With a combination of humour, honesty and an ability to understand some of the more idiosyncratic features of different national cultures, she has provided a text which should become essential reading for anyone hoping to do business abroad, and indeed anyone seeking to understand better people from other cultures."

—Mel Read MEP, Labour Member of the European Parliament
representing the East Midlands region of the U.K.

"*When in Rome or Rio or Riyadh . . .* is a delightful book to read. It combines deep insights into common everyday cross-cultural experiences with an engaging almost visceral style of narration. Though it offers practical tips in Q&A format, it is not just another cultural etiquette book; reading this book is like taking a perceptive journey, flitting across more than thirty countries. Ms. Olofsson has succeeded in giving a new depth and meaning to those day-to-day points of contact to a new culture—e.g., names, making conversation, working day, table talk, relating—which form the crux of cross-cultural experience and interaction."

—Dr Madhukar Shukla, Professor OB & Strategic Management,
XLRI, Jamshedpur, India

"As always, Gwyneth Olofsson gives her guidance on how to behave, dress, speak or write in a way everyone can understand. *When in Rome or Rio or Riyadh . . .* will come in handy every time you go on a business trip abroad, wherever your destination happens to be. Businesspeople everywhere should have this book in their possession."

—Christina Eide, Vice President, Volvo Information Technology AB

"I read *When in Rome or Rio or Riyadh . . .* with my daughter, and despite the fact that she is a university student and I'm a managing director, we both appreciated the true value of this book. As the number of people who work and travel internationally is increasing rapidly, we all need a book like this—well-structured, down-to-earth and helpful."

—Pavel Baranov, Managing Director, VSM Group, Moscow

"This is a most useful book for business travelers in the twenty-first century. It gives many useful tips, thanks to which I now understand (possibly too late) some of the mistakes I have made in the past."

—Philippe Divry, Senior Vice President,
Renault VI Powertrain Division

When in **Rome** *or* **Rio** *or* **Riyadh**...

Cultural Q&As for
Successful Business Behavior
around the World

Gwyneth Olofsson

INTERCULTURAL PRESS
A NICHOLAS BREALEY COMPANY

To Richard, Lizzy, and to all my students, past and present.

First published by Intercultural Press, a Nicholas Brealey Company, in 2004.

Intercultural Press, Inc.
PO Box 700
Yarmouth, Maine 04096 USA
Tel: 207-846-5168
Fax: 207-846-5181
www.interculturalpress.com

Nicholas Brealey Publishing
3-5 Spafield Street
London, EC1R 4QB, UK
Tel: +44-(0)-207-239-0360
Fax: +44-(0)-207-239-0370
www.nbrealey-books.com

Printed in the United States of America

08 07 06 05 04 1 2 3 4 5

ISBN: 1-931930-06-6

Library of Congress Cataloging-in-Publication Data

Olofsson, Gwyneth.
    When in Rome or Rio or Riyadh— : culture q&as for successful business
behavior around the world / Gwyneth Olofsson.— 1st ed.
        p. cm.
    Includes bibliographical references and index.
    ISBN 1-931930-06-6
    1. Business travel—Guidebooks. I. Title.
    G156.5B86O46 2004
    395.5'2—dc22   2004013522

Acknowledgments

The basis of this book lies in the questions, observations, and stories of many people I have met during the course of my work. It was their experiences of, and their questions about, encountering other cultures that first inspired me to delve into the fascinating area of interculturalism, a process which, many years later, led to my writing this book. In particular I'd like to thank my students at Volvo IT and SchlumbergerSema who shared their intercultural experiences with me. They provided the ideas and raw materials for much of the book, and I am very grateful to them.

Way back in the last century when I first started writing on intercultural subjects, Monica Rossing, the former editor of the Volvo Group's staff magazine, *Global*, was unfailingly supportive. Her successor, Susanne Hanssen, has been similarly positive and encouraging and has generously allowed me to use in this book some material that has already appeared in the magazine. I'd also like to thank Anna Cederberg Gerdrup of the Wilson Logistics Group's "Network News," and Anne-Cathrine Hartmann of Eka Chemicals' *Eka Echo* magazine, who have also given their permission for the use of articles I've written for their publications.

Writing *When in Rome or Rio or Riyadh . . .* has been a long process and different people have helped me at different stages. Nicholas Brealey set my feet on the right track when this book was a confusing jumble of letters and comments, and Charlie Bergman of Meridian Associates gave me much encouragement and good advice when it was most needed.

Meridian Associates also provided me with access to its wonderful GlobeSmart Internet tool.

I've also learned an enormous amount from two other excellent Internet sources, Intercultural Insights and the Delta Intercultural Academy's DialogIn. I'm afraid I have been only a passive member of both groups (as every spare minute of my time has been spent writing this book), but I'd like to thank the organizers and the contributors to these very different but fascinating sites. They have provided me with both information and inspiration.

Once I'd submitted the manuscript to Intercultural Press, Toby Frank's warmth and good sense provided me with the necessary guidance and inspiration to complete the book. I have learned an enormous amount from Judy Carl-Hendrick, the managing editor, who combines high standards of professionalism with a deep knowledge of the subject.

The last stages in the preparation of the manuscript involved a number of people. I'd like to thank Andrew Robinson for checking some particularly awkward facts; Douglas Lipp for his comments on Japan; Aslam Khan for some information on Islam; and my niece, Sarah Hogg, for information about France and Spain, as well as some suggestions about useful reading. The parents, staff, and children of the International School of the Gothenburg Region have been a real source of information about countries ranging from Ghana to Pakistan, from the U.S. to South Korea, and just about everywhere in between. Finally, Joan Holmedal has saved me many hours work in front of the computer, by ensuring that my commas, colons, and so forth are in the right place.

When in Rome or Rio or Riyadh . . . took a long time to write, and as I worked on it I let the dust gather in the corners of my home, didn't read a single novel, and neglected my friends. It's the last sacrifice on this list I regret the most. I'd like to thank my remaining friends, and my family in Sweden and England, for their support during the years it took me to finish this book. I hope you enjoy reading it!

Gwyneth Olofsson

Contents

Country-by-Country Contents

Venezuela

Introduction

My work as a language and intercultural consultant in Scandinavia has meant that I have spent a lot of time with businesspeople over the last fifteen years. Many hours have gone into listening to and correcting accounts (delivered with varying degrees of fluency) of meetings, sales campaigns, negotiations, development budgets, and the like. At the same time I have learned an enormous amount about how large and small companies work and about the problems individual employees face in their day-to-day work.

A growing number of these problems are a result of the globalization process. Over the last six years, the volume of world trade has risen by 50 percent, which has had enormous consequences for many corporations. All the companies I have worked with in the last ten years, whether large or small, whether in the fields of engineering, IT, or pharmaceuticals, have had greatly increased international contact. Some of this has been the result of mergers, takeovers, new markets opening up, or the growth of new suppliers in distant countries. Whatever the reason, employees often had to learn to deal with new ways of working and communicating, usually without the slightest knowledge of the customs and values of the people with whom they suddenly had daily contact. The consequences of this lack of preparation for increased intercultural contact have often been negative, and occasionally catastrophic.

A Wealth of Material

The people I meet work in a large number of companies in all sorts of different capacities. They include IT specialists, sales personnel, purchasers, trade union representatives, CEOs, and just about everyone in between. Many work for global organizations, and most have some degree of contact with people from other countries. Some travel widely, others stay at home but have extensive international phone and e-mail contact, while still others receive foreign visitors on a weekly basis.

It is people like these who have provided me with the material for this book, for during our meetings they told me about what they were working on and asked questions about the strange way foreign managers, customers, or suppliers acted. From there, it was a natural progression for me to start to look for answers to these questions. Eventually I began keeping a written record of the kind of questions I was asked and the answers I came up with. At the same time, when my students were out traveling, they would e-mail or fax me with inquiries or comments, so I began to amass quite a collection. Then I started writing cross-cultural columns in Volvo's internal magazine *Global*, the Wilson Group's magazine *Network*, and Eka Chemicals' *Echo*, and still more letters arrived. It is this material that forms the basis of this book.

The first books I consulted to help me answer these questions posed by my clients were the ground-breaking works of Geert Hofstede, Fons Trompenaars, and Charles Hampden-Turner. They were my guides when I set out to find answers to questions about how people from different cultures reacted to each other. I also consulted country-specific business guides for information as well as using my own network of business and professional contacts who had firsthand experience with the country in question.

The Internet was an invaluable resource, providing access to intercultural study groups, newsletters, and mountains of information on interculturalism in general and individual countries' cultural peculiarities in particular. One especially valuable source of information was Meridian Resources' GlobeSmart service, a Web-based tool that provides access to detailed, country-specific information on a wide range of topics.

Why Did I Write the Book?

Intercultural, or cross-cultural, studies is a relatively new subject. A few books appeared in the mid-1980s, and now, twenty years later, there is a steady stream of new publications and Web sites covering this area. This growth of interest reflects an increasingly global economy, which in turn has brought with it international contact for people who perhaps have never left their native country or even spoken to anyone from another culture.

The area of intercultural communication is a wide one, and this is reflected in the many types of books available. Some are etiquette books, giving lists of dos and don'ts to bear in mind when you are working abroad or with people from other cultures. Others take a theoretical approach and are equipped with impressive diagrams charting and grouping cultures that share common characteristics. A few look at the relationship between corporate and national cultures, while others have specific functions, such as preparing people for the psychological and social pressures of a foreign placement, and still others delve deeply into the history and culture of a particular geographical area. All approaches are valuable and add to the sum of human knowledge.

However, I wanted to produce a book putting "ordinary" businesspeople's cross-cultural experiences center stage. It is these thousands of daily person-to-person contacts, whether in the boardroom or on the shop floor, that determine how successful (or not) a multinational company is going to be. All individuals involved in cross-cultural contacts have found themselves in unexpected situations, and their observations and impressions, as well as their questions, deserve respect and attention.

In short, a combination of sorts, between the behavioral guides and the cultural and historical theory, is what began to emerge. To be successful while interacting in another culture means that you have to make the cultural and social cues around you and then behave appropriately in response. The old adage, "When in Rome, do as the Romans" puts this in a nutshell. It is also as insightful today as it was nearly 400 years ago when Cervantes first conceived it, and thus provides a fitting title for the book.

Secondly, I wanted to write a book that in some small way examined our potentially harmful human tendency to divide people into "them" and "us." The danger when a company suddenly experiences a greatly increased amount of international contact is that groups emerge with the "us" group being fellow nationals and "them" being those from other countries. Of course, you will find this "us" and "them" dichotomy in any company with more than ten employees—it is a natural part of human behavior. But "they" become easier to identify when they are from another country, or look, dress, or sound different from "us." Often executive management acknowledges the problem and tries to unite its workforce with mission and vision statements or with a corporate statement of objectives. These initiatives have varying degrees of success, but good managers feel compelled to do *something;* they know that where divisions widen beyond a critical point and when employees feel they have nothing in common, the company will start to suffer. Unfortunately, mission statements, however worthy, are not going to make a lot of difference if they ignore the underlying cultural differences of a company's workforce.

The best way to break down these divisions, or to stop them from arising in the first place, is of course to learn about the way your foreign counterparts usually do business. But just as important is to step back from your own national and corporate cultures and try to see them through new eyes—the eyes of someone who does not automatically share your beliefs and values. This can be an uncomfortable experience, but it is a vital one, because before you can make sense of another culture, you have to understand your own.

My third reason for writing this book was to give everyone the opportunity to learn from the uncomfortable situations in which other people have found themselves. This is, of course, a much more pleasant way of learning than by making all the mistakes yourself.

Who Is This Book For?

When in Rome or Rio or Riyadh . . . is designed to be read by open-minded people who are interested in getting the most out of their international business contacts and in learning how to avoid problems before they crop up. I believe potential readers fall into four main groups. Where would you put yourself?

1. *The pragmatist.* You are observant enough to see that people in other countries do things differently from you, but instead of putting these differences down to stupidity or deliberate wrong-headedness, you want to learn how to deal with them in the interests of the company. You may even adopt another culture's way of doing things—the "When in Rome, do as the Romans" method—if it is the best way of "getting the job done." You realize that a certain degree of intercultural awareness is good for the company, and perhaps even good for your own career.

2. *The inquiring mind.* In your business dealings with another culture you have come across some form of behavior, or a way of doing something, that you find puzzling. You cannot make sense of it within your usual terms of reference and have turned to this book for answers. You are a bit of a Sherlock Holmes and are interested in finding out the reasons why people from certain other cultures behave as they do.

3. *The victim of post-traumatic stress.* Perhaps you have firsthand experience of the most dramatic form of *culture clash*, when, for example, during an international project expectations have been dashed, taboos broken, and everyone involved left in a state of baffled resentment. If you have, you will want to understand what went wrong so you can avoid such a situation again.

4. *Finger-bowl phobic.* Your motive is fear, a pretty good motive for learning. You know you have an international trip in front of you and dread "putting your foot in it," whether that involves drinking out of the finger bowl, giving the wrong kind of present, or doing something unsuitable with your chopsticks, and etiquette questions like these are usually the ones people ask most frequently and are often answered quite simply. Also, if you make such a mistake, it is easily excused by the fact that you are from another culture. However, misunderstandings based on, for example, different ideas of what "honesty" or "as soon as possible" mean are more difficult to put right.

It is important that we try to continue to search for explanations for unfamiliar behavior, or else we risk attributing it to the peculiarities of a particular culture or the personal failings of an individual. And in difficult situations we might find ourselves drawing conclusions like this:

- They (those foreigners) work like that because they don't know any better.
- They finish things late because they are not sufficiently developed to understand the advantages of *our* method.
- They are lazy.
- They deliberately slow down to try to annoy us.

That way madness lies!

How Do I Find My Way Around?

When In Rome or Rio or Riyadh . . . is made up of letters I have received from different employees of varying nationalities. In many cases, however, people have not actually written to me, but have asked me questions or described situations when we have met face-to-face. In those cases I've tried to write down the question as accurately as possible. In yet other cases I've heard secondhand of situations that have arisen at a workplace, and I created a question that tries to pinpoint the intercultural problem area as accurately as possible. And on the subject of pinpointing, this is a good place to define a couple of the definitions I use.

When I write of *Latin America* I mean countries with Latin-based languages (e.g., Spanish and Portuguese), so this embraces Mexico as well as all the countries of Central and South America. By *Southern Europe* I mean Italy and Spain and the southern parts of France. I don't include Turkey here, even though Turkey may well join the European Union in the future.

Most of the questions ask about a specific country, but most of my answers include references to other cultures, usually to point out similarities. I believe that by broadening the scope of the answers this, in management-speak, provides "added value" for the reader. In other words, if you want to find out something about Brazil, with no extra effort you may also learn a little about Argentina, Norway, and Indonesia! E. M.

Forster, an English author who explored intercultural tensions in the novel *A Passage to India* before the word *intercultural* had been invented, has one of his wisest characters urge the others to, "Only connect." She, and perhaps Forster himself, meant that you had to apply experiences of your own life in order to interpret and understand those of other people. By the same token if we allow ourselves to think about what cultures have in common, or how they approach the same problems, we may well find that countries connect with each other in strange and unexpected ways.

This book is divided into three parts. The first part, "The First Steps," takes you through the "getting-to-know-you" process, from the initial introduction stage to the point in the relationship when people start to meet and socialize.

The second part, "Understanding Each Other," examines two areas that can cause problems from the first moment in a relationship to the last: communication and time. When working with people from other cultures, the message you convey may be quite different from the one you intend, and if you time it wrong, the message may be disregarded anyway.

The third part, "Working Together," explores even deeper waters. It looks at (1) how our personal profiles (as defined by our gender, age, ethnicity, and nationality) are molded by where we come from, and (2) what effect our culture has on our roles and relationships at work. The last chapter of this section deals with fundamental questions about what we believe are right, important, or natural ways to behave. So you could say that the book starts in the intercultural shallows of etiquette and progresses to the murky depths of ethics and assumptions, where potential misunderstandings can have bigger and more far-reaching consequences.

Each of the three parts is divided into related chapters, which in turn are divided into subsections. At the end of each subsection you will find a summary, "In a Nutshell," which summarizes many of the points raised in the letters, as well as adding a little basic information about each of the thirty-three key countries that the book focuses on. Sometimes I feel I should remind readers of certain rules of correct behavior that apply wherever they are likely to find themselves, and have included those under the heading "Global Business Standards." In other cases I've highlighted situations that might result in a sticky intercultural misunderstanding under the heading "Global Warnings." I have tried not to generalize too much when it comes to the comments in "Nutshells," but certain groups of countries do have a lot in common whether in terms of ethnicity, geography, or politics. I'm thinking of China, Hong Kong, and Taiwan, which form one group; Austria, Switzerland, and Germany, which form another; and the Scandinavian countries of Sweden, Norway, Finland, and Denmark that form a third. So in "Nutshells" I sometimes write one entry that applies to the whole group. Where I do this I make the reference clear.

These thirty-three countries have not been chosen at random; they make up the world's biggest economies as measured in Gross Domestic Product. (See *The Economist's Pocket World of Figures*, 2003 edition. There may be minor changes from year to year, but the list remains essentially the same.)

The World's Largest Economies in Order of Size of Gross Domestic Product (2003)		
1. U.S.	12. India	23. Turkey
2. Japan	13. South Korea	24. Denmark
3. Germany	14. Australia	25. Hong Kong
4. U.K.	15. Russia	26. Poland
5. France	16. Netherlands	27. Norway
6. Italy	17. Taiwan	28. Indonesia
7. China	18. Argentina	29. Saudi Arabia
8. Brazil	19. Switzerland	30. South Africa
9. Canada	20. Belgium	31. Finland
10. Spain	21. Sweden	32. Thailand
11. Mexico	22. Austria	33. Venezuela

By concentrating on the countries where most international business transactions and contacts take place, I kept the size of the book manageable. The exclusion of many countries, including most of Africa, says nothing about the richness of their cultures, but a lot about the inequalities of global economic performance.

I have tried to make my answers as objective as possible, taking into account that the letters provide us with only a quick glimpse of what may be a very complicated situation. Regard each letter as part of a tiny short story taken from someone's working life. By reading between the lines you can sometimes understand what prompted the letter (anger, surprise, curiosity) and as in literature, you do not need to have experienced the same situation yourself to identify with it. In these micro-situations there is very little background information and you cannot be 100 percent sure whether the problem has personal, corporate, or cultural roots. But, well, life is like that.

When you read the letters, please look at where the question comes from, as that often reveals a lot about the culture of the person doing the asking. As we all know, what is regarded as self-explanatory in one culture is a complete mystery to another. What you find strange about a culture depends on which culture you come from.

What Is Culture?

This brings us to the question, "What does *culture* mean?" In this book it has nothing to do with art, theater, music, or literature. One useful definition comes from *Riding the Waves of Culture* by Fons Trompenaars, in which he calls culture "the way in which a group of people solves problems." Karin Sharma in *Alla dessa Kulturer* calls it "A dynamic system giving rise to a shared means of interpretation."

This book focuses primarily on national culture. However, to answer the questions that people have asked, I have had to take into account other influences including regional, corporate, and industry cultures. It is obvious to any U.S. citizen, for example, that the culture of New York City is different from that of San Francisco, just as IBM's corporate culture is not the same as Microsoft's. And even when two people are both from the same city, if one works in the restaurant business and the other in a bank, they are going to be part of very different industry cultures.

Because it is so complicated, this whole area of culture can easily become a morass of sloppy thinking and soggy subjective opinion. But to be honest, that is why it is so interesting! Everyone who has had the slightest international experience has his or her own opinions on what successful intercultural contact means, and these opinions are often perceptive and shrewd. Despite attempts to turn intercultural studies into a science, with a plethora of theories based on surveys and painstaking investigations, and books full of tables and graphs, most businesspeople I know are less interested in theory than in working successfully on a personal level in intercultural situations. And that is still essentially an art, based on squishy and unquantifiable concepts, like "intuition" and "empathy," as well as on knowledge and facts.

What Does Culture Have to Do with Business?

Occasionally, perhaps even frequently, those of us who have dealings with other cultures have found ourselves in uncomfortable situations, where we recognize something has gone wrong but cannot put our fingers on it. The problem is that we can rarely trace the exact causes of the misunderstanding or dispute.

How about that nightmare meeting with a potential foreign customer last week? Was the agreement with the other company in the little-known country of Erkonia and Damique abandoned because the price of your product was too high, or the quality too low? Or perhaps it had nothing to do with either but it failed because you two just did not hit it off. And if that was the case, was the reason that

- Erkonians were occupied by the Damiquian army fifty years ago, and since then Erkonians have never trusted Damiquians (and you have a Damiquian family name)?
- Following the Erkonian custom, your contact addressed you by your given name although you had never met before, and she was twenty years younger than you were (and you thought this was very rude)?
- Your counterpart misunderstood a word you used? (You said "used to" and she thought you had said "usually." She heard, "We usually give credit," but what you actually said was, "We used to give credit.")
- Corporate policy meant that she offered you only a simple lunch in the staff dining room, in contrast to the luxurious dinner that you had offered her when she had last visited your company? (You felt

this showed that her company was mean-spirited, had no understanding of the concept of reciprocity, and was not showing you or your company the respect your reputation deserved.)
- You had a headache, had forgotten to pack the aspirin, and were in a foul mood even before the meeting?
- You were both having a bad hair day?

So was the contract rejected for cross-cultural, corporate, language, or personal reasons? It is impossible to tell, but probably for a mixture of all of them. But what about the participants' reactions to the failure of the meeting? They will vary, of course, but an inexperienced or uninformed Damique national, for example, may react in one of two ways:

- "Well, tomorrow's another day, and I'm sure she'll see reason then," which is the optimist's reaction.
- "Well, they're all like that. What can you expect from people from the Erkonian Republic? We'll never be able to work together," which is the pessimist's reaction.

Of course, both reactions are undesirable. The optimist shares a widespread human failing, that of assuming that his or her own views are automatically the right ones. This is so clear to her that she cannot imagine that any reasonable person can hold a different view. She may believe, for example, like many businesspeople, that making a good profit is the primary aim of a business. But who says that she is right? People can be motivated by loyalty to the workforce, by the aim of manufacturing the best widget in the world, or by creating a business to pass on to their grandchildren. And what is a "reasonable" decision anyway—one based on serving one's personal self-interest, on increasing production capacity next year, or on achieving a bigger market share over the next decade? In thinking that her own view is the only "reasonable" one, our optimistic friend reveals a lack of self-awareness that is likely to give her problems in future intercultural contacts.

The pessimist's reaction to failure is to find someone else to blame. We have all done it, although if we have any sense we fight against the inclination. But it is easy, and surprisingly common, even among widely traveled and experienced businesspeople, to employ cultural stereotypes of the "What can you expect from people from Erkonia? They've never been any good at R&D/logistics/working to deadlines" variety. Our Damiquian may easily accept that there are many people in his own culture with whom he has absolutely nothing in common, but, strangely, he may still conclude that all Erkonians are alike. This pessimist is nevertheless further along the road to cultural enlightenment, despite his worrying ignorance, because he at least acknowledges that cultural differences *do* influence behavior.

Culture affects how we think and act as individuals, and affects our relationships (business or otherwise), because the culture factor is of increasing importance in a world where international contacts are becoming more frequent and intense. This globalization of business has been aided by the spread of the Internet and by easy travel and communications, but (as yet) there is no software that automatically translates other people's behavior into terms you understand.

For the sake of our companies' futures (and our own as employees), we have to minimize the possibility of cross-cultural misunderstandings and start making the most of our different backgrounds. The benefits in terms of increased profits and market share as well as the "softer" ones of a happier workforce cannot be ignored.

What about Me?

So, what do we as individuals need to possess if we want to be equipped for the challenge of increased intercultural contacts? I would suggest the following four qualities.

1. *Awareness of your own national culture.* Solving problems where another culture is involved requires you to think in another dimension. And you have to know what your own perspective is before you can make sense of what you see. Even if we have not been there, most of us would recognize a photo of the Taj Mahal taken from the front, but what about from the side, or from a helicopter directly overhead? And if the camera were being held at a distance of a yard, the picture would look quite different from one

taken from a distance of fifty yards. You need to know where the camera is positioned and its angle in relation to its subject if you are to make sense of the picture it takes. Similarly, you have to learn to think about the angle on life and business taken by the members of your own culture, and what influences their (and your) attitudes, beliefs, and behavior at work.

2. *Awareness of the culture of your own company or corporation.* Two successful companies founded the same year, of similar size, and with headquarters in the same city may have entirely different corporate cultures if one, say, produces fire extinguishers and the other sells IT solutions. The culture of the company or corporation you work for is bound to have an effect on the way you treat your coworkers and your customers, and to influence everything from your expectations about job security to the way you dress. If you work for a global corporation, can you spot its "country of origin" in its mission and vision statements, or in the proportions of different nationalities in the membership of its top management? If you work for a national rather than a multinational company, how open is it to learning from similar companies operating in different countries or from employees with roots in other cultures?

3. *Awareness of your own personal cultural profile.* All countries are made up of subcultures. Divisions can be along geographical, religious, class, or ethnic lines, to name just a few, and sometimes differences between these subcultures cause serious tensions and rifts. But they are usually overridden by unifying factors such as a common language, a shared educational system, or loyalty to a royal family or system of government. Or perhaps you share with fellow nationals a preference for coffee served in a special way, or a certain long-running soap opera. We all have to be aware of the complexity of our own individual cultural heritage, whether we are a middle-class African American with a dash of Welsh blood, a working-class Irish Protestant with Jewish roots, or an Afrikaans-speaking South African of Indian extraction. This awareness of our cultural roots brings with it self-knowledge. Together with our cultural identity, our personal characteristics (gender, age, ethnicity) and social situation (married or single, white-collar or blue-collar,

manager or secretary) give us each a unique profile. This profile affects how we look at the world, and how we are regarded in return.

4. *Awareness of the culture you are going to meet, and a willingness to look at it in a spirit of interest and respect.* An interest in learning about the culture you are going to meet, and in what motivates and influences its members, makes an excellent start to a good relationship between people of different cultures. Possession of even basic pieces of information can help remove some of the stumbling blocks that act as barriers in intercultural relations. This book aims to provide some of this information, as well as inspire you to discover more for yourself.

I expect that if you work in business or industry you will be able to identify with the problems described in the book even if you aren't, I sincerely hope, likely to experience all of them personally! I also hope that by raising questions and sharing concerns, businesspeople all over the world will come a little nearer to understanding each other—and themselves.

To the Global Businessperson

You may well have had uncomfortable, amusing, or irritating experiences when doing business with people from other cultures. Let me know about them, and I may share them with others in my next book!

Gwyneth Olofsson
experiences@communico.o.se

PART I

The First Steps

CHAPTER 1

Getting Acquainted

Getting to know a place, like getting to know an individual, takes time. Even new names can be confusing. Fifteen years ago I was on a ship in the middle of the North Sea on my way from England to Sweden, where I had a job waiting for me. On the ferry I met a few Swedes and we started chatting. I asked one where she came from and she told me, "Yutterborry." She must have seen the look of incomprehension on my face. "You know—where this ship lands."

But I thought we were bound for *Gothenburg*. I must be on the wrong ship! Well, actually I wasn't. The Swedish name for Gothenburg is Göteborg, which when pronounced correctly appears to your average English speaker to have no connection whatsoever to its written form.

There was a lot I had to learn about Sweden—not only the language. The next lesson followed quickly. During the bus trip from the ferry into the center of the city on that dark January night, I came to the conclusion that I'd had no inkling there were so many Jews in Sweden. Unlike my home country, England, people in Sweden don't draw their curtains at night, and I could see clearly into houses and flats as I drove past. To my surprise, an illuminated seven-branched candlestick was shining in every window. The only other menorahs I'd ever seen were through the windows of the local synagogue back home in England.

It turned out, of course, that I was wrong—the candlesticks were simply a traditional Swedish Christmas decoration. (This was before the Swedish furniture company IKEA had become a household word; ten years later my [non-Jewish] parents in England had bought their own seven-branched Swedish Christmas candlestick at their newly opened local branch of IKEA.)

The day after my arrival in Sweden, I went for a walk around town to get my bearings and do a little shopping. During the course of the morning, I decided that Gothenburg shop assistants must be the rudest in the world. They simply refused to serve me or, indeed, to pay any attention to me at all, whether I went to the liquor store to buy a bottle of the local *snapps*, or tried to pay for a pair of socks. I was beginning to think that the shop assistants had made some sort of anti-British pact when, on my third attempt to make a purchase (this time in the post office), I noticed a ticket dispenser in a corner. I discovered that everyone who wanted to be served took a ticket and waited for the number to be flashed up on a little screen (a bit like bingo without the prizes). By the way, this system is now widely practiced at the delicatessen counters in English supermarkets, another example of the globalization process in action.

Getting acquainted with a new country or making sense of a whole new culture takes considerable time. But meeting an individual from an unfamiliar culture does not have to be a difficult experience if you get to know the relevant customs first. In every culture there are well-defined conventions and rituals surrounding the process, which make the exchange of names and greetings with strangers relatively straightforward.

Naturally, it is good to be aware of these before traveling outside the borders of your own country, but there are times you might try a bit too hard, like the North American businessman who, determined to make a good impression on his first visit to Japan, learned how to bow in the correct Japanese fashion. However, his counterpart knew all about the Western habit of shaking hands, so he stepped forward with his hand outstretched just as the American brought his head smartly down. The resulting impact made them both see stars. Perhaps that's one concrete example of "culture clash."

◆ **Moral**
Getting acquainted with a new country or making sense of a whole new culture takes considerable time, so don't trust your first impressions.

Names and Address

When Juliet asked, "What's in a name?" Romeo told her that it meant nothing. Of course, Romeo was a teenager in love, so he couldn't be expected to think clearly. And as events turned out, the Montagues and the Capulets believed that there was quite enough in a name to kill for.

Names *are* important. Most people have at least two, not counting nicknames or pet names, and in some cultures the number is far higher. They are an integral part of our personal and social identities, and they can give others an enormous amount of information about us.

For a start, one of our names usually indicates which family we belong to. But the size of families varies greatly. There are only a handful of Featherstonehaughs, for instance. It's a very old name with origins going back to the 1200s, to the border country between England and Scotland. It can be pronounced in a number of ways, including, strangely enough, Fanshaw. This may explain why there are so few left with this ancient name. The most sensible members of the family probably got tired of not being able to spell their own name and changed it to Smith long ago. On the other hand, there are many Chans and Hos; a staggering 90 percent of the nearly 1.3 billion Chinese share a paltry one hundred family names.

Most given names and some family names indicate gender, like the *a* Russian women add to their family names and patronymics (father's first name plus an ending), and the *dóttir* (daughter) that Icelandic women add to their father's (or sometimes their mother's) given name.

A name can be an indicator of marital status, too. Some women change their family name to their husbands' on marriage, while others, including the Chinese and Icelanders, keep their own. Yet another group, which includes Spanish women, use both.

Your name will also say something about your nationality, although what it implies won't necessarily be true. For example, my name, Gwyneth Olofsson, tells the world of my Welsh and Swedish connections, but says nothing about my being English, which in fact I am. In a world where national boundaries are becoming less significant and people are traveling more, it is no longer unusual to encounter a Dane named Mohammed or an Argentinean called Vladimir.

What you are called may also say something about your religion, or even about your political affiliations. In Northern Ireland, which has areas that are predominantly Catholic or Protestant, having a typically Irish Catholic name like Patrick Murphy might be enough to earn you a beating if you find yourself on the wrong side of the line in Belfast. Billy Brown might suffer a similar fate if he ventured into a Protestant area. And Sunni and Shia (Shiite) Muslims may also be able to identify each other by their names. Omar and Abu Bakr, for example, are often used by Sunni Muslims, whereas typical Shia names are Hasam and Ali.

Your name can even reflect your racial background. In the U.S., there is a group of relatively new names that have become fashionable in the African American community. There are now books specifically targeted at expectant mothers from this group to help them choose a name for their baby. Orienta, Aneisha, and Shaniqua are examples of girls' names. In the same way, Wesley in Britain is associated with men and boys with an African Caribbean background.

Names can tell an enormous amount about you, including your parents' social status (e.g., there are few working-class people named Nigel or Simon in the U.K.), to the month of your birthday, (April, May, and June being the ones that "spring" to mind in the English-speaking world, and Noel and Noelle in France). Your name can even give a clue as to how old you are: there are few Tracys and Sharons under twenty or over fifty in the U.K., and in Sweden the only men called Albert are over seventy or younger than ten.

Because names carry so much personal information, it is essential to get them right. If you're meeting people from another culture for the first time, try to get a list of their names in advance. Check that you understand which order they are in (given or family name first) and have at least a rough idea of how to pronounce them.

Once you know what someone is called, you need to know how to *use* this information, that is, how to address individuals. Even if you have memorized all the six names of your potential customer, you wouldn't be well advised to use them all at your first meeting. Indeed, in certain circumstances you may be better off not using names at all but confining yourself to titles. "Frau Doktor Professor," for example, should be enough for anyone! A lot depends on the degree of formality regarded as appropriate in the culture you are visiting.

And just think: If Romeo had called Juliet "Joan" the second time they met, that probably would have finished the relationship on the spot. So make it a priority to remember the names of people you have met.

LETTERS 1–4

Names come in all shapes and sizes, from the micro, like Bo Ek from Sweden or Ms. Ng from Singapore, to the magnificent, like Señora Ana Maria Vasquez Fernandez de Martinez from Argentina. In the latter case, knowing which name to use can sometimes be difficult.

Which name?   Letter *1*

FROM INDIA ABOUT **ARGENTINA**

I requested and received the list of people I will meet on my first visit to Argentina. However, I got a shock as they seem to have about five names each and I really don't know what I should call them when we meet.

Yes, many Spanish-speaking countries are "name rich." First of all, it's common for both men and women to have two given names, as in Juan José or Ana Maria. Then it gets complicated. In formal situations, or when they write their names, Spaniards, Argentineans, Mexicans, and Spanish-speaking Central and South Americans will give their father's surname followed by their mother's. When speaking to a person, use the father's name preceded by the person's professional title or "Señor" or "Señora"; therefore, Juan Carlos Lopez Garcia would be addressed as "Señor Lopez." Married women usually add their husband's name to their maiden name, so when Señorita Ana Maria Vasquez Fernandez marries Señor Juan José Martinez Andreani, she becomes Señora Ana Maria Vasquez Fernandez de Martinez. The husband's family name is usually preceded with *de*, but both the *de* and the husband's family name may be dropped in everyday speech. So the individuals above would be addressed in everyday situations (much to the relief of people with poor short-term memories) as "Señor Martinez" and "Señora Vasquez."

In nearby Portuguese-speaking Brazil, people are often on first-name terms quite quickly, but as in Argentina, that name may be the first of six or seven. Unlike the rest of South America, the father's name is last on the list and is the one that follows "Senhor" and "Senhora" in everyday situations. But in Brazil, some people with several names (but not much confidence in foreigners' ability to remember them) have taken matters into their own hands. When they present their business card to you, they will underline one or two names, indicating which one(s) they want you to use, and cross off a title and those names which you should perhaps be aware of but don't need to use.

Given or family name?	Letter *2*

FROM THE NETHERLANDS ABOUT **INDIA**

I don't know whether to address my Indian colleagues by their given or family names, and in fact I can't even tell which is which.

This is tricky, as there are so many religious and regional customs in India. Historically, Hindus did not have family surnames, and this is still true in the south of India. However, in the north, people usually have a family name after their given names; these family names sometimes indicate which caste the person belongs to. A Hindu man following more traditional practices will probably have two initials preceding his given name, K. R. Narayananan, for example, but no family name. The first initial stands for the name of his hometown, and the second is the initial of his father's given name. A Hindu woman will often follow her own given name with her husband's name.

Christian Indians and Eurasian Indians often have given names followed by family names, some of which may be of British and/or Portuguese origin, such as Mary Rozario. The woman in question would be addressed as "Mrs. Mary" or "Mrs. Rozario" (the "Mrs." being less an indication of marital status than a respectful title applying to all mature women). You can address Indian Muslims by putting a "Mr." or "Mrs." in front of the given name. If in doubt, ask your colleague what he or she would like to be called, and if you're meeting a stranger, it's not a catastrophe if you do use someone's given name rather than the family name, as long as you precede it with "Mr." or "Mrs."

Mr. Who? Letter 3

FROM THE U.K. ABOUT **CHINA**

I've just returned from China and wonder why everyone called me Mr. Kevin (Kevin is my given name). Why didn't they use my surname?

They probably thought that was what they were doing. In China, as in Vietnam and Korea, the family name comes first, followed by two others: Lee Wu Yew, for example, is Mr. Lee. The surname is usually only one syllable long, can be spelled in many ways, and is shared by many thousands of families, so it is rarely used on its own.

The middle name may be a generational name, which siblings and cousins share to show they belong to the same generation. The generational name and given name used to be separated by a space or a hyphen, but nowadays are usually written as one word, for example, Fu Chinfanda. This applies to most Chinese if they live in Asia, whether in China itself or in Singapore, Indonesia, or Malaysia. However, some Chinese, especially those with Western given names, put them first, for example, Sylvia Lau.

One final thought: if your surname is Braithwaite or Riddell or something equally difficult for the Chinese to pronounce, they may have chosen your first name simply because it was easier.

What's your patronymic? Letter 4

FROM BELGIUM ABOUT **RUSSIA**

I'll be going to Russia soon and have heard that they use the "patronymic" name. What exactly is this, and how should I use it?

Russians generally have three names: the first is the given name, the second the patronymic (the father's first name plus an ending), and the third the surname, for example, Sergei Alexandrovich Popov. A woman adds a female ending, the letter *a*, to her patronymic and her husband's surname, as in Anna Sergeyevna Odintsova. Some Westerners are not aware of this and drop the *a*, which is a bit like calling your female guest "Mr." This is not likely to win you many friends.

Russians who are acquainted often address each other by using the first name and patronymic, which shows a mixture of friendliness and respect. If all goes well, you may be invited to do the same, but wait to be asked.

LETTERS 5–6

The level of formality regarded as "normal" varies enormously from culture to culture.

How formal?   Letter *5*

FROM CANADA ABOUT **GERMANY**

I'm about to visit Germany for the first time on business. I know first impressions are important, and Germans have the reputation of being very formal. Is there anything special I should be aware of?

A lot depends on which business area you work in and the ages of the people you are going to meet. Banking, for example, is known as being more traditional and formal than, say, information technology, and older people tend to be more formal than younger ones.

When you speak English in Germany or Austria, you should be prepared to speak it with a German degree of formality. You should certainly call your colleagues "Frau" or "Herr" (or their title) plus their surname, unless they take the initiative and address you by your given name. The same is the case in Spain, France, or East Asia, where it's a good idea to use title and surname.

You should also be prepared to establish your academic qualifications, so make sure your business card lists your degrees as well as your job title. If you look at any German telephone directory, you'll see names followed by the details of the subscriber's academic qualifications, which demonstrates how seriously they are taken. If you have a Ph.D. (a doctorate), you can expect to be addressed as "Frau Doktor" or "Herr Doktor" (which may or may not be followed by your family name), and you'll be expected to address German colleagues who possess such a degree in the same way. Professional titles are also important in the cases of, for example, lawyers, engineers, and teachers. So a teacher with a doctorate should be addressed as "Herr Doktor Professor." See if you can get a list of the names and titles before you go and try to memorize them. The same applies in Argentina and Italy, where academic and professional titles are taken especially seriously.

How informal?   Letter 6

FROM VENEZUELA ABOUT THE U.S.

On a recent visit to Los Angeles I was surprised to hear a secretary calling her boss by his first name. It sounded rather disrespectful to me. Was it just this particular firm?

This was not a sign of disrespect, but simply evidence of a more egalitarian relationship between boss and secretary, for a boss will almost certainly call a secretary by her first name. In fact, this job often isn't called "secretary" any longer. The job titles Personal Assistant (PA), Administrative Assistant (AA), and Executive Assistant (EA) are ways of attempting to define her duties (they are usually female) and emphasize the fact that she's on the managerial team. Many secretaries in the U.S. are far more computer literate than their bosses are, others are highly qualified linguists, and most control their managers' schedules. So many will resent any hint that they are in any way less worthy of respect than their bosses simply because they are secretaries. They will regard being addressed by their first names by someone who insists on "Mr." or "Señor" as patronizing.

In cultures where hierarchies tend to be more pronounced, as in South and Central America, and in Southern Europe and India, people may find this rather egalitarian approach disturbing (as you did). In these countries the relative status of boss and subordinate is made very clear, and it is usually taken for granted that secretaries address bosses by their title and surname, while secretaries are addressed by their given names. However, many secretaries in English-speaking cultures find this very marked difference in the way of addressing managers and secretaries rather old-fashioned, even rude. So even if the manager and his or her secretary are on first-name terms, it is only courteous that you address her as "Ms." (for married and unmarried women) and her surname, if you expect to be addressed as "Mr." or "Ms." She'll soon let you know if she wants you to call her by her given name.

LETTER 7

Your title, in some cultures, is just as important as your name.

| Mr. Haji? | Letter 7 |

FROM NEW ZEALAND ABOUT **INDONESIA**

On my recent trip to Indonesia, there were many times when I heard the word Haji *used to address someone, but I was told the word* Bapak *or* Pak *meant "Mr."*

Bapak ("Pak" for short) does indeed mean "Mr.," and *Ibu* means "Mrs." or "Miss" in Indonesia. As introductions tend to be lengthy and formal, it's a good idea for you to be formal as well. So what about "Haji?" Muslims comprise about 87 percent of the population in Indonesia, and this title is given to any man who has completed a pilgrimage to Mecca.

The female equivalent is "Hajjah." (Incidentally, when people have made the pilgrimage, the same titles apply in other Muslim countries and regions, like Pakistan or Malaysia, as well as the Middle East, North Africa, and parts of West Africa and India.) However, these religious titles may not always be used in business circles, especially by younger people who have worked internationally.

Titles are generally considered important in Indonesia, and you should use professional titles when you address someone; for example, "Doctor" for those with a Ph.D. and "Engineer" for anyone with an engineering degree. When being introduced to someone for the first time, the order goes as follows: "Bapak" or "Ibu," then the person's academic title if he or she has one, the given and family name, and finally the business title; for example, Bapak Engineer Babang Kusumaatmaja, Vice President. If in doubt, you can always ask the person you are meeting how he or she would like to be addressed. If your own name happens to be a combination like Billy Joe Smith Jr., you will probably be asked to do the same.

LETTERS 8–9

The conventions governing the use of names are so complicated that the occasional misunderstanding is bound to arise.

Oh dear! Letter 8

FROM ITALY ABOUT **INDIA**

I've recently come back from India and only now realized that I was addressing my Indian counterpart incorrectly the whole time. I guess he was too polite to tell me.

I see from the rest of your letter that your counterpart is called Mr. Singh. I guess he is a Sikh (usually easy for foreigners to recognize, as the men traditionally wear a turban to cover their long hair). The word *Sikh* in the Punjabi language means "disciple," and all Sikh men have a given name followed by *Singh* to show their Sikh identity. After that often comes a clan or subsect name, for example, Gobind Singh Mansukhani. A Sikh woman's given name is followed by *Kaur* or *Singh*.

Your mistake was understandable, because in the West *Singh* is often used in the place of a surname, but in India it often comes as the second of three, as in Ranjit Singh Chahal. When you called your counterpart "Mr. Singh," it was the equivalent of calling a Catholic or Protestant "Mr. Christian." However, he doesn't appear to have been too upset by this. Anyone who has regular contact with other cultures has to develop a high degree of tolerance, plus a sense of humor, to deal with the inevitable misunderstandings that are bound to arise. In formal situations your contact may be addressed by his given name preceded by "Mr." and followed by Singh, as in Mr. Sandeep Singh.

His or Hers?   Letter 9

FROM MEXICO ABOUT **POLAND**

I've been sending e-mails to a Polish colleague for several months now, but I can't tell if I'm writing to a man or a woman. He or she replies to my e-mails with just an initial and surname. Now my colleague is coming here on a visit, so I really need to know who is going to arrive at the airport! Is there any way I can tell by the name?

I guess that electronic messaging systems have their advantages: You can begin an e-mail with "Hello" and avoid the problem of how to address your correspondent. In your case, you've been able to ignore the question for a while, but now it's come to a head. If there isn't any way to establish the gender, the best idea would probably be to admit your ignorance in advance and ask openly if you should expect a man or a woman.

But I can see from the name you sent me that your future visitor is a woman. Her surname ends with an *a*, which indicates that the "owner" is female, as it does in Russia (see Letter 4). She hasn't included her full first name in her e-mails but has used an initial. That is not unusual, because in Poland business contacts almost always address each other as "Mr."

or"Mrs." followed by the professional title and/or family name, and not by their first names.

But even when first names are used, they may cause more problems than they solve. Nicola, for example, is a male name in Italy but female in the U.K.; Conny is a male in Sweden but female in Germany; and Toby is a male in Britain but female in the U.S. Life can be difficult at times!

IN A NUTSHELL: *Names and Address*

GLOBAL BUSINESS STANDARD

Mr., Mrs., or Ms. plus family name.

GLOBAL WARNINGS

Names in one language can have unfortunate meanings in another. If you know or find out that your name causes laughter or embarrassment when you introduce yourself, use another name, use only your initials, change the pronunciation, or simply ignore the giggles.

In most countries, the use of the given name is reserved for children and perhaps other family members. It is not accepted in business situations. Exceptions: Given names are widely used in business in the U.S., Canada, the U.K., Australia, N.Z., and Scandinavia. (But even in these countries it can depend on age and status.)

- **Argentina:** People inherit both their mother's and father's family names. When written, the father's name comes first, and in ordinary situations, after "Señor," "Señora," or a title. Only the family name is used when addressing an individual. (See Letters 1, 5, and 6.)

- **Australia:** Given names are regularly used, irrespective of position or status.
- **Austria:** Use "Frau" or "Herr" and the family name. "Dr." and "Professor" titles are also widely used. Two or (occasionally) three titles may still be used for the same person, for example, "Herr Direktor Doktor." (See Letter 5.)
- **Belgium:** With Flemish and German speakers, use the Global Business Standard. With French speakers, use "Monsieur" or "Madame" plus surname. Flemish family names may be in two parts, for example, De Bakker or Van Gastel.
- **Brazil:** Brazilians almost always go by first names (sometimes preceded by a title, such as "Doctor" or "Senhor" or "Senhora"). (See Letters 1 and 6.)
- **Canada:** Given names are used readily, irrespective of position or status. French Canadians more often use the titles "Monsieur" or "Madame" plus surname. ("Mademoiselle" is used infrequently in business, as it is used only for very young, unmarried women.) (See Letter 5.)
- **China:** The family name is followed by the generation name and then the given name. Titles are important, for example, General Manager Li, or Madam Wu. Women keep family name after marriage, and use the title "Madam." (See Letters 3 and 5.)
- **Denmark:** Usually given names are used from the first meeting, but use the Global Business Standard if in doubt.
- **Finland:** Given names are used frequently, but use the Global Business Standard if in doubt.
- **France:** It is best to use the titles "Madame" or "Monsieur" plus the family name, even after a long acquaintance. ("Mademoiselle" is used infrequently in business as it is used only for very young, unmarried women.) (See Letters 5 and 6.)
- **Germany:** See Austria.

GLOBAL BUSINESS STANDARD

Younger people with international experience are more likely to drop titles and use given names from the word *go*.

- **Hong Kong:** See China.
- **India:** For Muslims, use "Mr." or "Mrs." plus the given name. Hindus in the south use place initial and father's initial followed by given name. Hindus in the north use a family name, which may be indicative of caste. "Singh" is used by all Sikh men, and is the equivalent of "Mr.," so use "Mr." plus the given name. (See Letters 2, 6, 7, and 8.)
- **Indonesia:** When meeting someone for the first time, introduce him or her as follows: "Bapak" or "Ibu," then the person's academic title, then the given name and family name, and finally the business title. (See Letters 3, 5, and 7.)
- **Italy:** Use "Signore" (Mr.) or "Signora" (Mrs.) and the family name. Academic titles are used frequently. "Dottore" is used for all levels of university graduates. (See Letters 5 and 6.)
- **Japan:** Use family names first, followed by given names, but be aware that some may introduce themselves to Westerners with their given name first. Use the Global Business Standard; otherwise, add *san* to the surname. (See Letter 5.)
- **Mexico:** Use "Señor" or "Señora." Usually people have two given names, and often two surnames (father's family name first, then mother's). Married women replace their mother's name with *de* and husband's surnames. Titles are important, for example, "Licenciado" for university graduate. (See Letters 1 and 6.)
- **Netherlands:** See the Global Business Standard.
- **Norway:** Usually given names are used from the first meeting.
- **Poland:** Use "Pan" for men and "Pani" for women, followed by the family name or a professional title. Surnames ending with an *a* indicate females. (See Letter 9.)
- **Russia:** Use a professional title and family name at the first meeting. The usual order is the given name followed by the patronymic (derived from first name of father) and then the family name. Women have a female version of the patronymic, and a female version of the husband's surname, both ending in an *a*, for example, Raisa Maximovna Gorbacheva. (See Letter 4.)
- **Saudi Arabia:** Saudi names are difficult to translate to other alphabets. Spelling may vary. The order is title, given name, patronymic starting with *bin* (*bint* for women), family name. (See Letter 7.)

- **South Africa:** See the Global Business Standard. Both Afrikaner (similar to Dutch) and British family names are common, as are family names indicating tribal or ethnic origins.
- **South Korea:** Use the family name, followed by the generation name, followed by the given name. Women retain own name upon marriage. Work titles are very important and routinely used. (See Letter 5.)
- **Spain:** See Argentina. Married women often choose not to adopt their husband's surname, but they do become "Señora." (See Letters 1, 5, and 6.)
- **Sweden:** Usually given names are used from the first meeting. Names may start with, or include, the letters Å, Ä, and Ö, which do not appear on non-Scandinavian keyboards. These symbols give the names a completely different pronunciation, and are found after Z in the Swedish alphabet.
- **Switzerland:** See the Global Business Standard or a title where appropriate. Depending on which language area you are in, see Austria, France, or Italy for details.
- **Taiwan:** See China.
- **Thailand:** Given names are followed by family names (although family names are not widely used). Nicknames are frequently used. Individuals usually addressed by "Khun" or "Mr." or "Mrs." and then the given name. (See Letter 5.)
- **Turkey:** Use the family name (which comes after one or more given names), followed by "Bey" for a man and "Hanim" for a woman (equivalents of "Mr." and "Mrs."). Or use the Global Business Standard.
- **UK:** See the Global Business Standard. "Dame" is a title awarded by the British monarch to distinguished women. If people have a title (e.g., Lady Thatcher, Lord Tebbit, and Sir Mick), use it.
- **US:** Given names are used readily, irrespective of a person's position or status. (See Letter 6.)
- **Venezuela:** People inherit both their mother's and father's family names. When written, the father's name comes first, and in ordinary situations is the only family name used when addressing an individual (after "Señor" or "Señora" or title.) Married women usually go by husband's surname. (See Letters 1 and 6.)

Meetings and Greetings

If you live in a city, the chances are that you see hundreds, if not thousands, of people in the course of a day—on the train to work, in the restaurant at lunchtime, and in the movie theater in the evening. You see these people, but you don't meet them. The moment when two strangers become visible to each other, when they reveal their identities, when they *meet,* is an important moment. This moment marks the transition from the role of stranger to that of acquaintance and is accompanied by rituals in all parts of the world.

Although there are enormous differences, two main aspects of meeting a new person are common to nearly all cultures: There is usually a special set of phrases and the exchange of names, and also some sort of symbolic physical movement, like the offering of a hand to be shaken or the lowering of a head. This is the moment when, if we were dogs, we'd start sniffing each other. As we are humans, we have to make do with our "social antennas." We might not be conscious of doing so, but we notice the clothes of our new acquaintance, the firmness of his or her grip, the tone of voice, or the depth of the bow. We immediately begin to form our first impression.

The rituals associated with meeting someone for the first time are many and varied, even within the same culture. In the U.K., for example, you would probably expect that your first meeting with a senior manager in your company would be accompanied by a handshake and the formal greeting, "How do you do?" But if you were later introduced to the members of the team you were going to work with, depending on their ages and your own, you might feel that a nod, a smile, and a "Hi" were introduction enough.

The "meeting and greeting" procedure is initially about the exchange of basic personal information, but it is also about the establishment and outward statement of an individual's status. So, although your egalitarian hackles may rise at this, it's the subordinate who bows lower than the manager in Japan or Korea, and much gentle probing may take place before an introduction to find out the relevant statuses of the people to be introduced. The depth of the bow will be determined by one's job title, by how many people one supervises, or even which university one attended. Etiquette books in Europe and North America also take the subordinate/superior roles seriously; these explain that it's the person with lower status who is always introduced to the person of higher status. Assuming that you want to impress some particularly old-fashioned superiors with your "savoir faire" and that you need to introduce two people to each other, one male and the other female, then the man (unless he's much older or has a particularly high status) should be introduced to the woman rather than vice-versa.

Just how formal the whole process is varies enormously from country to country. The U.S. has a reputation for being a place where people make social contacts easily, often without the need for a third party to get involved. Americans find it easier to introduce themselves, even to complete strangers, than do the Scandinavians, French, or South Koreans. Whereas the latter group may question whether it is worth getting to know people with whom they might have nothing in common, and might never see again, North Americans find it natural to introduce themselves, ask a few personal questions, and strike up a conversation. One explanation is historical. In the comparatively short history of the U.S., hundreds of thousands of people moved to the New World, and many of them continued across the American continent to build a new life. They came from a wide range of countries and backgrounds, were often on the move, and had to rely on their own resources for making new business and personal acquaintances. They were forced to develop the skill of making new contacts quickly and easily.

Whatever the procedure entails, the moment you meet someone new, you take the first step toward establishing a new relationship. However long- or short-lived the relationship turns out to be, it is a good idea to be aware of the unwritten rules and rituals surrounding the process in different cultures.

LETTERS 10–11

First meetings usually consist of some sort of physical acknowledgment of the other person, whether that's a handshake, a bow, or a simple nod. However, what you do when meeting someone is just as important as what you say.

Just passing through   Letter *10*

FROM GERMANY ABOUT THE **U.S.**

I'm a receptionist working in a multinational corporation and never know what to say to American visitors who say, "Hello. How are you?" as they walk past. Actually, by the time I've decided how to answer, they're usually out of range anyway.

The problem here is that although the greeting is in the form of a question, no answer is really required. In this respect it's on a par with the British "Good morning" and "Good afternoon" and the Australian "Good day." If the same question is asked as part of an introduction, the answer is, "Fine, thanks, and you?" In the situation you mention, however, you don't have a chance to say anything meaningful, so a nod and a smile or a simple "Hello" will suffice.

A similar question is the British, U.S. American, and Canadian greeting "How do you do?" This is used in more formal circles and only when being introduced to someone for the first time. The correct answer, which confuses everyone (including many native speakers), is to respond with the same phrase, "How do you do?" However, this form of introduction is becoming less common and is considered old-fashioned on both sides of the Atlantic, and is being replaced by "Pleased to meet you," or even (and here we come full circle) "Hello, how are you?"

Small talk—small mind?   Letter *11*

FROM THE U.S. ABOUT **VENEZUELA**

I work a lot with Venezuelans, and feel that whenever I meet a new business prospect I spend half my time answering questions about my family, mutual acquaintances, my trip there, and so on. This means I have to make three visits to the country in order to do something that should really only take one. Is there any way around this?

In a word, no—that is, not if you want to do business there, or anywhere in Latin America, for that matter. Venezuelans take a long time to greet each other; their numerous polite questions are a sign of respect for and interest in the individual. They want to get to know you not only because you doubtless have a charming and interesting personality, but also because for them it makes sound business sense to know and trust the person they are doing business with. If something goes wrong with the deal, most Latin Americans want to know their contacts will do their best to solve the problem personally, for it is often a time-consuming and expensive process to enforce contracts or to get legal redress through the courts.

This preference for doing business with people you know can be a barrier for U.S. Americans, Canadians, and some Northern Europeans. They have to be prepared to invest the time to make long-term relationships in Latin America, India, Southern Europe, and most of the Middle East if they want to work successfully there. So it's time for you and your similarly task-oriented colleagues from, among others, Australia, Germany, Switzerland, and Austria to stop looking at your watches and start using some of your social skills to help build the long-term relationships that will benefit you in business terms, and possibly enrich you as people.

LETTERS 12–13

Handshaking is accepted as a friendly greeting almost everywhere. However, that's not to say that all handshakes are alike.

Bone-crunchers   Letter *12*

FROM THAILAND ABOUT THE **U.S. AND PARTS OF EUROPE**

Why do some American and European men treat the handshake as some sort of competitive sport? What are they trying to prove? There have been times when my hand has been quite sore after such greetings.

I agree. There's nothing more off-putting than extending your hand to greet someone and finding yourself engaged in something that feels like a trial of strength to see who has the stronger grip! In the U.S. and Russia, and to a lesser extent Germany and the U.K., a firm handshake, accompanied by a direct look into the other person's face, is regarded as a reflection of a strong and sincere personality. However, that's about as sensible as believing that everyone who wears spectacles is intelligent or that you're bound to have a quick temper if you have red hair.

The purpose of handshaking is to establish friendly relations, not to impress someone with the force of your personality. In cultures where women shake hands, they are far less likely to be knuckle-crushers than their male colleagues. And in many Asian cultures, such as Japan, Indonesia, Vietnam, and Thailand, where simply touching a stranger may be a slightly uncomfortable and unfamiliar experience, handshakes are often tentative and gentle, although they may last longer than the North American or European variety. In these Asian countries the handshake is a foreign import rather than a "home-grown product," and a very firm handshake may be regarded as a bad-mannered attempt to impose the force of your personality on others. Having said all that, when you *do* take someone's hand, yours shouldn't feel like a dead fish—floppy and limp. That would imply that you found the contact distasteful. Take your cue from your fellow-shaker and shake with sensitivity.

A whole lot of shaking . . .   Letter *13*

FROM THE U.K. ABOUT **FRANCE**

What are the conventions about shaking hands in France? My impression is that they shake hands much more frequently than we do here in the U.K.

You are quite right: In France, more hands are shaken more often. In the U.K. and the U.S., a casual wave or a general "Good morning, everyone" is probably enough to start the day, but this is not typical of Europe as a whole. There, greetings are both more personal and formal. A French office manager will, for example, greet all colleagues by name and shake hands with each of them at both the beginning and the end of the day. The same will happen in Spain, where it is also common even for colleagues working for the same firm to shake hands on both entering and leaving a meeting room. When it comes to social events in the majority of both Eastern and Southern European countries and in Central and South America, the host and other guests will shake hands or exchange hugs on both arrival and departure. Not to do so would be regarded as a sign that something was wrong.

Also, handshaking is not confined to a business environment in France. Even on a beach you can observe whole families, children included, greeting each other in this way. However, in the U.K. and the U.S., handshaking is associated primarily with meeting people for the first time, usually in a business environment. But as a rule of thumb, it's better to offer your hand too many times than too few.

LETTERS 14–15

There are alternatives to handshaking, of course. In some cultures you bow, while in other cultures old acquaintances may kiss each other.

Bow and bow again?   Letter *14*

FROM BELGIUM ABOUT **JAPAN** AND **SOUTH KOREA**

I have had contact with some Japanese people here in Europe and will soon be visiting them in Japan. I know they usually bow to one another. Should I do the same, and if so, how?

It would be appreciated if you did bow, as it shows respect for the country's customs as well as for the individual you are greeting. In Japan, the general rule is to bow from the waist (with the arms at the sides for a man, and resting on the thighs for a woman) while avoiding eye contact.

As a general rule, the individual with the lower status should bow lower and more often than the person with the higher status. As a guest, you should start the ball rolling by bowing, but not too deeply. If you wish to emphasize your respect for a certain individual, for an older person, for example, give an extra bow.

Some Japanese businesspeople may initiate a handshake when introduced to a foreigner because they may assume that foreigners don't know about, or are uncomfortable with, bowing, so be prepared for them to stick out their hands. Other Japanese businesspeople will shake your hand if you offer it, but they may be as unfamiliar with this procedure as you are with bowing.

In South Korea, people also usually greet each other with a bow, although South Koreans are familiar with the Western-style handshake. If you're introduced to a Japanese or South Korean and he or she bows, do the same, saying your own name softly at the same time. Afterwards, business cards are usually exchanged (which is just as well, as probably neither of you could understand what the other said).

Kiss kiss   Letter *15*

FROM THE U.K. ABOUT **RUSSIA**

I shall soon be off to Russia on my first business trip. I've seen on TV that Russian men often kiss each other. Will I be expected to do this? I would feel really uncomfortable—I don't even kiss my father!

What you have probably seen on TV is foreign political leaders arriving in Moscow and being greeted by the Russian president with a hug and a kiss. But as we all know, politicians are not "normal" people, and their behavior is not duplicated in the business world. Russians are usually quite formal at a first meeting and appreciate courtesy and patience from visitors. However, as the relationship progresses over time and you get to know each other better, male Russians might express their friendship for another man with a hug and a kiss on the cheek when meeting or saying good-bye. This is an expression of friendship and is not likely to happen to you until you get to know each other well, and not always then. The same applies in Latin American and Southern and Eastern European cultures, where friends and family of both genders greet each other with a kiss on the cheek.

Don't be concerned that hugging and kissing in these circumstances have any homosexual overtones. Think how many male players and spectators (gay and straight both) react at sporting events when someone scores—they are wrapped in each other's arms before you can say "Goal!" and nobody turns a hair.

IN A NUTSHELL: *Meetings and Greetings*

GLOBAL BUSINESS STANDARDS

Businesspeople shake hands (with the right hand only), but women should note the Global Warning below.

Businesswomen greeting business acquaintances should stick to bowing and/or handshaking rather than kissing.

GLOBAL WARNINGS

In Hindu and most Muslim cultures, cross-gender handshaking is frowned on. Foreigners of either gender shouldn't initiate such a handshake.

If you come from a culture where kissing and hugging are common, be aware that acquaintances and friends from other cultures may find this close proximity uncomfortable.

- **Argentina:** The meeting and greeting process takes longer than in North America or Northern Europe, because participants want to know a lot about individuals before doing business with them. Colleagues who know each other may follow a handshake with an *abrazo* (embrace). (See Letters 11, 13, and 15.)

- **Australia:** Style is informal. It is acceptable to introduce yourself rather than wait for an introduction. Handshaking is the usual business greeting, although less so between women. (See Letter 11.)
- **Austria:** See the Global Business Standards. Shake hands at beginning and end of meeting. Occasionally older men may kiss a woman's hand. (See Letter 11.)
- **Belgium:** For French-speaking parts of Belgium see France; otherwise, see Global Business Standards.
- **Brazil:** See Argentina.
- **Canada:** Style is quite informal. See the Global Business Standards. For French-speaking Canada, see France. (See Letter 10.)
- **China:** A slight bow or nod is customary, and a handshake may accompany this. Grip is usually softer than in Europe or the U.S. Eyes are often lowered when meeting someone, as a sign of respect. Greet oldest/most senior person first.
- **Denmark:** See the Global Business Standards.
- **Finland:** See the Global Business Standards. Note that Finns often don't smile.
- **France:** Introductions are not usually accompanied by a smile. Handshaking is very frequent, even among colleagues at start and end of day. It's important to greet everyone (even strangers) on entering a public space with *Bonjour*. (Double-cheek kiss is the custom between friends and relations.) (See Letters 11 and 13.)
- **Germany:** Introductions are not usually accompanied by a smile. See the Global Business Standards. Shake hands at beginning and end of meeting. (Letters 11 and 12.)
- **Hong Kong:** See the Global Business Standards. Also see China.
- **India:** Bows may be accompanied by a "prayer" gesture of the palms of hands together (called *namaste*). Foreigners are not expected to reciprocate in kind. Handshake is usually softer. The meeting and greeting process takes longer than in North America or Northern Europe, as participants want to know a lot about individuals before doing business with them. (See Letters 11 and 12.)
- **Indonesia:** The grip is usually softer, and may continue for a longer duration than is customary in Europe or North America. It may also be accompanied by a slight bow. (See Letter 12.)

- **Italy:** See the Global Business Standards. On occasion, men may kiss a woman's hand. (See Letters 11, 13, and 15.)
- **Japan:** The lower status person bows deeper. If shaking hands, grip is usually softer. (See Letters 12 and 14.)
- **Mexico:** See Argentina.
- **Netherlands:** Both genders shake hands on meeting, and names are said at the same time.
- **Norway:** See the Global Business Standards.
- **Poland:** See Italy. (See Letters 13 and 15.)
- **Russia:** Friends and relatives (including men) often greet each other with a hug and a kiss. Otherwise use the Global Business Standards. (See Letters 12, 13, and 15.)
- **Saudi Arabia:** If a handshake is used, the grip is usually softer and may go on longer than in Europe or the U.S. The meeting and greeting process takes longer than in North America or Northern Europe. Traditional greeting between male friends involves embrace and kiss. A man should not greet a veiled woman. (See Letter 11.)
- **South Africa:** Black South Africans may take a long time over the meetings and greetings as a sign of courtesy, and handholding is a sign of friendship. Otherwise, U.S.-style firm handshakes are the norm and eye contact essential.
- **South Korea:** Introductions by third-party people are the rule. Each partner must know the other's status before relationship is established. Slight bow is combined with "weak" handshake. (See Letter 14.)
- **Spain:** Handshaking is frequent, even among colleagues at the start and end of each day. May greet everyone (even strangers) on entering a public space with "Hola." (See Letters 11, 13, and 15.)
- **Sweden:** See Netherlands.
- **Switzerland:** See the Global Business Standards. (See Letter 11.)
- **Taiwan:** The grip is usually softer and the handshake may go on longer than in Europe or the U.S.
- **Thailand:** A bow may be accompanied by a "prayer" gesture of the palms of the hands together. Foreigners are not expected to reciprocate in kind. (See Letter 12.)

- **Turkey:** See the Global Business Standards. The meeting and greeting process takes longer than in North America and Northern Europe.
- **UK:** Handshaking is less common than in mainland Europe. Introduce a junior to a senior, a man to a woman, a colleague to a customer. (See Letters 10, 12, 13, and 15.)
- **US:** An informal style is used. Strength of handshake sometimes seen as reflecting strength of character (so you do get some "knuckle crushers"). Introduce a junior to a senior, a man to a woman, a colleague to a customer. (See Letters 10 and 12.)
- **Venezuela:** See the Global Business Standards. Otherwise, acquaintances and friends embrace and kiss freely on meeting. (See Letters 11 and 15.)

Business Cards

Business cards are an indispensable help to people with a bad memory for names. However, most don't have a picture of the person, so it is quite possible to end up with a pocketful of business cards and no idea of which card belongs to which face. You can avoid this by taking your time over the exchange, studying the card carefully, and checking the pronunciation with the person. (Unfortunately, I have personal evidence that even these measures are no guarantee against "senior moments.")

The exchange of business cards is part of the meeting and greeting ritual and thus has a certain symbolic function. It's a ritual tied to giving and receiving, and it is equally as important as the exchange of gifts is at a later stage in the relationship. In this case, the "gift" is written information about an individual and a company, and as such it is extremely important that it is treated respectfully.

There is no global standard for how a business card should look or which language it should be written in. In the Netherlands, for example, many business cards have only the initial of the first name followed by the family name, while in Spain there are likely to be at least four names. Then there's the question of job titles. If you have worked for a large organization, you know the hours spent after every reorganization trying to decide upon new job titles. The fine differences between "Information

Officer" and "Information Manager" and "Systems Developer" and "Systems Programmer" can occupy people for days. But when these same people have to travel to a country where their native language isn't spoken and they need to get their cards translated, the translator isn't aware of these fine distinctions. All sorts of mistakes can occur. It makes sense to get any translations checked by a native speaker familiar with your company to ensure that the cards are accurate, but it may be hard to find such a person. In fact, I heard recently that it was so difficult to ensure that cards written in English were translated correctly into Japanese and Chinese that one company had given up trying and simply presented the English-language version.

That's a pity, in part because the Japanese appreciate the effort of the Western businessperson to get business cards translated accurately, and because the main virtue in the exchange of cards is that they have great practical value. In the case of Japan, even if you have to omit the job title, having your name written in Japanese phonetic symbols is enormously useful to your Japanese counterparts. Ideally, cards eliminate the need for time-consuming questioning to find out exactly what your new acquaintance does for a living or his or her position in the company. But even if you are sure that the information contained is correct, what does it *mean*? If your visitor is a department manager, does that mean she has ten or one hundred employees? And although a division manager in your company may be part of the executive management team and just marginally lower than vice president in the divine order of things, in the company on the other side of town, people with the same job title may be much further down the corporate ladder.

So as a rough guide, treat the exchange of business cards with the greatest respect and courtesy, but remember that the information on them may be open to interpretation.

LETTERS 16–17

Exchanging business cards raises three questions: *who* you give them to, *when*, and *how*.

Who to give them to, when . . .   Letter *16*

FROM THE U.K. ABOUT **JAPAN**

I know that the giving and receiving of business cards is important in Japan, but who do I give them to, and do I have to wait until someone offers me one first?

You don't have to wait for someone else to take the initiative. Protocol says that the person of lower rank should offer his or her card first, but being the first to offer can also simply show that you are keen to continue the contact. You can offer your card to any new business acquaintance without causing offense. The procedure of presenting and receiving is similar to that for China (see the next letter), but in Japan the giver only needs to use one hand to give the card.

It's very important to have a business card holder that keeps the cards you receive separate from your own, so you avoid any frantic juggling of cards. In Japan the cardholder should be made of dark leather, not of metal, and should have two pockets.

One person you should always give a card to is the receptionist or secretary (usually female) of the person you are going to meet. Take the time to help her pronounce your name and your company name correctly, and she'll be able to help her boss do the same.

. . . and how   Letter *17*

FROM THE U.S. ABOUT **CHINA**

I'll be traveling to China in a few months. Can you tell me something of the procedure surrounding business cards?

Get your cards printed in both English and Mandarin Chinese, and be sure that a native from mainland China does the translation to avoid embarrassing mistakes. Hong Kong and Taiwan use a different style of characters, so if you're following your trip to mainland China with a visit to one of these places, get two versions of your cards printed, and make sure they don't get mixed up.

When you present your card, check that the side with the Chinese writing is facing the person you're giving it to. Present the card formally with both hands, holding it by the two top corners; if you are presenting your cards to a group of people, be sure that you start with the most senior person first. Receive cards with both hands and read them carefully before putting them away. You may want to take this opportunity to ask how to pronounce a name.

Wherever you are, the idea behind the whole procedure of exchanging cards is to "break the ice," so don't rush things, and treat the individual and his or her card with respect. Don't write on a card you've been given, don't put it in a wallet and then place it in your back pocket, and never leave it behind after the meeting. All three actions would be regarded as very rude—not the impression you want to leave after a first meeting.

LETTERS 18–20

What information to include on your card is an important decision.

Showing off? Letter *18*

FROM AUSTRALIA ABOUT **EUROPE**

I'm getting new business cards printed before my next trip to Europe and have been advised to include my academic qualifications (I have a doctorate). I've never bothered to include my title before, and I don't want to appear to be "showing off."

Your uncertainty shows just as much about the country you come from as the countries you're going to. In egalitarian Australia, and indeed in the U.S., the U.K., and Israel, there may be a reluctance to appear to be an "egghead," and in cultures where the practical is regarded more highly than the theoretical, someone with a Ph.D. may be regarded with a certain degree of suspicion! But even in these countries, if you work in an area (e.g., pharmaceuticals or IT) that relies on cutting-edge technology or being first on the market with new developments, it would be a good idea to include postgraduate degrees and other professional qualifications.

If your itinerary includes German-speaking countries, France, or Southern and Eastern European nations, you should definitely include academic titles, especially any higher than an undergraduate degree, along with your job title. In France and the U.K., graduates may include the names of especially prestigious universities on their cards no matter what industry or business area they work in. In these countries education is highly regarded, and a higher degree may mean that you will be listened to with greater respect—always a pleasant position to be in!

Consider taking two sets of cards along, both with the basic information of your name, company, and job title, but one with your academic title and one without. This way, you can judge the situation and act accordingly. For example, if you feel that the site foreman is not going to be interested in your doctorate in archaeology, you don't have to inform him of it.

Print in Polish?	**Letter** *19*

FROM IRELAND ABOUT **POLAND**

I'm getting business cards printed before my first visit to Poland. I'd like to know if they should be in Polish as well as in English.

If you're thinking of doing long-term business in Poland, your Polish partners may appreciate your thoughtful gesture if you have one side printed in Polish. But do make sure that the translation is a good one, and get it double-checked. If you're having your job title translated, make sure your translator understands exactly what it entails (*Ass. Manager*, for example, can cause problems for an inexperienced translator), and that words such as *manager* or *executive* are included where appropriate, as these help establish your status.

In some countries, like Belgium and Switzerland, there are two or more local languages, neither of which is English. There, an English-only card is a good solution, so that you don't get into the "Why Flemish but not French?" or "Why French but not German?" sort of argument. Where English is one of two official languages, as in Canada, make sure your cards are printed in both languages, and present the card with the appropriate language the "right" way up for the recipient.

Soft focus	Letter *20*

FROM THE U.S. ABOUT **EUROPE**

> *In the U.S., I have a business card with my photo on it, but my friends in Europe tell me they don't have cards like this. Should I use the cards anyway, or get new ones?*

Business cards with photos are not as common in Europe, but that isn't an automatic reason not to use them there. One disadvantage I can think of is that stuffy individuals might regard it as carrying the cult of the personality too far, and if your face overshadows the company logo, it might create a negative impression.

I can also see some practical disadvantages. You just have to look at many people's passport photos to see that some of us, although charming souls, are not photogenic. You don't want to scare off your customers!

More seriously, I think the photo idea is practical and sensible, but it's probably better to err on the side of tradition and not use photos unless you have a special reason for doing so. For example, if you need to send a card ahead of you and your name could be read as male or female, a photo would eliminate needing to write "Ms." or "Mr." in front of your name.

IN A NUTSHELL: *Business Cards*

GLOBAL BUSINESS STANDARDS

Business cards should include the company name and website address, your name, job title, address (including e-mail), and phone and fax numbers preceded by the area codes.

When giving cards, make sure the appropriate language is facing the recipient.

If your given name does not clearly indicate your gender, consider including "Mr.," "Mrs.," or "Ms." before your full name (unless you prefer to make use of the element of surprise!).

GLOBAL WARNINGS

Don't present or receive a card with your left hand in a Muslim country.

Don't accept a card and put it away without looking at it. Don't write on a card, bend it, put it in your back pocket (where you are going to sit on it), leave it behind, or generally "hurt its feelings!"

- **Argentina:** No great weight is attached to the exchange of business cards. Cards usually show full (often very long) name. Have business cards printed in Spanish with the English translation on back.
- **Australia:** No great weight is attached to the exchange of business cards. Including degrees on your card may be regarded as unnecessary or even pretentious, depending on the industry you work in. (See Letter 18.)
- **Austria:** Include titles beyond your bachelor's degree on your card. If you are from a well-established company, include the date when

your company was founded. It's not necessary to translate business cards from English. (See Letter 18.)

- **Belgium:** Business cards in English only will solve problems about whether to use French, Flemish, or German. (See Letter 19.)
- **Brazil:** Cards from Brazilians will contain all names and titles, but the giver may underline the name(s) he or she wants to be known by and cross out the others. If you are providing translation on reverse side, make sure it is in Portuguese, not Spanish.
- **Canada:** Has two official languages. Have your card printed in both French and English. (See Letter 19.)
- **China:** It is very important to present a card to everyone at the beginning of your first meeting. Take plenty. Cards should be in both English and Chinese. Make sure a native speaker from China does the translation (rather than Taiwan or Hong Kong). Have the translation double-checked. (See Letters 16 and 17.)
- **Denmark:** English-only business cards are acceptable because many people know English. Often given at end of first meeting.
- **Finland:** See Denmark.
- **France:** In formal settings, when you give your card to a person of higher rank, you might not receive one in return. The French include academic credentials as well as other appropriate titles on their cards. Graduates from the top universities may include this information on their cards. (See Letter 18.)
- **Germany:** See Austria.
- **Hong Kong:** See China (but make sure a native of Hong Kong does the translation). (See Letter 17.)
- **India:** People commonly include all of their educational degrees, titles (current and previously held), and current position in the company on their business cards. Foreign businesspeople should include their university degrees, as well as the names of any prestigious educational institutions attended.
- **Indonesia:** Cards in English-only are sufficient. If you know you will be dealing with Chinese Indonesians, have a Chinese translation on reverse side. If dealing with ethnic Indonesians or government officials (usually Muslims), be sure translation is in Bahasa Indonesian. Include all titles and academic qualifications.

- **Italy:** Some Italian businesspeople have three cards: one with all degrees, titles, and contact information; another without the titles but including contact information, to use when a less formal relationship has been established; and a calling card with name and possibly personal contact information to use in social occasions. (See Letter 18.)
- **Japan:** It's very important to present a card to everyone at the beginning of your first meeting. Present the card with one hand, and with a bow. Take plenty, with English on one side and Japanese on the other. Double-check that the translation is correct. Your name written in Japanese phonetic symbols will be appreciated. (See Letter 16.)
- **Mexico:** Have business cards in English with the Spanish translation on the other side. Present on first meeting.
- **Netherlands:** English-only business cards are acceptable. It's common that their business cards may only have the initial of given names. Often given at end of first meeting.
- **Norway:** English-only business cards are acceptable. Often given at end of first meeting.
- **Poland:** Take plenty of business cards, and have them in Polish on one side and English on the other. It may be difficult to get new ones printed there. (See Letters 18 and 19.)
- **Russia:** Take plenty of business cards, and have them printed in Russian on one side and English on the other. Titles are important in Russia to know with whom one is dealing. Be sure to have your title (not just your department or functional area) displayed clearly on your card.
- **Saudi Arabia:** Cards should be printed with English on one side and Arabic on the other.
- **South Africa:** See Netherlands.
- **South Korea:** Exchange cards immediately after formal greetings. In groups greet the most senior member first and work your way toward the most junior. (The senior person will usually greet you first.) Use two hands to present card.
- **Spain:** Cards usually show full (often very long) name. Good to have Spanish on one side and English on the other. (See Letter 18.)

- **Sweden:** Including degrees on your card may be regarded as unnecessary or even pretentious, depending on the industry you work in. Often given at end of first meeting.
- **Switzerland:** See Austria.
- **Taiwan:** Cards should have an English and a Chinese side. Make sure a native speaker from Taiwan (rather than China) does the translation. (See Letter 17.)
- **Thailand:** Cards should be printed with English on one side and Thai on the other.
- **Turkey:** Cards are usually exchanged at the end of the first meeting.
- **UK:** No particular ritual. Graduates from one of the top universities may include this information on their cards. Usually exchanged at end of first meeting. (See Letter 18.)
- **US:** Including degrees on your card may be regarded as unnecessary or even pretentious, depending on the sector you work in. Usually exchanged at end of first meeting. (See Letters 18 and 20.)
- **Venezuela:** No great weight is attached to the exchange of business cards. Good to have Spanish on one side and English on the other.

CHAPTER 2

Making a Good Impression

So, what happens after the introductions? Whether you engage in social pleasantries or get right down to business, you will spend a lot of time observing your new acquaintances, and they will be observing you too. We may or may not be conscious that we are doing this—that is just the way we are. This ability to observe each other evolved so we could make vital decisions on which our survival depended. "Is the new member of the tribe going to be an asset in the next mammoth hunt or is he going to club me when my back's turned so he can be the new chief?"

Even when we are on our home turf, we tend to keep a close eye on new people until we feel we know them. Because the parameters are familiar, we are better able to judge if someone is being friendly or unfriendly, or whether our new acquaintance's colorful Hawaiian shirt marks him as a free-thinking, creative type with the sort of individuality that our company is looking for or a dangerous freak with an ego problem. When we meet people from another culture the process of assessment is even more complicated because we don't share the same background, and if we use the same standards to make judgments, we run the risk of coming to the wrong conclusion.

Essentially, after the introductions we are trying to establish the basis for a relationship, and to do that we need to be aware of what we have in common and what we don't. We use external clues like dress, manners, and body language to decide whether we can get along. We also ask ourselves questions like these: Is he reliable? Is she generous? Is he interested in my way of looking at things, or is he sloppy, lacking in respect for my culture and me, and interested only in the next deal and the bottom line? And, because we're only human, we sometimes jump to the wrong conclusion and are misjudged in our turn.

One of my friends told me the following story. An Englishwoman she knew had returned from a couple of years in the Middle East with an Iranian husband. Back home, her girlfriends thought her choice of husband rather exciting and romantic and did their best to make the new arrival feel at home in his wife's country. They were friendly and open and treated him from the first like "one of the gang." But my friend, Carol, never liked him. She found him arrogant and snobbish and couldn't understand what had possessed her friend to marry the man. As a result, she hardly ever spoke to him.

As the months passed and the young couple moved from the honeymoon phase to the more mundane phases of marriage, they started to have the occasional quarrel. In the course of one of these, the husband said he thought that his wife's friends were loose women of bad moral character. They had flirted shamelessly with him, and they would obviously have gone further if he had made a move. The only respectable one among them was Carol, who had behaved toward him in an appropriately modest manner.

Seen through a different cultural filter, behavior intended to be warm and friendly was seen as dangerously provocative. And as a final irony, Carol's unfriendliness had created a favorable impression, because it had been interpreted as showing the appropriate degree of reserve and respect that should mark relations between the genders in the husband's culture.

Then there is the case of a foreign visitor who made a hit in Argentina. When he met his potential customer for the first time, he greeted him in Spanish, gave him a quick firm handshake, and looked him in the eye. He got quite close to his listeners to deliver his sales pitch, and spoke expressively and with great enthusiasm about his product. During the coffee break, he answered questions about his family and children and made similar inquiries himself. He even joined in the discussion about soccer and asked a few questions about the local team, which got him invited to the next match.

This man behaved in the same way during his visit to Japan, but he made a very negative impression there. He was perceived as loud, brash, and arrogant, and as attempting to dominate his Japanese counterparts. The same behavior was judged according to different standards.

There are many ways of making cultural faux pas, of creating the wrong impression. However, in the very first stages of a relationship there are some easy guidelines to follow that can help you get off on the right foot.

◆ MORAL

We don't always create the impression we are striving for, but being conscious of some of the unwritten rules of behavior of another culture can help us do just that.

Dress

Clothes fulfill a number of functions: they protect us from the climate; may indicate what our occupation or nationality is; and inform others about our wealth, status, and personal taste. Finally, they keep us from ending up in the local jail, charged with gross indecency.

How we dress is an integral part of our culture, and as such is influenced by local traditions and customs. But at the same time the world of international fashion seems to have developed what can be termed the "global uniform" for teenagers and young adults, consisting of blue jeans and T-shirts for both sexes and which is accepted leisurewear from Copenhagen to Cape Town. So, right now a call center operating in Delhi has some of its Sikh employees dressed in *salwar kameez*, the traditional baggy trousers and long tunic worn by women for centuries, while other colleagues, both male and female, are clad in regulation jeans.

Our choice of clothes is influenced by such national cornerstones as politics, religion, and big business, as well as the more lightweight vagaries of fashion. The birth of the People's Republic of China in 1949 was marked by the abandonment of the embroidered robes worn by the middle and upper classes, and the adoption of simple jackets and trousers by everyone. These clothes were designed to eradicate the outward indications of class, occupation, and gender, which were no longer regarded as worthy of notice in the new state. Thirty years later in Iran, Islamic fundamentalists insisted that God required women to wear long, shapeless garments and veils so that men wouldn't be led from the path of virtue by the sight of an uncovered face.

The founding father of IBM, Thomas J. Watson Sr., was almost equally insistent on a dress code. His directive to new managers was, "Be careful with people, don't swear, and wear a white shirt." The "uniform" that Watson and other American business leaders insisted on was seen as an outward guarantee that its wearers possessed the sterling qualities of reliability, respectability, and responsibility. Watson's legacy was long-lasting. As late as the 1980s, if you saw two or three young men together with short hair cuts, dark suits, white shirts, black lace-up shoes, and darkish socks and tie, you could be pretty sure they either worked for IBM or were evangelical Christians making house calls. I can't imagine that Mao, Khomeini, or Watson—international leaders with global power—paid particular attention as to whether pink was in or out of fashion; nevertheless, they did have strong views on clothes.

The fashion industry may decide on skirt lengths and whether trousers will have cuffs or not this year, but how we dress also reflects what is going on in the wider world. Thirty years ago, a small minority of top executives working for multinational corporations might take work home with them. If necessary, they could read a report and make a few phone calls in the evening or over the weekend, although in a pre-cell phone society there was no guarantee that they would reach who they wanted. As a rule, most people performed one kind of activity at the office and another at home. Now it's not that simple. In the last ten years, with the advent of the personal computer and the Internet (not to mention the cell phone), people have been able to work more from home on a regular or an irregular basis.

At the same time that these divisions between work and home have become more blurred, it is becoming more difficult to differentiate between work and leisure clothes. A number of companies in some countries have followed the U.S.: good-bye three-piece suit, hello corporate casual. Yet many people who come from countries that prefer to keep work and home life separate like to keep their clothes separate too. In

Spain, for example, people change their clothes when they come home from work, shedding their work roles and reassuming their family or private roles.

Of course, all my readers are sensible and broad-minded people who know how unwise it is to judge a person solely by his or her appearance. However, when you want to make a favorable impression, it is probably a good idea to assume the people you are going to meet are not similarly "enlightened." Make an effort to ensure that your dress conforms to local standards of what is practical (especially in extreme climates), respectable, and in good taste. This may be boring advice, and following it may repress the real vibrant creative you, but do it anyway. Business is business.

LETTERS 21–23

Appropriate business dress varies enormously from country to country, region to region, and individual to individual.

Uniform informality? Letter *21*

FROM GERMANY ABOUT THE **U.S.**

I've heard about the American trend to "dress down" on Fridays. What does that mean exactly, and is this still the case? And finally, should I follow their example?

In the 1990s, many newly established computer companies in the U.S. initiated relaxed dress codes. Instead of wearing a dark suit to work, young people in creative or technical jobs were allowed to come to work in the sort of clothes they wore in their free time. Well-established companies in other fields looked at the phenomenal success of these companies and decided that even if they couldn't imitate them in anything else, in the matter of dress they could. They took as their role models the young laid-back IT tycoons who showed it was possible to be a multimillionaire and still not wear a tie.

These bigger companies decided to introduce *casual Friday*, when employees were allowed to abandon their work "uniform" one day a week. Then the trend took off, and "year-round casual" became the company policy for many organizations. Employees were encouraged to adopt a more relaxed dress style in the belief that it would give the company a more go-ahead image, encourage its employees to get more personally involved with their work, and stop staff thinking in "old-fashioned," hierarchical terms.

However, there were times when this resulted in problems, because some people's ideas of casual wear meant cut-off shorts and a scruffy T-shirt, and this caused some raised eyebrows during customer meetings. So HR departments decided to issue complex guidelines describing what "business casual" meant. Now the pendulum is swinging back, and many individuals are discovering they can be just as creative in a suit as in a sweatshirt.

As a visitor to the U.S., it's probably better to err on the side of formality rather than to dress down too far. But don't be surprised if the manager you're meeting is wearing a sweater and slacks rather than a white shirt and dark suit.

Trousered Amazons?   Letter 22

FROM DENMARK ABOUT **BRAZIL**

I'll be traveling to Brazil soon, and I wonder if trousers are acceptable in a business context? (I'm female, by the way!)

Although trousers on women are increasingly accepted in the workplace in North and South America and in Europe, it's generally better not to wear trousers on business trips if you are not sure whom you are going to meet. If you are unlucky, you may end up in an important meeting with the last of the dinosaurs who believes that a women's place is in a pair of seamless nylons. You may decide to ignore that possibility, but you should at least be aware of it. Of course, it makes sense to wear trousers if you're visiting factories, building sites, or whatever, where you may have to climb into trucks, inspect foundations, and so on. Trousers are also practical in colder countries. However, they should not be too tight, and if they're being worn to a meeting in the office rather than for a factory tour, they should be part of a suit, preferably one with a long jacket—unless, of course, you have a beautiful bum (and to be honest, how many of us do?).

In some countries, women in trousers attract criticism. People see them as trying to imitate men and attempting to usurp their roles. In more traditional Muslim societies particularly, skirts with modest hemlines are preferable to masculine-style trousers, unless your trousers are accompanied by a tunic-length blouse that covers your hips. In these countries it is best to avoid sleeveless dresses and tops, shorts, low necklines, and high hemlines entirely. Actually, the last three taboos apply to all business trips if you want to be taken seriously.

Porker problem	Letter 23

FROM THE U.K. ABOUT **SAUDI ARABIA**

This isn't really a question, but an experience I'd like to share with you so no one else will make my mistake. On a recent visit to Saudi Arabia I took my usual lightweight suit and a selection of ties, one of which had tiny pictures of animals as part of the design. Before the start of my first meeting, I was taken aside by our local representative and told to go back to the hotel to change. One of the little animals on my tie was a pig, and the rep warned me that if my Saudi counterpart noticed this, it would be interpreted as an insult, and any possible deal would be off.

Thanks for sharing your story. It's easy to underestimate religious sensitivities if we are not particularly religious ourselves, but of course they must be taken into account when meeting people from other cultures. The pig is considered to be an unclean animal to Muslims as well as to Jews and Hindus, so pictures of the porcine variety are not a good idea on any clothing if you're going to Saudi Arabia, Indonesia, or India, for example. Furthermore, in addition to not eating pork, Muslims will not touch pigskin and certainly don't want to see pictures of their least favorite animal. The area of religion is probably the most sensitive area of all, and a lack of awareness of or a lack of respect for someone else's beliefs will lose you business—perhaps permanently.

Some more things about ties and colors . . .

On the subject of ties in general, it's better to be dull and boring than to run the risk of offending anyone. I know that some men see ties as their only chance to express their individuality because they're otherwise limited to the "uniform" of the dark business suit, but on occasions it's wiser to keep the wilder aspects of your personality a secret until you get home again. So don't take animal or other "jokey" ties (even if your daughter did give you a fetching Mickey Mouse creation for Christmas).

Avoid single color ties for the simple reason that your favorite color is bound to mean something inappropriate somewhere! Depending on where you find yourself, both white and black ties may be associated with funerals, red with weddings or the Communist Party, green with Muslim sympathies, pink and lavender with your sexual preference, and so forth.

LETTER 24

Even your taste in colors is affected by your culture. Diana Vreeland, the American fashion writer, wrote on a visit to India in the 1970s that "pink is the navy blue of Asia," meaning you do not stand out in the crowd in shocking pink in Delhi in the same way you would in Dublin or Detroit.

Where wear white?   **Letter *24***

FROM ITALY ABOUT **CHINA**

I'm planning a business trip to China this summer and am considering what to wear. I've heard it isn't a good idea to wear a white dress. Is that correct? (I have a really nice one in that color, which is why I am asking.)

Even so, I'm afraid it still isn't a good idea. In China, and places with an ethnic Chinese population like Taiwan and Hong Kong, white clothes are associated with funerals, and immediate families are traditionally supposed to wear white for seven weeks after a family member has died. It's not a good idea to be dressed head to toe in red either, as it's a color associated with people getting married, and bright yellow robes are worn by Buddhist priests. If you're wearing dresses, most patterned fabrics are fine, and otherwise a skirt (at least below the knee and not too tight) and blouse are business-like. Trousers and a long blouse in some cool fabric are a good idea if you are visiting factories or farms, in which case you should also take rubber-soled shoes.

LETTERS 25–26

Our clothes reflect the image we want to project. Pop stars and actors know this very well, but to some businesspeople this seems a difficult concept to grasp.

Scruffy seniors   Letter 25

FROM BRAZIL ABOUT THE U.K.

I am a secretary at a large international firm in Rio de Janeiro, and my company was recently visited by a group of suppliers from England. It included a number of quite senior managers, and we found them pleasant and easy to get on with. However, I was surprised by their appearance. Their trousers were baggy and weren't pressed, their shoes were obviously cheap, and some of them needed a good haircut. Don't they realize that these things are important?

The British generally aren't noted for their elegance when it comes to clothes. Most British children between the ages of eleven and sixteen (or even eighteen) wear a uniform to school, which means that for several of their most formative years they don't need to think about what they are going to wear. I sometimes feel that British men secretly look back wistfully to those days when the choice of clothes was made for them. British women, like women the whole world over, usually pay more attention to their clothing than their male counterparts do.

In their defense, it can be tricky to know how to dress in an unfamiliar climate. Because the British summer is so short, many businessmen don't have lightweight summer suits, although they'll have a number in heavier material. British people in general associate warm weather with vacations, and may have lots of clothes in their wardrobes suitable for a barbecue or the beach but not for a business meeting when the temperature is over 85 degrees F. In Latin American and Mediterranean countries, your appearance reflects your status, taste, and even education, so most people take great pains to look good. Although appearances are important all over the world, in Britain, Scandinavia, and North America how you look is not regarded as an infallible indicator of how you are going to speak and act. In New York or London, for example, a cab driver is as likely to get a large tip from a man in torn jeans as from one in a good suit. So don't judge a book by its cover.

Unpopular uniform   Letter 26

FROM JAPAN ABOUT **FRANCE**

> *We have offered our factory workers here in France fashionable free clothing (shirts and windcheaters) with their own names on the front and the company's logo on the back. We believe that it helps good communication by making employees easily identifiable. We are very surprised that so few of our French staff have ordered these garments. Back in Japan, everyone is proud to wear our logo.*

Appearance is important to the French—they take it seriously—and that's not to say that your clothing isn't attractive. Company attire is unusual in French companies, because employees see their choice of clothes as reflecting their individuality. The Walt Disney Corporation got a similar surprise when it opened "Euro Disney" outside Paris. Its thirteen-page dress code, which gave clear rules about what staff should and should not wear, and which had been accepted without problems in the U.S. and Japan, was received first with incredulity and secondly with hostility by its French employees, who saw these rules as an infringement of their personal liberty.

The French also prefer a certain degree of privacy, even in the workplace, which means that they don't particularly like clothing that tells the whole world their names or who they work for. You'll find the same love of privacy reflected in offices too, where French middle managers prefer the privacy of their own individual offices to the open floor plan favored in many East Asian companies.

LETTER 27

Shoes stay on your feet in most places of work, but in some cultures, when your host takes you to dinner or on a special visit, you should be prepared to remove them.

Removing shoes   Letter *27*

FROM POLAND ABOUT **JAPAN**

We've heard the Japanese remove their shoes indoors. As foreigners, will we have to do the same?

An American I met who worked a lot with Japanese in the U.S. said he could always tell when Japanese colleagues were approaching his office: he could hear them shuffle along the corridor because they always changed into slippers at work.

As a visitor you certainly won't have to remove your shoes in offices, but if you are visiting Japan, South Korea, or Thailand and see shoes lined up outside a public building or private home, take yours off too and line them up neatly with the others. Another clue is the presence of slippers lined up and ready to wear. You should also remove your shoes if you visit mosques and many temples or shrines in North Africa, the Middle East, or

Asia. As shoes and hosiery are going to be so much on display, it's a good idea to make sure that yours will stand up to inspection. Sometimes when you've taken your shoes off, slippers will be provided for you to borrow, but you can't be sure of this. And a final note on the fascinating subject of socks—the Japanese have a super-smart type that separates your big toe from the others so you can wear them with flip-flops. Isn't that a cool idea?

IN A NUTSHELL: *Dress*

GLOBAL BUSINESS STANDARDS

Being neat, clean, and well-groomed is a must. It's a sign of self-respect, and respect for the people you meet. (Being quietly fashionable and elegant would be nice but for some of us, despite our best efforts, this remains merely a distant dream.)

Men: Suit and shirt. Tie may be optional in some cultures.

Women: In non-Muslim and moderate Muslim countries, a suit with knee-length skirt and modest blouse is a safe bet. Variations on this theme are infinite.

GLOBAL WARNINGS

Women should not assume trousers will be accepted (or fashionable) everywhere. To be on the safe side, take a skirt and pantyhose with you and see what women are wearing when you get there.

Shorts: No, they are not acceptable, not even knee-length "city shorts," and even if you have a beautiful bottom. Shorts are for the beach and playing tennis.

Jeans: They are best avoided unless it's your day off and you're still young.

- **Argentina:** Appearances are very important. Elegant and good-quality clothes and shoes confer status. (See Letter 25.)
- **Australia:** See the Global Business Standards. Clothes reflect a tendency to informality.
- **Austria:** See the Global Business Standards. There is a tendency to formality in dress and good quality is important.
- **Belgium:** See the Global Business Standards.
- **Brazil:** Clothes, especially women's, are a little more informal than in some other South American countries. Executives, especially in big cities, dress more formally. Much weight is given to your appearance. (See Letters 22 and 25.)
- **Canada:** Extreme cold in winter means it is essential to take warm clothes and footwear. However, fur coats may be regarded with disapproval.
- **China:** See the Global Business Standards. Solid white is traditionally worn at funerals, solid red at weddings. (See Letter 24.)
- **Denmark:** See the Global Business Standards. The usual style is informal, and the priority is comfort rather than elegance. (See Letters 22 and 25.)
- **Finland:** The priority is warmth and comfort rather than elegance. (See Letter 25.)
- **France:** Appearances are very important. Elegant and good-quality clothes and shoes reflect and confer status. (See Letter 26.)
- **Germany:** See Austria.
- **Hong Kong:** See the Global Business Standards. (See Letter 24 and China.)
- **India:** Heat means that jackets and ties are often abandoned in the summer. Leather jackets, ornate leather belts, and so on are not acceptable to many Hindus (the cow is sacred). Avoid pictures of pigs or dogs on T-shirts or ties because they are offensive to the Muslim minority. (See Letter 23.)
- **Indonesia:** Adhere to the Global Business Standards in large cities (a jacket is usually optional). Dress is less formal outside urban areas. Modest dress is especially important for women in this largely Muslim country. (See Letters 23 and 27.)

- **Italy:** Appearances are very important. Elegant and good-quality clothes and shoes reflect your status. (See Letters 24 and 25.)
- **Japan:** Very conservative/formal business attire is the norm. Remove shoes in private homes and traditional restaurants. Women wearing short or tight skirts will have a problem sitting on the floor in traditional restaurants. (See Letters 26 and 27.)
- **Mexico:** (See Letter 25.)
- **Netherlands:** See the Global Business Standards.
- **Norway:** See the Global Business Standards. Standards of dress are relatively informal. The aim is comfort and warmth rather than elegance. (See Letter 25.)
- **Poland:** See the Global Business Standards.
- **Russia:** Extreme cold in winter means it is essential to take warm clothes and footwear.
- **Saudi Arabia:** Pictures of pigs or dogs on T-shirts or ties are inappropriate. Pigskin articles offend Muslim sensibilities. Westerners should not try to adopt Saudi dress, but dress extremely modestly. Long, loose skirts and tops are advised for women, not trousers. Buttoned shirts (and no neck jewelry) are standard for men. (See Letters 23 and 27.)
- **South Africa:** Dress conservatively, including long-sleeved shirts and ties for men, skirts for women. Trousers for businesswomen are not very common. In winter take warm clothing, because houses can be cold.
- **South Korea:** There is a South Korean joke that all South Korean males are born in three-piece suits. Foreign businessmen should wear a dark, conservatively tailored suit, white shirt, and tie. Women should wear a conservative suit, skirt, and blouse. Remove shoes in private homes and restaurants. (See Letter 27.)
- **Spain:** See Argentina. (See Letter 25.)
- **Sweden:** Businesspeople generally dress less formally than in Southern European or South American cultures. The aim is comfort rather than elegance. In private homes most people remove their shoes. (See Letter 25.)
- **Switzerland:** See Austria.

- **Taiwan:** See the Global Business Standards. Jackets may be optional in summer. See China. (See Letter 24.)
- **Thailand:** Appearance is seen as a reflection of status. Conservative business dress is expected, although a jacket may be optional in summer. You should remove your shoes in private homes and restaurants, so make sure your socks are hole-free. (See Letter 27.)
- **Turkey:** See the Global Business Standards. Businesswomen should dress modestly, especially away from the main cities (this is a Muslim country). (See Letter 27.)
- **UK:** See the Global Business Standards. Appearance is not seen as a reliable reflection of status. Dressing inconspicuously is a priority for men. (See Letters 23 and 25.)
- **US:** See the Global Business Standards. Appropriate business attire depends on the job, the industry, the particular company, and on the region. Informality increases as you move westward. Appearance is not seen as a reliable reflection of status. Unlike in Europe, women usually wear pantyhose to work when wearing skirts and dresses, even in high temperatures. (See Letter 21.)
- **Venezuela:** See the Global Business Standards. (See Letter 25.)

Manners

Being well-mannered is not simply learning a lot of "dos and don'ts." It is not just about etiquette, which to me conjures up pictures of maiden aunts discussing the correct way to hold a teaspoon. The whole question of good manners is a much more important issue, for in essence it is about showing consideration for the feelings of others, about putting yourself in someone else's shoes (or sandals), and respecting their ways of thinking and behaving, especially if you are in their country and even when they are in yours.

You can't talk about good or bad manners in isolation, because they impinge on many aspects of life. For example, is it polite or impolite to show an interest in an individual by asking personal questions? Does it show good manners and consideration for fellow participants' valuable time to get straight down to business at a meeting, or is it a sign of rudeness and lack of respect for the people you hope to do business with? Your answer will depend on your cultural background.

You are always going to run the risk of breaking some unwritten rule when you visit a foreign country. (I have lived in Sweden for fifteen years, but I never remember to take off the paper before presenting flowers to someone. Somehow I've never been able to accept that it is good manners to press a bunch of slimy stalks into someone's hand.) Luckily, most people will not worry about such minor breaches of etiquette.

However, there are some sure-fire ways of upsetting people, and they are the same wherever you find yourself. Directly or indirectly criticizing someone's country—its customs, its food, its efficiency, and the appearance of its citizens would be pretty certain ways of putting an end to any business plans. Another example of bad manners guaranteed to annoy is to display a complete lack of knowledge of, or interest in, your hosts' country or culture. Consequences of this ignorance can have practical consequences. For example, your letters addressed to the city formerly known as Bombay may not be delivered, as the name has been changed to Mumbai. Such mistakes can also result in a rapid cooling in relations if, for example, you assume the businessman from Karachi is from India rather than Pakistan, and your visitor from Vancouver is from the U.S. rather than Canada.

Even less acceptable than ignorance is arrogance. Never assume your culture has possession of the moral high ground, or that the citizens of another country are any less proud of their culture than you are of your own. The attitude that "we do things better where I come from" is easily detected and very much resented. It is also the ultimate in bad manners.

LETTERS 28–29

Being well-mannered implies having at least a basic knowledge of the country and people you are doing business with. There are so many websites devoted to the culture, history, and news of every country that there is no excuse for ignorance.

Is the U.K. UnKnown? Letter 28

EGYPT ABOUT THE **U.K.**

We had a visitor from the U.K. recently, and before his presentation I introduced him as an Englishman. He corrected me and said he was a Scotsman. I felt I'd put my foot in it, and would like to know what I'd said wrong.

There's quite a big difference. Despite being so small, the United Kingdom is divided into four countries: England, Scotland, Wales, and Northern Ireland. Although the traditions that bind them are very strong, each country has a separate identity, and this sense of national separateness has been strengthened recently as political power has passed from London to the national assemblies.

Scotland has always had its own legal and education system, and in the shops you can spend both English and Scottish money. In Wales, the national identity is very much tied up with the ancient Celtic language of Welsh, while until very recently Northern Ireland's bloody history has set it apart both from the rest of the U.K., and its neighbor, Ireland. The term *Great Britain*, by the way, refers only to mainland Britain and doesn't include Northern Ireland.

People from the U.K. are very proud of where they come from and will usually correct you if you get their nationality wrong. They can spot nationals from other parts of Britain by their accents, but this isn't easy if your native language isn't English. So if you don't know exactly where your visitor comes from, you can always avoid the problem by calling him or her "British."

American miss? Letter 29

FROM JAPAN ABOUT THE **U.S.**

I've heard that people from Brazil and Canada may be offended if I use the term American *to refer only to the people who live in the United States. Is this so?*

What we call each other is a sensitive matter. When many people use the term "American," they mean someone from the U.S.—which is strange when you think about it, as many countries make up the two American continents. After all, if we refer to someone as "European," we are aware that he or she can come from one of many different countries and cultures.

Even the term *North Americans* is not specific enough, for that includes Canadians and Mexicans. Latin Americans often call people from the U.S. and Canada *gringos*, which no longer carries the anti-American tone that it had in the past. (And some Latin Americans even use this term to describe people from Germany and the north of Europe.)

In Britain, we often refer to people from the U.S. as *Yankees* or *Yanks*, and in contrast with most of the rest of South America, Argentineans and Uruguayans will often use the term instead of *gringo*. However, the terms *Yankees* and *Yanks* are not popular in the U.S., because people from the southern states don't regard themselves as "Yankees" at all!

I've heard a Canadian say that citizens of the U.S. should really be called *Usians*, but somehow I don't think it will catch on. Instead, if you talk about U.S. Americans, Canadians, Brazilians, and so on, nobody should be offended.

LETTERS 30–31

How you should talk to customers or colleagues and what it's acceptable to talk about are aspects of communication that people from different cultures have very different ideas about. (You can read more about how we communicate, and the language we use to do so, in Chapter 4.)

Just too loud?   Letter *30*

FROM JAPAN ABOUT THE **U.S.**

I was very surprised on my first visit to the United States to be spoken to as if I was a very stupid child by people who do not seem to be able to moderate their voices. Why do they speak so loudly?

What is regarded as an acceptable vocal volume varies enormously from culture to culture. Americans do tend to make themselves heard more than some other people as they are up-front communicators who aren't used to hiding their feelings. They put a value on self-expression and on an individual presenting his or her ideas clearly, and they want to be heard when they speak. But they are not alone in this. Germans may speak more loudly than some fellow Europeans like Finns or Swedes, and the volume of an animated discussion in Italy can also be pretty high. In other cultures where quietness and modesty are valued, such as Japan, Indonesia, or Thailand, loud voices are seen as a breach of good manners, and speech is usually more moderated. But don't confuse loudness with rudeness. Where loud voices are the norm they are simply regarded as a reflection of the speaker's involvement in the subject.

But a final thought has struck me. English speakers faced with foreigners whose native language is not English may wonder if they are being understood. Perhaps the Americans you met spoke as they did in the (mistaken) belief that the louder they spoke the easier you would find it to understand them. And to turn to the point you make about being spoken to as if you were a child: I think this can be a mistaken way to help non-native speakers of English understand the language. In an effort to "simplify" the language people sometimes remove key articles of grammar, or speak what amounts to baby talk to foreign visitors. The intention is to be helpful but the speaker comes across as patronizing.

Horror, shock!   Letter *31*

FROM THE U.S. ABOUT **SPAIN**

I was recently in Spain and commented after a meal how much I disliked bullfighting. I realized from the reactions of my Spanish counterparts that they didn't agree, but I feel I have a right to my opinion.

Of course you have a right to your opinions, but not a heaven-made right to express them if you know they are going to upset other people. A wonderful English noblewoman, Lady Mary Wortley Montagu, wrote in a letter in 1755, " . . . fig leaves are as necessary for our minds as for our bodies, and 'tis as indecent to show all we think as all we have."

That doesn't mean you have to lie about your convictions, but try to avoid getting into discussions that could become heated. When faced with a question that could lead to trouble, there is usually a diplomatic answer if you can think quickly enough. I hope you can select the preferred alternative in the example below.

Question: "Don't you think that our health service is the best in the world?"

Alternative answer 1: "No, I don't. Ours is obviously much more efficient, and our nurses are prettier too."

Alternative answer 2: "Luckily I haven't been ill during my time here, so I really don't have much firsthand experience. But I passed an impressive white building on my way from the airport. Was that a hospital? Does it have a good reputation?"

The ultimate bad manners are to criticize, directly or indirectly, the country where you are a guest. If you do—expect fireworks!

LETTERS 32-35

Rude behavior in your culture is not necessarily rude in another. The "rules of the game" may be quite different to what you are used to.

Just too busy . . .   Letter *32*

FROM SPAIN ABOUT THE **U.S.**

We have a new colleague from the U.S. in our office. Naturally we want to be friendly, but he only talks about work and does not seem to want to take the time to get to know us. Some of us think he's rather rude, but is this a cultural thing?

It's hard to say how much it is the individual's personality that affects his behavior and how much it's the culture he comes from. It's quite a stressful situation finding oneself in a new culture, especially if you are the only foreigner in the workplace, and individuals react to stress in different ways. Some mask their uncertainty with an overly confident manner; others hide themselves away from social contact.

However, there may be cultural differences at the root of what you perceive as rudeness. U.S. Americans, like the Germans, take their work very seriously, and it is important to them that they are seen as efficient and hard-working. During the working day socializing will often take a backseat to work, whereas in your own culture and in those of Southern Europe and Latin America socializing is an integral part of the job. American culture is sequential, meaning that people prefer to do one thing at a time, and for Americans business comes first and then pleasure. Where they do try to combine the two, at a "working lunch," for example, the emphasis will be mostly on the business at hand and less on the social or culinary aspects.

So don't take his seeming lack of interest in you as a sign of rudeness. Include him in your lunchtime meals, and tell him jokingly that when he leaves his desk talking shop is forbidden. There are few people of any culture who do not appreciate genuine friendliness.

. . . or too tired?   Letter *33*

FROM FRANCE ABOUT **JAPAN**

On my recent visit to Japan, the top manager at the meeting where I presented my proposal appeared to sleep during my entire speech. He didn't have any comments to make or questions to ask afterwards, so I doubt he heard a word I said. I found his behavior very disconcerting and indeed rude. Do you have an explanation for it?

Unless he was snoring loudly, you don't actually know he was asleep. In Japan, sitting with one's eyes closed in meetings is quite common. It usually means that you are listening carefully, not that you are tired or bored. The Japanese are good listeners, and it's likely that he was simply concentrating deeply on what you were saying. If you were speaking in English, and not his native language, he may have needed to listen particularly intensely. Or he may not have understood any English at all and was concentrating on what the interpreter said. It is quite common for senior managers not to play an active role in business discussions, but to leave the practicalities to their subordinates, who may have a better command of English and a more detailed knowledge of the business under discussion. It would be wrong to interpret his behavior as reflecting lack of interest or deliberate rudeness.

This also underlines the need to socialize with the Japanese and not to place so much value on the midday meeting or presentation. It would be a good idea to invite the manager and his subordinates to dinner, as it's often during these "social" occasions that senior Japanese open up and become more receptive to new ideas.

Yuck . . . no thanks!   Letter 34

FROM THE U.S. ABOUT **SOUTH KOREA**

On my first visit to South Korea a few years ago I made a real mistake. I was offered tea a couple of times before a meeting, but I refused because I don't like tea (or coffee either, come to that). I found out later that I had created a very negative impression and was regarded as a rude foreigner. Let that be a warning to others!

The act of eating and drinking with another person is not simply about the simultaneous consumption of calories, but it provides an opportunity to help build or strengthen a relationship. In individualist cultures like yours, you expect to gratify your own specific tastes, which is why going to U.S. fast-food restaurants is such a stressful experience for many Europeans, who find it difficult to choose between twenty different types of coffee. In the majority of other cultures, the offering and acceptance of food and drink has a symbolic value, and if you reject the offered coffee or candies out of hand, you are also rejecting the person who is doing the offering. When traveling anywhere abroad, try to forget some of your likes and dislikes if you can and accept offers of food and drink, for acceptance can be the first step to getting to know someone better. (And after all, we aren't talking about eating monkey brains here.)

By the way, visitors to your office in the U.S. would probably appreciate being offered refreshments. They might even think that *not* being offered anything was rude. So even if you can't offer the full spectrum of beverages and cold drinks, do remember to offer something simply as a friendly gesture.

To queue or not to queue? Letter 35

FROM ENGLAND ABOUT **GERMANY**

Why is it that in some countries queuing is respected and others it's not? I find it very irritating when I travel to Germany and other people barge ahead of me in queues for the elevator or for a table at a restaurant.

You've got me there! I really can't explain the origins of queuing, and can think of no historical reason why the British, Canadians, and U.S. Americans should take so naturally to it while the Germans, Italians, Japanese, and South Koreans, and the peoples of North Africa and the Middle East, for example, avoid it wherever possible. Italian friends tell me that in many cases queuing is considered a slow and cumbersome way of getting things done, although being British I find the alternatives worse. In England, one of the few times people become angry in public (except at football matches) is when someone tries to jump a queue. It's regarded as a sure indicator of lack of moral fiber. The Swedes are also queuers. As I mentioned in Chapter 1, when you go into any kind of shop in Sweden, whether you want to buy half a pound of cheese or a fur coat you have to take a numbered ticket and wait for your number to come up before you go up to the counter to do your business.

But we have to accept that what is a rule of polite behavior in one country does not automatically apply in another one. There are no global absolutes when it comes to what is polite, and the best we can do when we're traveling is to keep an open mind on the subject.

IN A NUTSHELL: *Manners*

GLOBAL BUSINESS STANDARDS

Good manners mean you:

Give people from other cultures the benefit of the doubt if they break *your* rules.

Stay open-minded. Be prepared to modify your behavior and your preconceptions when further information or evidence becomes available about the manners of your target country.

Show an awareness of and interest in the history, customs, and so on of your "target" country.

Be prepared to explain and/or apologize if you break their rules.

Take time to listen to people; pay close attention to what they say and do not say.

Thank people when they are helpful.

Try to learn at least a little of the language.

Reciprocate as far as you can (hospitality, favors, gifts, and compliments).

Keep in touch after you have gone home.

GLOBAL WARNINGS

Never directly or indirectly criticize any aspect of a foreign country to a native of that country.

Never believe for a minute that only your culture has all the right answers.

Below you will find (usually) only one example of good and bad manners for each country. There are, of course, many more.

- **Argentina:** Good manners: showing personal interest in a new acquaintance. Bad manners: pointing with a finger; when indicating something, use the whole hand. (See Letters 29 and 32.)
- **Australia:** Good manners: not mistaking good manners for formal manners. People do not stand on ceremony. Bad manners: "talking big," boasting.
- **Austria:** Good manners: being punctual. Bad manners: being very informal; moving to first name terms at the start of a relationship.
- **Belgium:** Good manners: being aware of the two main language groups, Flemish and French. Bad manners: an outsider approaching an individual employee without checking with his or her manager first.
- **Brazil:** Good manners: showing personal interest in a new acquaintance. Bad manners: rushing business. (See Letters 29, 30, and 32.)
- **Canada:** Good manners: having material written in French when dealing with French Canadians. Bad manners: assuming that Canada is just like the U.S. (See Letters 29, 30, and 35.)
- **China:** Good manners: showing special respect for older people. Bad manners: losing your temper in public under any circumstances. (See Letter 30.)
- **Denmark:** Good manners: arriving punctually. Bad manners: disparaging the royal family.
- **Finland:** Good manners: arriving punctually. Bad manners: interrupting a speaker.
- **France:** Good manners: allowing the most important person to enter a room first. Bad manners: asking personal questions that may be regarded as intrusive; drinking too much. (See Letters 30 and 33.)
- **Germany:** Good manners: being punctual. Queuing is *not* a sign of good manners as it is in many other countries. Bad manners: being very informal; moving to first name terms at the start of a relationship. (See Letters 32 and 35.)

- **Hong Kong:** See China.
- **India:** Good manners: allowing time for things to develop and not rushing. Bad manners: questioning or challenging people senior to you.
- **Indonesia:** Good manners: speaking in a low and modest voice. Bad manners: rushing the getting-to-know-you process and getting down to business too fast. (See Letter 30.)
- **Italy:** Good manners: showing generosity to new acquaintances and visitors, and reciprocating to such behavior. Bad manners: drinking too much. (See Letters 32 and 35.)
- **Japan:** Good manners: speaking in a low and modest voice. Bad manners: "talking big"; losing your temper. (See Letters 30, 33, and 35.)
- **Mexico:** Good manners: taking a personal interest in others, acknowledging they have an identity outside of work. Bad manners: shying away from physical signs of friendliness, for example, backslapping or a pat on the arm. (See Letters 29 and 32.)
- **Netherlands:** Good manners: knowing that Holland is not another name for the Netherlands but is just a part of it. Bad manners: treating subordinates in a less than egalitarian way.
- **Norway:** Good manners: being on time. Bad manners: not understanding that silence may mean that a Norwegian is considering a point (has not really finished speaking) and interrupting.
- **Poland:** Good manners: displaying generosity wherever possible, and reciprocating in kind. Bad manners: criticizing "sexist" attitudes in the country.
- **Russia:** Good manners: see Poland. Bad manners: addressing someone by first name only; asking someone not to smoke.
- **Saudi Arabia:** Good manners: ignoring any veiled women not introduced to you by someone else. Bad manners: refusing offered refreshment; asking about the health of someone's wife or daughter. (See Letters 30 and 35.)
- **South Africa:** Good manners: praising the natural beauty of the country. Bad manners: raising your voice or adopting an aggressive manner.

- **South Korea:** Good manners: allowing the most important person to enter a room first. Bad manners: refusing an offer of refreshment. (See Letters 34 and 35.)
- **Spain:** Good manners: avoiding direct confrontation or blunt refusals. Bad manners: criticizing bullfighting. (See Letters 31 and 32.)
- **Sweden:** See Finland. (See Letter 35.)
- **Switzerland:** See Austria.
- **Taiwan:** See China.
- **Thailand:** See Japan. (See Letter 30.)
- **Turkey:** Good manners: showing respect for older people. Bad manners: directly confronting a fellow worker in the workplace and risking open conflict.
- **UK:** Good manners: being aware that only citizens of England are English. Inhabitants of England, Wales, Scotland, and Northern Ireland are all British. Bad manners: not joining in social conversation (small talk). (See Letters 28, 30, and 35.)
- **US:** Good manners: being punctual. Bad manners: smoking without asking permission. (See Letters 29, 31, 32, 34, and 35.)
- **Venezuela:** Good manners: starting conversation with inquiries about health of family. Bad manners: wandering into the kitchen to help with a meal. (See Letters 29 and 32.)

Socializing

For anyone with a job, the days and weeks divide themselves neatly into working days and weekends, working hours and leisure time. However, what we call the *working day* in fact contains a fair amount of non-working activity. People who work from home with the aid of a PC and Internet access often complain that it is the social aspect of working life which they miss most. That includes the chat in the elevator up to the office, the shared coffee break, the trip to the cafeteria, or walking to the garage at the end of the day. All of these give opportunities for social interaction with colleagues, getting to know others, and building relationships. Where work ends and socializing begins is difficult to say. In some cultures it is taken for granted that groups of (male) employees will meet after work, and in Japan and South Korea, for example, drinking after work is vital if you are going to be accepted as one of the team, for there is no work without people, and people are social animals.

It's even more difficult to draw the line in an unfamiliar culture. Is the ten minutes of small talk and gossip at the beginning of a meeting in a Southern European or Latin American company a waste of time, as the Germans, Swiss, and Finns tend to believe, and a social activity better suited to after work? Or is it instead an effective way for employees to share important information that will improve the internal communication process at the company and reduce the time people would otherwise have to spend writing e-mails to each other? (In certain British companies, the management has prohibited the sending of internal e-mails on Fridays and has encouraged employees to speak to coworkers on the phone or face-to-face. They consider it more cost-efficient.) Or perhaps sitting and chatting before the meeting strengthens employees' interpersonal relationships, thereby helping to reduce the possibility of conflicts. All of these interpretations are possible.

It is asking for trouble if a foreigner tries to change the way local people socialize at work, as many expatriate managers have found. Foreign managers in unfamiliar cultures are quick to see the savings in time and money that removing opportunities for social contact would bring, but they aren't as good at identifying the reactions of their employees. Trying to change or get rid of the tea break in a British factory, discontinuing the *nomunication* parties in Japan (see Chapter 3), and shortening the lunch breaks in France in the name of productivity were all measures made by new foreign bosses that revealed a lack of understanding on their parts of what was important to the local workforce. The measures also created a lot of resentment, and resentful employees, as every HR boss knows, do not usually give their best to their jobs.

Wherever we work, there are few jobs that do not require at least some contact with others. To put it simply, the better the contact, the more smoothly work proceeds—it's not rocket science. And when you spend time socializing, whether with colleagues or customers, you're more likely to be able to discover the individual behind the job, and ironically, perhaps, achieve a better working relationship.

LETTERS 36–38

Social occasions are intended to bring people together and can help establish a good relationship with new colleagues, customers, or suppliers. However, these occasions may not be entirely anxiety-free.

Karaoke complex   Letter 36

FROM BRAZIL ABOUT **CHINA**

I will be traveling to China soon to visit one of our customers, and have heard from people who've been there that I'm likely to have to sing karaoke. I have a terrible singing voice, and the thought of singing in front of a lot of people terrifies me. What on earth shall I do?

Karaoke clubs originated in Japan, but have now spread to the rest of the world, and are especially popular in China, Taiwan, and Southeast Asia. The clubs provide a microphone and music videos with the background music to popular songs, but you have to provide the vocals to accompany them. Not knowing the words to Chinese songs will be no excuse, as most bars have some popular English or U.S. American songs and you should be able to recognize at least a few tunes.

Don't worry about making a fool of yourself. The important thing is not how you sound but that you join in, and in doing so get to know your hosts better. It's often difficult to make friendly contact with people from other cultures, especially if you don't speak their language, but singing for each other is a way of doing this. Of course, you can try to get out of singing, but your hosts will appreciate it if you show you are prepared to let them see your more human side by joining in and performing (even at the risk of embarrassing yourself). Even if you're dreadful, you'll still get a round of applause, and if you've warned them that you're not a good singer, they only have themselves to blame if they go home with headaches!

Sauna suspicion   Letter *37*

FROM SPAIN ABOUT **FINLAND**

Is it true that if you want to do business in Finland you have to be prepared to visit a sauna?

It's certainly not required for foreigners to take a sauna with business partners, but for Finns it is a natural way to get to know each other or to spend time relaxing with family or friends after a day at work. There are absolutely no sexual overtones in its use in Finland as there may be in other countries. You'll find saunas everywhere; you'll find them at all hotels and swimming pools, in nearly all apartment buildings, and in many private homes. There is even a story that the first thing that Finns did after arriving to work on an engineering project in equatorial Africa was to build a sauna!

If you are invited to share a sauna, don't worry: The sexes are usually segregated, and although Finns and Scandinavians in general are quite relaxed when it comes to nudity, nobody will think it strange if you wear a towel or a swimsuit.

No go go-cart   Letter *38*

FROM INDIA ABOUT **SWEDEN**

My company is collaborating with a Swedish company, and when I was there recently I was invited out by the manager to share in a departmental social evening. I was very surprised to find that we were to spend the evening go-cart racing, and that everyone in the department, men and women, young and old, were expected to join in. I found it an uncomfortable experience.

Business socializing usually reflects both national and corporate cultures. In Sweden, social equality is a powerful concept, both politically and in the workplace. A manager is a manager behind the desk, but after working hours is neither better nor worse than his or her subordinate.

Indeed, even the word *subordinate*, implying a strict hierarchy where some are higher than others on the corporate ladder, is regarded as rather old-fashioned in Sweden. To be good at your job as manager, you also have to be a team player.

Coming from a society like India, with a very strict hierarchy both inside and outside the workplace, you might find this free mixing of bosses and workers rather an uncomfortable experience involving a loss of prestige on your part. And both workers and managers alike will probably share this feeling of unease.

However, in egalitarian Scandinavia, and on the other side of the world in Australia and New Zealand, any lingering shreds of hierarchical status disappear when away from the workplace, and if you ride go-carts, enter the company orienteering competition, or attend the annual picnic, no attention will be paid to whether you're vice president or a junior technician, male or female, young or old. The important thing is that you join in. If you lose the race or get grass stains on your trousers, nobody will think the worse of you.

LETTER 39

Building a relationship involves giving and taking, whether time, gifts, or hospitality. But sometimes the relationship becomes unbalanced and someone does all the taking, or just as bad, all the giving.

Generosity requires reciprocity   Letter 39

FROM SWEDEN ABOUT **ITALY**

My job frequently takes me to Italy, where I'm constantly surprised by the generosity shown me by Italians. They not only buy me coffee, but they invite me for drinks and dinner and then drive me to my hotel. When I offer to pay for myself they just shake their heads. I'm not quite sure how to react.

To pay for oneself or split the bill is very un-Italian, so forget it! However, it is important to understand the Italian attitude, which is not simply one of generosity but also of reciprocity. If an Italian pays for you today, it's expected that you'll pay for both of you next time. It can be difficult to get your wallet out before an Italian, and the same applies in other Southern European countries and in Mexico and South America. In a restaurant you can perhaps have a quiet word with the waiter between courses and ask for the bill. When the Italian takes out his wallet, whisper, "Già fatto," which means *already paid*. At the bar the magic words are "Pago per tutti," which means that you pay for everyone.

This can take some getting used to if you are accustomed to splitting the bill, which happens routinely in Scandinavia, the U.S., and the Netherlands. But don't simply accept generosity and not return it or you'll end up with a reputation as a skinflint and a "taker." You will also find that invitations become fewer and personal contacts cooler. Don't risk it!

Note that women may find it harder to reciprocate directly, because Italian gallantry may have difficulty with women picking up the bill. Instead, take a present on your next visit. A box of chocolates for the whole department would be appropriate, or give individual presents from your own country to the people you have had the most contact with.

LETTER 40

*A **satisfactory balance between working life** and private life is something most of us want. But how it is defined varies from culture to culture.*

Business is pleasure?   Letter *40*

FROM MEXICO ABOUT **U.S. MULTINATIONALS**

I find the insistence of some large multinationals on after-work and weekend social activities all in the name of "team building" a threat to family life. Work is work, but employees need time with their families too, and evening meetings and residential and weekend courses can weaken family relations. They can also lead to infidelity and divorce, all for the sake of "building relationships at work."

In countries where people are brought up to believe that the family, their personal interests, and their social network are more important than work, where who you *are* is more important than what you *do*, encroachment on employees' free time is not welcome. This may go against some multinationals' corporate cultures, which seem to require that work comes before all else in their employees' lives. This insistence on work above all is certainly part of the Protestant work ethic (although of course not all multinationals have roots in Protestant countries) and is particularly strong in the U.S, the U.K., and Scandinavia. Work, and socializing with colleagues and customers, also has a high priority in Japan, South Korea, Hong Kong, and China. However, Catholic countries in Latin America, European countries in the Mediterranean region, and Muslim cultures have different traditions, and work is not given the same, almost semi-religious, status.

Most companies realize that building relationships between employees is good for business, and one way to do this is to run employee-only courses and workshops that encourage colleagues to socialize and get to know each other better. However, companies must also realize that they will lose staff if they are seen as unsympathetic to their employees' families and their needs. I know of one large Scandinavian company that, when it opened subsidiaries in Belgium, another Catholic country, organized weekend courses for its employees. That all ended, however, when the irate spouses of these employees wrote a series of complaints to the executive management making the same case that you did.

Corporate policies regarding human resources management and staff training are often made at a headquarters located on the other side of the world, with roots in a culture that has little in common with their employees' cultures. You should follow the example of the Belgian wives and husbands and make your opinions felt to those in authority. It's in the interests of the company to have a happy workforce, and management won't have that if employees' spouses feel antagonistic to their partners' employers.

IN A NUTSHELL: *Socializing*

GLOBAL BUSINESS STANDARDS

Eating at a restaurant with a new business acquaintance is a widely accepted way of getting to know one another. (See also Chapter 3.)

Don't leave visitors in their hotel rooms with nothing to do night after night. (Would you like it?)

If you are a male entertaining a female visitor, she may be more comfortable if you include your wife or a female colleague in any after-work invitations.

When you have established friendly relations with someone, remember to keep in touch.

Send greetings on important local holidays, the occasional postcard from your hometown, and an e-mail or a phone call now and again just to keep the relationship alive.

GLOBAL WARNINGS

When entertaining foreign guests, do not offer or be persuaded to provide prostitutes.

Do not go to shady bars or clubs. As well as being unethical, such visits will cause you and your company untold trouble if the authorities or the press find out.

- **Argentina:** Soccer matches are popular opportunities to socialize. Cafés are centers of social life. (See Letters 39 and 40.)
- **Australia:** A common way of building relationships among customers and suppliers is attending sporting events together. It is not uncommon to be invited home for a meal. (See Letters 38 and 39.)

- **Austria:** Time with family and friends is likely to take priority over socializing with colleagues after work or on weekends. On their birthday, they take in a treat to share with their colleagues.
- **Belgium:** Time with family and friends is likely to take priority over socializing with colleagues after work or on weekends. (See Letter 40.)
- **Brazil:** Soccer matches are popular opportunities to socialize. Informal patterns of socializing, including barbeques, are popular. Having fun is important. (See Letter 3.)
- **Canada:** Time with family and friends is likely to take priority over socializing with colleagues after work or on weekends. Climate will limit social activities in winter months, especially at night.
- **China:** As well as "ordinary" visits to restaurants, Chinese banquets may be held for important foreign visitors. Everything from visits to karaoke clubs to classical Chinese opera may be offered to visitors. (See Letters 36 and 40.)
- **Denmark:** Many restaurants and pubs, even in small towns, act as social centers. (See Letters 38, 39, and 40.)
- **Finland:** A visit to a sauna is a popular way for friends and business acquaintances to relax. (See Letters 37, 38, 39, and 40.)
- **France:** Visits to events like opera, ballet, or concerts reflect the French interest in culture.
- **Germany:** See Austria.
- **Hong Kong:** See China.
- **India:** Indian cities do not offer much nightlife outside the international hotels. Visitors may be entertained at Indian homes. Male and female colleagues will not socialize together outside work. (See Letter 38.)
- **Indonesia:** Most corporate entertaining is in restaurants. (See Letter 40.)
- **Italy:** Sociability is a highly prized personal quality. Italians in towns spend much time out walking, chatting, and meeting friends in the evenings. Soccer matches are popular opportunities to socialize. (See Letter 39.)
- **Japan:** Business and social lives mingle. Singing in karaoke bars after work is popular. During visits to traditional restaurants, make

sure you remove your red "toilet slippers" before returning to table. Female spouses are rarely invited. (See Letters 36 and 40.)

- **Mexico:** Soccer matches are popular opportunities to socialize. Mexicans in towns spend much time out walking, chatting, and meeting friends in the evenings (as in the south of Europe). Much socializing is with others of the same sex. (See Letters 39 and 40.)

- **Netherlands:** Time with family and friends is likely to take priority over socializing with colleagues after work or on weekends. When it is their birthday, the Dutch take in a treat to share with their colleagues. (See Letter 39.)

- **Norway:** See Canada. (See Letters 37, 39, and 40.)

- **Poland:** Social activities often include the copious consumption of vodka.

- **Russia:** See Poland.

- **Saudi Arabia:** Social activities never include the copious (or otherwise) consumption of vodka or any other form of alcohol—it's illegal. The host's duty of hospitality is taken very seriously. Female visitors are rarely included in invitations, unless it's to meet other women. (See Letter 40.)

- **South Africa:** Sporting events, like cricket and rugby matches, give opportunities to socialize.

- **South Korea:** Business and social lives mingle. Cafés and restaurants are popular places to socialize. *Salons* are expensive drinking places, and a group hires a room. Much socializing is with others of the same sex. (See Letters 36 and 40.)

- **Spain:** Bullfighting and soccer matches are popular opportunities to socialize. (If you can't stand the sight of blood, politely decline an invitation to a bullfight rather than risk fainting and having to be carried out in the midst of the spectacle. It has happened.) Spaniards in towns spend much time out walking, chatting, and meeting friends in the evenings. (See Letters 39 and 40.)

- **Sweden:** Visitors may be left very much to their own devices in the evenings. When it is their birthday, Swedes take in a treat to share with their colleagues. (See Letters 37, 38, 39, and 40.)

- **Switzerland:** See Austria.

- **Taiwan:** See China.
- **Thailand:** Consideration for others and generosity (with time and invitations) are highly prized. They should be returned in kind. (See Letter 36.)
- **Turkey:** The host's duty of hospitality is taken very seriously and generosity can be overwhelming. Visitors should try to reciprocate. (See Letter 40.)
- **UK:** Working after hours and on weekends is widely accepted, which limits time for socializing with colleagues, customers, and family. Pubs are important places to meet and talk at both lunchtime and after work. (See Letter 40.)
- **US:** Informal socializing patterns are widespread. Working after hours and on weekends is widely accepted, which limits time for socializing with colleagues, customers, and family. There are strict rules about giving and receiving corporate hospitality. (See Letters 39 and 40.)
- **Venezuela:** It is important to spend time after work in face-to-face contact with colleagues and customers to maintain relationships. (See Letters 39 and 40.)

Gift Giving

What's the idea behind giving someone a present? Whether it's giving Great-Aunt Maud a box of lace hankies or your customer a bottle of twenty-year-old whisky, the purpose is the same. It's about cementing a relationship, and in business it often marks the end of the first stage in the getting-to-know-you process. Of course, once a personal relationship is established gifts may continue to be exchanged. Birthdays are taken seriously in some countries, and the sixtieth birthday in South Korea and Japan or the fiftieth in Sweden is a good time to show you remember a colleague or business contact. Festivals like Christmas, the Lunar New Year, and the Russian New Year are occasions when local populations exchange gifts, and even if these festivals are not part of your own tradition you can show your interest in another culture by joining in.

Gifts are also exchanged at company level. Sometimes this takes place at the initial meeting and at other times to mark the signing of a contract, the completion of a project, or the anniversary of a merger. These gifts, as well as the gifts you give to foreign business acquaintances, should show your own country and company in a favorable light. Company-level gifts tend to be large and expensive, for example, works of art, furniture, crystal, or silverware, and usually become the property of the company rather than of the current CEO. However, they can be on a less grand scale and still be greatly appreciated. One international corporate headquarters in Europe looks forward to the annual delivery of a large box of the finest grapefruit from an Israeli company, while a certain Indian company enjoys the exotic gift of six boxes of shortbread cookies from Scotland every December.

But receiving presents is not always a simple pleasure. It may make you feel that you should respond by giving a gift too, by providing some sort of service, or by doing someone a favor. We're not talking about bribery and corruption here (unless the presents are particularly expensive and accompanied by expectations of advantage) but about reciprocity, about giving as well as receiving. The balance here is very fine; generous hospitality, great food, or thoughtful gifts are unlikely to be purely and simply expressions of friendship, but may also be a way of putting you under an obligation which, at some time in the future, you will be expected to repay.

In cultures where people put a great weight on doing business with individuals they know well and have long-standing relations with, as in China, Japan, and South Korea, frequent and generous present-giving is more common than in countries where "business is business" and where agreements are regarded as being between institutions rather than the people who represent them. Businesspeople from the U.S, the U.K., Scandinavia, and Australia often dislike being put under obligations, believing like the U.S. economist Milton Friedman that "There is no free lunch." The solution, of course, is to repay the giver in kind, giving gifts of a similar value to the ones received, but that can be expensive, or even impossible if corporate rules limit the expenditure on gifts or entertainment.

When exchanging gifts on a personal or corporate level, the present itself shouldn't be the point of the exercise. Like your mother always said, "It's the thought that counts." Presents should be an outward symbol of inner feelings, whether the feelings are of respect, gratitude, or simple goodwill. (And if you cannot claim to feel at least one of these emotions, you shouldn't really be trying to establish a relationship, let alone be giving gifts.)

But if a gift is a symbol of something deeper, it should be chosen with care. At the very least it should be inoffensive. That doesn't sound like much of a requirement, but it is surprisingly easy to choose an inappropriate gift. You couldn't go far wrong with a key ring, you would assume, but if it is made of leather or pigskin it would be offensive to practicing Hindus or Muslims. And don't give a desk set to a superstitious Chinese colleague, for if it includes a paperknife, this suggests the severing of a friendship. Illustrated books about your own country would appear to be an excellent gift, as indeed they are, but check that there aren't any pictures of the porcine variety in them if you are sending them to Muslim countries like Saudi Arabia, Indonesia, or Pakistan. Anything in a set of four (the word *four* in Japanese sounds like *death*) is to be avoided in Japan, and if the front cover has a photo of that famous nude statue in your capital city, the book may be considered pornographic in more straight-laced societies.

At its best, a personal gift should reflect an interest in and knowledge of the recipient's tastes and preferences. The Japanese are masters at finding out this sort of information, so they can send the right type of monogrammed golf balls, or tickets to the most sought after ballet. Once you know what to give there only remains to find the gift, and the Internet provides all sorts of gift-giving services to make the process easier. You can send books and CDs, already gift wrapped, reserve tickets, order ties or scarves, or (my personal favorite) have enormous bars of chocolate bearing your logo or photo delivered to individuals you want to impress.

Choosing presents is not an easy task, whether they are Christmas presents for relatives you see every day or gifts for people from a culture that is not your own and who you may not even have met. You do not want to be judged as either a skinflint or a distributor of bribes. The exchange of gifts should be about giving and taking, and sharing thoughts and experiences. It's a ritual that deserves to be taken seriously.

LETTERS 41–44

Choosing a suitable present can require a certain degree of knowledge of the recipient's culture as well as his or her personal tastes.

Beautiful booze   Letter *41*

FROM THE U.S. ABOUT **EUROPE**

Does alcohol make a good present when traveling overseas? It's always convenient to buy at duty free shops or on the plane, but I don't want to offend anyone.

It all depends on the sort of contact you have with your European colleague. I wouldn't take alcohol to anyone I didn't already know quite well, for you may find you cause offense. Your foreign colleague or customer might come from a long line of teetotalers, be a reformed alcoholic, or have religious reasons for not drinking.

However, if you're invited to someone's home, flowers and a bottle of wine or liqueur are usually acceptable, although alcohol is forbidden to Muslims, Buddhists, Hindus, and Sikhs. If you're invited to a French or Italian colleague's home, it's probably best not to take wine because it's like carrying coals to Newcastle—they have plenty of their own, thank you. It's also probable that if your host is French, he or she will know a lot about wine and may have chosen the wines to accompany the food. If you do want to take a bottle, take some drink (not wine) produced in your own country; in your case, bourbon would be appropriate. If you want to leave a present for a group of people, a bottle of booze is not a good idea. I mean, on the practical level, short of drinking it in the office, how are they going to divide it fairly?

Meaning of flowers

FROM SWEDEN

I travel quite widely to different countries, and I have always hesitated about giving flowers because I've heard there are many superstitions about their number or color. Yet as there are flower shops all over the world they would make a convenient gift.

You're right about the superstitions surrounding flowers. Every country seems to have one or two flowers that are associated with death or funerals and that are not suitable as gifts. Unfortunately, these flowers differ from country to country. In Thailand, for example, you shouldn't give marigolds or carnations, while in Japan it's camellias, lotus blossoms, and lilies that are taboo. There you should also be careful not to give flowers in groups of fours or nines, numbers that are considered to bring bad luck. In China, all white or yellow flowers are unlucky. Frangipani blossoms are associated with funerals in India, but in Italy and France it's chrysanthemums. In these European countries you should also give an odd number of stems for good luck. This can be very confusing, so consult a local florist for advice before making your selection.

But in fact you should consider whether flowers make a good gift in a business context. In many countries in Europe and Latin America, for instance, flowers are usually given only to women, and in Taiwan and many other Asian countries they are given mostly to sick people. However, when invited to someone's home they are usually acceptable as a present to the hostess. In some countries, like Sweden, Poland, and Germany, it's customary to remove the paper before handing over the flowers. (This raises the awkward question of what to do with the paper. The accepted solution seems to be taking the crumpled damp paper home with you.)

Holiday goodies?

FROM ARGENTINA ABOUT **SAUDI ARABIA**

I'd really like to send a present to some people in our office in Riyadh to mark the end of Ramadan. When is this and what should I send?

At the end of Ramadan comes the Eid al-Fitr, one of the two Islamic holidays. During Ramadan, which is a very special month for the world's billion Muslims, including those in Saudi Arabia, Indonesia, and Turkey, most believers fast from dawn to dusk. The purpose of this long fast is to teach self-control and to give Muslims a greater understanding of what it means to be poor and hungry. The end of Ramadan, as you would expect at the end of a long fast, is marked by feasting and lots of get-togethers.

In the case of the Eid, it can be tricky to know when to send something; the date changes from year to year because the Islamic calendar is lunar-based. However, a phone call to your nearest mosque or a look at a few Internet sites should provide you with the information you require. As a general rule, the date for the start of Ramadan moves ten or eleven days forward every year in the international calendar.

The idea of sending a small present, perhaps of something edible like candy or cake (making sure it's well packed and not going to arrive as a soggy mess or a heap of crumbs) to acknowledge this important occasion is a really nice thing to do. It shows an awareness of, and an interest in, what is important to other people.

Thank you all . . .   Letter *44*

FROM SPAIN ABOUT **CHINA**

> *I'll be traveling to China for the first time soon and don't know what to do about presents. I'll probably be involved in meetings with the whole company (ten people). Should I give them each a present?*

Sometimes it's easier to give a present to a whole group rather than to individuals, especially if you haven't had much contact previously. Also, gift giving can be a sensitive issue in China, so presenting a gift to an organization rather than an individual is a good idea. If you want to leave a present for a group of people, a whole department, for example, something edible like a basket of fruit or a large container of candies or cookies from your own country is a good choice. You could also buy something for the office, like some flowering plants or a set of cups and saucers. Alternatively, pens with your company logo or books (in the appropriate language) also make good presents. Make sure you present the gift to the most senior manager and only after business has been concluded.

In China, it is common for business acquaintances to dine out together, and an invitation to a meal may be a suitable gift; in this case, include everyone in the company. Ask for advice about suitable Chinese restaurants at your hotel, or invite them (and an interpreter if necessary) to a Western restaurant for a change. With a gift like this you'll have the chance to get to know each other on a personal level, which will be a plus.

LETTER 45

Receiving a present—the process of receiving and opening a gift—also requires some thought.

For me? You shouldn't have . . .   Letter *45*

FROM THE NETHERLANDS ABOUT **JAPAN**

I know the Japanese take the exchange of gifts very seriously, and if I'm presented with something I want to make sure I know how to act graciously.

In Japan, as in many other countries in East Asia and South America, you usually don't open the gift in front of the giver. Bow and thank him or her, then put the present to one side. Open it only if urged to do so, and in that case don't tear the wrapping off wildly like a seven-year-old on his birthday but show some restraint. In fact, don't tear the paper at all if you can help it, as this may give the impression that you lack self-control, which is a shortcoming most Japanese find hard to accept. Remember that the symbolic aspect of gift giving is far more important than the present itself, and showing too much haste or over-eagerness to see what you've been given doesn't reflect well on your attitude to business relationships.

The Japanese take gift giving seriously and may try unobtrusively to find out about the individual's hobbies or interests to ensure that they give an appropriate gift. If you have the chance to do some similar intelligence work and give your Japanese contacts presents that reflect their personal tastes, this would reflect well both on you and your company.

LETTERS 46–47

Declining a gift (or not offering one) can be difficult. However, there are times when, for various reasons, people feel they have no choice. But this is not a step to be taken lightly.

Reconsider?   Letter 46

FROM JAPAN ABOUT THE U.S.

I was extremely surprised when the special present I had given to a manager in the U.S. was returned to me with a note saying that the recipient regretted that he was unable to accept it. Is this simply a formality, and should I present the gift a second time?

No, the recipient means what he says (as most U.S. Americans do), although you must not take his refusal personally. There can be a number of explanations. Many countries have laws that expensive gifts must be declared for tax purposes, while some companies have very strict rules governing the cost of the presents that their employees can accept or give. In the cultures of the U.S., Australia, and New Zealand, and indeed most of Europe, there isn't the same emphasis on gift giving as a symbol of a growing relationship between individuals and companies that there is in Japan. Instead, there is a fear of finding oneself under an obligation to someone if one accepts expensive gifts, especially if company rules forbid reciprocating with gifts of the same value.

In other countries, like Russia, China, Hong Kong, Taiwan, and Thailand, your gift may at first be politely refused so that the recipient doesn't appear greedy. However, both parties know that the gift will be offered a second and perhaps even a third time, and then the recipient will usually "give in," but this is not the case in the U.S.

Present or bribery?   Letter 47

FROM AUSTRALIA ABOUT **INDIA**

My company is building a factory in India and the red tape is a nightmare. We have heard that if we give a small "present" to a local official this will save us a lot of bureaucratic problems. This sounds suspiciously like bribery to me. What do you think?

That's hard to say. In India you may pay for a service before rather than after, receiving it. Would your objections be less if the services you mention were described as "consultants' fees" or "advisory services"? It may not affect the ethics of the situation you find yourself in, but the fact is that the official involved will probably be earning a fraction of what you earn in a country without the safety net of social benefits. This is his way of making a decent living, and the giving of such "presents" for services is a widely accepted and expected custom in many relatively poor countries in Africa, Asia, and Latin America. Most people from the more affluent countries of Western Europe, Canada, the U.S., Singapore, and Australia, where laws to prevent bribery and corruption are rigorously enforced, can manage to provide for their financial needs in other ways.

I'm not condoning the practice of bribery; I'm just saying that it's all too easy to judge others by the alien standards of one's own culture. On the other hand, paying this "fee" might give the signal that the company is going to be a ready source of "backhanders" to unscrupulous entrepreneurs. It's a good idea for a company intending to operate in a "foreign" culture to think carefully about which local customs it is going to adopt *before* it decides to do business there. (See Chapter 8, the section on "Ethics," for more discussion.)

IN A NUTSHELL: *Gift Giving*

GLOBAL BUSINESS STANDARDS

It is risky to say the following are *always* acceptable gifts; if you really try it *is* possible to find a pen with an offensive motif or a thoroughly unsuitable book. They can also be too expensive or too cheap. However, if you exercise a bit of commonsense the following are acceptable everywhere: pens, books, local handicrafts (e.g., crystal, pewter, wood), key rings, electronic devices (calculator, radio, CD player), and gifts for children (when visiting someone's home).

GLOBAL BUSINESS STANDARDS

The following are *usually acceptable* gifts: music (CDs and tapes); candy; flowers (see Letter 42); invitations to a meal; tickets to a show, sporting event, etc.; and stamps.

Gifts to mark local festivals show a respect for another culture/religion: Christmas, New Year, the Lunar New Year, Diwali, Eid al-Fitr, and Hanukkah are all marked by gift giving. If you want to send something, check the dates (some move from year to year) and that the gift and/or greeting card is appropriate.

Say "thank you" as if you mean it—even if the gift is not to your taste. Always phone or write a thank you note, and reciprocate with a gift of similar value.

GLOBAL WARNINGS

Inappropriate gifts include the following: personal items for members of the opposite sex, anything that offends religious sensibilities (e.g., alcohol for many Buddhists and most Muslims, pigskin for Muslims and Jews), and anything manufactured in an "unfriendly" country (e.g., China/Taiwan, Japan/South Korea).

In any country it may be difficult to tell the difference between a present and a bribe. Make sure you stay on the right side of the law.

Don't go empty-handed if invited to someone's home.

- **Argentina:** See the Global Business Standards. Knives symbolize the severing of a relationship, so they don't make good presents. (See Letters 42, 43, and 45.)
- **Australia:** Gift giving does not have an important role in business. They won't expect anything (except perhaps something with a company logo) unless they invite you to their homes. Overly expensive gifts can cause embarrassment. (See Letters 46 and 47.)
- **Austria:** Overly expensive gifts can cause embarrassment. Giving cheap or shoddy presents with logos is worse than giving nothing at all. (See Letter 47.)
- **Belgium:** See Letter 47.
- **Brazil:** Knives symbolize the severing of a relationship, so they don't make good presents. Clocks and watches are not popular either. (See Letters 42 and 45.)
- **Canada:** Overly expensive gifts can cause embarrassment. (See Letter 47.)
- **China:** Clocks, handkerchiefs, and cutting utensils do not make welcome gifts. Presents may be refused at first, to be accepted on the second or third time offered. (See Letters 42, 44, 45, and 46.)
- **Denmark:** Overly expensive gifts can cause embarrassment. Handmade articles are usually appreciated. (See Letter 47.)

- **Finland:** See Denmark.
- **France:** Avoid gifts with large logos. Choose gifts that imply the recipient has cultivated tastes, for example, books, tickets to some cultural event, or a good liqueur from your own country. (See Letters 41 and 42.)
- **Germany:** (See the Global Business Standards. See Letters 42 and 47.)
- **Hong Kong:** See China.
- **India:** Expensive gifts aren't usually exchanged. (See Letters 42 and 47.)
- **Indonesia:** Gifts are important. They're usually opened in giver's presence. Refusing a gift may be seen as an insult. If given an expensive gift, reciprocate with something of similar value. (See China if dealing with Chinese-Indonesians.) (See Letter 43.)
- **Italy:** See France. (See Letters 41 and 42.)
- **Japan:** Gift giving is an important part of a business relationship. Anything in groups of four symbolizes bad luck. Gift should be presented with both hands, and be tastefully and neatly wrapped. Hotels often provide a gift-giving service. Don't use white, black, or blue—colors associated with funerals—to wrap presents; use red, pink, or yellow instead. (See Letters 42, 45, and 46.)
- **Mexico:** Gift giving does not have an important role in business. They will not expect anything (except perhaps something simple with the company logo) unless the relationship has already become quite friendly. Overly expensive gifts can cause embarrassment. (See Letter 42.)
- **Netherlands:** Gift giving does not have an important role in business. Overly expensive gifts can cause embarrassment. (See Letters 45 and 47.)
- **Norway:** See Denmark.
- **Poland:** (See the Global Business Standards. See Letter 42.)
- **Russia:** Gifts are given on holidays and special occasions. Birthdays are important and you should know the birthdays of your important business contacts and colleagues. Usually gifts are not given until the end of a transaction or meeting, and they are not usually

opened in front of the giver. Most Russians will refuse the offer of a gift at first, but accept when urged. (See Letter 46.)

- **Saudi Arabia:** Don't admire something too enthusiastically—Saudis are generous and may give it to you. You are not expected to take a gift to a Saudi home, but a personal one for your host (not hostess) will be appreciated. (See Letter 43.)

- **South Africa:** Do not go empty handed if invited to someone's home (which is not unusual in South Africa). Personalized gifts after the relationship is established are appreciated.

- **South Korea:** Gifts are important, but they don't need to be expensive. They will not be opened in the giver's presence. The sixtieth birthday is very important and requires a present. (See Letters 42 and 45.)

- **Spain:** Gifts are never presented at a first meeting, but are given after the relationship has developed. Articles with large logos are not generally appreciated. (See Letters 44 and 47.)

- **Sweden:** See Denmark. Fiftieth birthdays are important and call for presents. (See Letter 42 and 47.)

- **Switzerland:** Do not give watches or clocks as they make the best there. (See Letter 46.)

- **Taiwan:** See China.

- **Thailand:** See Indonesia. (See Letters 42, 45, and 46.)

- **Turkey:** Gifts should be presented to older/more senior people first. (See Letter 43.)

- **UK:** Gift giving does not have an important role in business. People won't expect anything (except perhaps something simple with the company logo) unless they invite you to their homes. Overly expensive gifts can cause embarrassment. (See Letters 46 and 47.)

- **US:** See U.K. There are strict corporate rules and regulations regulating the value of gifts offered and received. Overly expensive gifts can cause embarrassment. (See Letters 41 and 46.)

- **Venezuela:** See the Global Business Standards. (See Letters 42 and 45.)

Chapter 3

Eating and Drinking Together

On one level, eating and drinking is simply about survival. But on another level, sharing food and drink is a social activity, an experience that forges links between people and brings them closer together.

It's not surprising, then, that when businesspeople are trying to make new contacts or cement old ones that eating and drinking come into the picture. This is especially true in cultures that put a lot of emphasis on interpersonal relationships, including the countries of the Middle East, Asia, Latin America, and Southern Europe. A formal dinner or banquet means that people have to spend at least a couple of hours in each others' company without talking business, which in high-tech, fast-moving Western cultures like the U.S. and Canada is in itself a novelty. The food provides the perfect topic of conversation; it gives people something to discuss without the risk of upsetting anyone (unless you are tactless enough to make disparaging remarks about a local delicacy).

Formal dining, like all rituals, entails strict patterns of behavior. For example, at a dinner in Japan or South Korea you should fill your neighbor's glass but not your own (see Letter 52), and when taking afternoon tea in England you should eat your scone after your sandwich but before your cake. These actions are not important in themselves, but as a part of a shared ritual they bring people closer together, and they may even mark a change in the relationship between host and guest—from stranger to acquaintance or acquaintance to business partner.

The opposite of the formal dinner or banquet (slow food?) must be fast food, and for people who take food and the rituals surrounding them seriously, like the French and Chinese, fast food may be seen as a threat to a whole way of life. To some French people, a McDonald's opening in town is no less than a menace to civilization as they know it! We can all get passionate about what we eat and drink, but if you don't come from the culture in question, the excitement generated is incomprehensible. The English can actually quarrel about whether it's better to put the milk in the cup *before* the tea is poured or *after*. Malaysians wait in eager anticipation to taste the first durian fruit of the season (an experience one Westerner described as "like eating *blancmange* in a toilet"), and the first ripe fruits fetch sky-high prices.

When you are abroad, accompanying a colleague to a local restaurant can mark a step forward in your relationship, but there are also pitfalls, especially if you are offered a local delicacy. For example, in Sweden there is a traditional Thursday lunch offered by most restaurants every week of the year. To non-Swedes it may seem like a rather bizarre combination: A thick pea and ham soup served with mustard, accompanied by *punsch*, a sort of sweet liqueur (although at workplaces the *punsch* is usually omitted from the menu), followed by pancakes served with jam and whipped cream. Actually, it tastes better than it sounds, and if it's really cold outside this is a wonderful way of keeping warm!

A U.S. businessman I know was visiting a large company for a week, and every day he accompanied his manager to the staff dining room, where there was self-service. On Thursday, the traditional fare was on the menu and he decided to try it. Being a polite man, the manager let his guest go before him in the queue, but unfortunately there was no indication on the food counter of the order in which the food was to be eaten. So naturally enough, the American poured the pea soup over his pancake. His Swedish manager, seeing too late what had happened and not wanting to embarrass his guest, said nothing and simply did the same. I believe they both enjoyed the meal.

I like this story because it shows that the manager had grasped the point of sharing a meal and building a relationship. In this context it wasn't really important what they ate, but that the two of them shared some non-business time and started to get to know each other. When you are eating and drinking you temporarily stop being an employee and remember that underneath the business suit you are simply a person with the same need of food and drink as everyone else. This need, and the wish to eat and drink in the company of others, is one of the common denominators of being human.

However, I do hope that as their relationship progressed the Swede felt able to tell his guest about the mistake—pancakes really do taste better with jam and cream!

◆ MORAL

Eating and drinking together is a reminder of our common humanity. It is a chance for a relationship to move from the purely business level to the personal.

Food

Food can be a challenge for everyone when traveling abroad. It may be a positive challenge: "How can I find room for another one of those delicious squid sandwiches/strawberry bonbons/sheeps' eyes?" Or it may be a negative one: "How can I possibly stomach that disgusting cheese soufflé/goat curry/chocolate cake?"

In short, one man's meat is another man's poison. There are all kinds of reasons why people find a food distasteful. There are religious taboos, of course, that can never be ignored, as McDonald's found to its chagrin when it fried French fries in beef fat without revealing this fact to its Hindu and vegetarian customers. Generally, though, international food chains are forced to take local tastes and religious prohibitions into account, so in India your hamburger is likely to be made of mutton instead of beef, and in France you can order a glass of wine with your Big Mac. There are also ethical questions that can affect food habits. Many younger people in North America and Europe who are concerned about animal welfare are becoming vegetarians, and foods like veal and *foie gras* provoke strong reactions because they are perceived as causing animals unnecessary suffering.

However, the main reason we are dubious about sampling food when we are traveling abroad is simply that it is new to us.

Local people have a tendency to present their foreign visitors with local delicacies to sample (usually from the best of motives), so you may be faced with an unfamiliar food whose taste or texture you find odd or unpleasant. Many Asians, for example, think that cheese, especially the strong smelling kind, is strange tasting stuff, whereas many Europeans wonder how Indians and Thais can manage to eat such fiery dishes. The British are amazed that Swedes can eat meatballs with jam rather than ketchup, while Belgians can't understand how the British can put vinegar instead of mayonnaise on their French fries. In short, the world is full of foods that people from other cultures find bizarre.

What I find most exotic is where the culinary traditions and tastes of one culture get transposed onto another. In England, the local fish and chip restaurant (a staple dish for the last century—cod in batter with chips, otherwise known as French fries in the U.S.) near my parents' home now offers egg rolls and chips. The egg roll is a vaguely Chinese-ish concoction of bean sprouts wrapped in a crispy coating. I've heard you can buy pizza topped with squid or seaweed in Japan, while the specialty of the corner pizzeria here in Sweden is *Pizza Indienne*, which combines the more traditional tomato and onion base with a topping of curried chicken and banana. I haven't tried it yet—I don't think my palate could stand the excitement.

If you simply can't avoid tasting a local delicacy that doesn't appeal to you, the recommended course of action is to cut it up small and swallow it quickly (and make sure you don't ask what it is!). However, if you really can't stomach something you've been offered you can always blame a food allergy: "Sorry, I'm allergic to squid/dog/ buttermilk/Coca-Cola." This is one of those situations when a "white lie" is better than the truth.

LETTERS 48–49

The links between specific foods and certain religious traditions are strong ones. While some foods are associated with celebrations, others are forbidden to groups of believers.

Acceptable to all?   Letter 48

FROM ARGENTINA REGARDING **GLOBAL EATING HABITS**

We're organizing a large conference here with participants from around the world and of every possible religion. I don't want to offer food that some of the participants can't eat for religious reasons, and I was wondering if you could recommend some foods that everyone can eat without problems.

As you probably know, pork is forbidden to Jews and Muslims, and many Hindus find it distasteful too, so don't expect many orders for bacon and eggs at breakfast. For Hindus, the cow is sacred, so they are not allowed to eat beef or veal. From the point of views of religious prohibitions, chicken is fine with most people—even if chicken feet, which are a delicacy in China, are not equally prized elsewhere. Lamb is also acceptable to meat-eaters of all faiths. However, the more religious followers of Judaism and Islam only eat meat from animals slaughtered in a special way; this meat is called *kosher* and *halal* meat, respectively. Jews who keep kosher will not eat dishes that contain both meat and milk, so they won't eat lamb and beef served in a creamy or cheesy sauce. And similarly for many Jews, a meat dish followed by ice cream would be a forbidden combination. In addition, Jews who keep kosher use separate dishes for meat and dairy, so disposable paper or plastic plates would be a good option.

Fish (but not shark or the kind of shellfish that has claws) is acceptable to the people of most faiths, but remember that eating fish dishes that contain bones requires considerable skill with the knife and fork and your visitors may be used only to chopsticks. Finally, as many people of all nationalities are vegetarian for religious, moral, or health reasons, it is a good idea to check that there is an option for them at every meal. The golden rule, especially if your visitor can't read the menu, is to explain what ingredients are included in a dish so he or she can make an informed choice. If this is a large conference and you expect a lot of people, you may consider having the menu translated into a number of key languages and having them available for those who are interested.

Forecasting fasting   Letter *49*

FROM RUSSIA ABOUT **INDONESIA**

The last time my colleague was in Indonesia, he arrived in the middle of a Muslim fast, which caused some problems. I don't want to do the same. Can you tell me when it is?

Indonesia is a predominantly Muslim nation, although there are substantial numbers of Hindus, Christians, and Buddhists too. The fast you refer to takes place in the Muslim month of Ramadan and as the Islamic calendar is lunar-based, and the start of Ramadan is marked by the first visible appearance of the crescent moon, an event that is very difficult to predict exactly. However, as a general rule, the date for the start of Ramadan moves ten or eleven days forward every year in the international calendar, so you should check on the Internet or call the Indonesian embassy before you go.

During Ramadan, most believers fast from dawn to dusk (exceptions are made for children and the sick, among others). If you're doing business in the afternoon with people who haven't eaten since sunrise, don't expect them to be at their best. Also, make sure that when *you* eat lunch, or even nibble on a mid-morning snack, you don't do so in front of people who have empty stomachs. That would be bad manners, to say the least.

It's also probably a good idea to avoid doing business on the last days of Ramadan, when the final preparations are being made for the big feast that marks its end.

LETTERS 50–51

People may avoid eating certain foods for a number of reasons, and not only religious ones.

One man's meat   Letter 50

FROM TURKEY ABOUT **GERMANY**

We've had a lot of visitors from Germany at our office over the last few years, and my colleagues and I have noticed that when we've been out to restaurants not one of them has ever chosen our national dish, lamb.

Lamb isn't a popular meat in Germany as, for reasons best known to themselves, many Germans and Swedes believe that mutton tastes like socks. This probably accounts for the avoidance of lamb you noticed in your German guests. I'm glad that you had the tact not to force your guests to sample something they really didn't like, even if you find (as I do) their distaste very odd.

Every country finds some of its neighbors' culinary preferences inexplicable. In France, horsemeat is widely eaten, while many people in other cultures find it distasteful. And while most Australians wouldn't dream of eating horse, they consider kangaroo fine. Dog in some parts of China and in South Korea, snake in China, and grasshoppers in South Africa are all delicacies in their own countries, but most foreigners would hesitate to try them.

But the fact remains that refusing food or drink (unless for religious or moral reasons) can be regarded as rude. An answer like, "I'm sorry, I don't like tea/coffee" is not an acceptable answer in a business situation when you are offered a cup of either, even if you never touch the stuff at home. And the same goes for food. If urged, and especially if it's a national specialty, always accept a taste of everything, and do your best to swallow as much as possible. To do so not only shows a degree of determination that most business partners will appreciate, but it also displays an openness to your host's culture.

Sweet temptation   Letter 51

FROM THE U.K. ABOUT **JAPAN**

When we have groups of Japanese here at our hotel we try very hard to introduce them to English specialties, and generally we have had great success, especially with our fish and beef dishes. The exception is our puddings. The British are famous for their hot desserts, usually served with cream or custard, and our chef provides a wonderful selection. However, our Japanese guests won't touch them.

Japan is hardly the dessert capital of the world. The Japanese, like the South Koreans and Thais, aren't too keen on sugary or creamy puddings (and indeed the only egg custard dish the Japanese eat contains fish and vegetables), although tastes are slowly beginning to change. Ask your chef to provide a selection of fresh fruit, both home grown and from farther afield, for dessert. He can also offer small cookies or cakes to accompany coffee or tea. I'm afraid, though, you'll have to ask him to keep jam roly-poly, spotted dick, and bread-and-butter pudding for home consumption.

IN A NUTSHELL: *Food*

GLOBAL BUSINESS STANDARD

A vegetarian dish should be available on all occasions when you invite guests to eat.

GLOBAL WARNINGS

Many of your fellow beings find the following foods distasteful, so don't force them down your guests' throats, however delicious you find them yourself: horse, dog, snake, frogs, insects, and dairy products.

Foods forbidden to followers of some religions include:

Islam: Non-halal meat, pig meat, and shellfish that have claws.

Judaism: Non-kosher meat and milk, pig meat, rabbit, shellfish, frogs, shark, and meat and milk in same meal.

Hinduism: Beef and pork.

Buddhism: Meat and fish (vegetarianism is promoted but not demanded).

- **Argentina:** People are proud of the quality of home-produced meat. *Mate*, an herb drink with a caffeine kick, is popular. (See Letter 48.)
- **Australia:** Barbeques of home-produced meat are very popular. (See Letter 50.)
- **Austria:** Pork and pork products (like sausage) are very popular. Lamb is not. They pride themselves on their coffee and cakes. (See Letter 50.)
- **Belgium:** They may be even better cooks than the French, and they take food very seriously. They eat French fries with mayonnaise. Sterilized milk, and not fresh, is the norm.
- **Brazil:** A lot of meat is eaten here. Barbeques are very popular.
- **Canada:** There is a Gallic influence in French-speaking areas.
- **China:** There are many different cuisines because China is so big. Visitors may be served unexpected delicacies, like snake, dog, or sea slugs. Food is taken very seriously and people are knowledgeable about it. (See Letters 48 and 50.)
- **Denmark:** Danes are great fish eaters and avid coffee drinkers.
- **Finland:** See Denmark. Game, including reindeer, may be on the menu.
- **France:** Food is taken very seriously and people are knowledgeable about it. Sterilized milk (not fresh) is the norm in supermarkets. (See Letter 50.)
- **Germany:** See Austria.
- **Hong Kong:** See China.
- **India:** There are many different cuisines because India is so big. Food can be very spicy. (See Letters 48 and 49.)
- **Indonesia:** *Nasi goreng* (fried rice with shrimp, meat, and spices) for breakfast takes Westerners a bit of getting used to. Durian, an exotic fruit with a distinctive taste, is popular there. (See Letters 48 and 49.)
- **Italy:** Food is taken very seriously, and pasta is an important staple. This is a Mediterranean country, so typical ingredients include eggplant, onions, garlic, vine leaves, peppers, and tomatoes.

- **Japan:** People are great fish eaters and meat is not as popular. Dairy products are not common. Overly sweet desserts are not popular. (See Letter 51.)
- **Mexico:** Indigenous foods may be eaten along with foods introduced from Europe. Hot and spicy food is common.
- **Netherlands:** The Dutch are great fish eaters and coffee drinkers. Because of their colonial past, there are many Indonesian restaurants in the cities.
- **Norway:** Norwegians are great fish eaters and coffee drinkers. Game, especially elk, is often on the menu.
- **Poland:** Live carp are bought for Christmas dinner and usually kept in a bathtub until the big day.
- **Russia:** Russia produces world-class caviar and champagne (usually for export). However, choice is limited at restaurants. They eat a lot of ice cream, even in the depths of winter.
- **Saudi Arabia:** Dates may be served at business meetings. These may be stuffed with almonds (be careful if you are allergic) or they may not be pitted (be careful of your teeth). During the month of Ramadan, Saudis fast during the day and may even abstain from drinking water, so it would be considered rude to eat or drink in their company. (See Letters 48 and 49.)
- **South Africa:** Barbeques of home-produced meat are very popular. (See Letter 50.)
- **South Korea:** Food is often very spicy. Dog and snake may be on the menu. (See Letters 50 and 51.)
- **Spain:** Sterilized milk (not fresh) is the norm. They are great fish eaters, and the national dish of *paella* incorporates fish and shellfish. A Mediterranean country, typical ingredients include eggplant, onions, garlic, vine leaves, peppers, and tomatoes.
- **Sweden:** Some adults may drink milk with meals. They love salty licorice but usually dislike lamb. Game, especially elk or reindeer, is often on the menu. (See Letter 50.)
- **Switzerland:** Seeing the Swiss eat French fries with mayonnaise will shock ketchup fans.
- **Taiwan:** See China.
- **Thailand:** The food is very, very spicy. (See Letter 51.)

- **Turkey:** This is an eastern Mediterranean country, so typical ingredients include lamb, rice, eggplant, onions, garlic, vine leaves, peppers, and tomatoes. Turks are well known for their sweets, including specialties like *baklava*. (See Letters 48 and 49.)
- **UK:** *Tandoori chicken masala* is now the nation's most popular dish (according to a politician). The Empire strikes back with Indian, Pakistani, and Chinese restaurants on every Main Street. Tea is still the national drink. (See Letter 51.)
- **US:** Foreigners may find the portions served at restaurants enormous. The wide choice of cuisines in cities reflects the ethnic origins of immigrants to the country. Drinking Coca-Cola with meals is seen by the rest of world as an eccentric habit.
- **Venezuela:** Grilled fish and meat (beef and chicken) are popular. Goat is preferred in certain areas. Fried corn pancakes are a local specialty.

Drink

As you might expect, this section doesn't deal with the question of carbonated as opposed to non-carbonated drinks; few people get involved in discussions of the relative merits of soda versus lemonade. However, feelings can run very high when the subject turns to alcoholic drinks.

People get passionate about drinks—the Spaniards and Italians love their wines, the French call brandy *eau de vie* (the water of life), while the Scots can talk for hours about the relative merits of single malt and blended whiskies. However, to certain Christian sects, as well as to Sikhs and Muslims, alcohol is absolutely taboo. Its sale and possession are outlawed in several countries, such as Saudi Arabia and Iran, and from 1919 until 1933 the manufacture, transportation, and sale of alcoholic beverages was illegal in the United States. Why?

One reason is that people "under the influence" of alcohol do not follow the rules of normal behavior of their culture or religion. They may temporarily forget the usual constraints on the way they think or behave, and this can cause trouble. You just have to think of the behavior of drunken English soccer fans in Europe or the deaths and injuries caused by drunk drivers in most countries of the world to understand what I mean. Alcohol abuse can also be a major problem for companies and can result in accidents at work, reduced efficiency, and absenteeism when someone has a hangover. However, these financial losses pale when you consider the damage to a company's reputation that can result from a representative over-indulging during a social occasion. Irreparable damage can be done to both individual reputations and customer relations. And I know of few large corporations where this *hasn't* happened at one time or another.

Yet this lowering of normal barriers can also have positive results. Otherwise reserved, shy, or and inhibited people may feel it easier to express themselves once they've had a glass of wine or a pint or two of beer. The ancient Romans had a saying, *in vino veritas* (there is truth in wine), and alcohol can help people break out of the constraints imposed by work or social roles to speak more honestly and behave more openly than they would normally. Because of this, in countries as far apart as South Africa, South Korea, and Russia, social drinking is regarded as a good way for people to relax and get to know each other. It's a matter of degree, though. The boundary between behavior that is warm and frank and offensive and aggressive is a fine one, and individuals vary greatly in how they act when they have been drinking.

Unfortunately, this happy state of affairs, where colleague or customers learn to get to know each other over *saki* or scotch, applies only to half of the population. Businessmen who drink a lot with suppliers or customers are usually regarded as being sociable, while a businesswoman doing the same thing is regarded in many, perhaps most, societies as showing a lack of judgment and even poor moral character. This is grossly unfair, of course, but businesswomen, whether working at home or abroad, are used to being judged more critically than men (but this doesn't mean they like or accept it).

LETTERS 52–53

Specific rules and traditions are often associated with social drinking.

Pass the glass   Letter *52*

FROM BELGIUM ABOUT **SOUTH KOREA**

I know that drinking is an important part of both social and business life in South Korea. I've also heard that there are quite strict rules involved. Can you give me some of the more important ones?

Most South Korean men believe that the best way to get to know someone is to drink with him. (I say men, as businesswomen, whether South Korean or not, are not included in such drinking parties.) There are several well-kept rules, one of which is that the host of the event will first offer a glass to the most honored person. If this guest is much older, or very senior, the glass will be offered with two hands or with the right hand supported by the left. The person receives the glass in the same way, that is, either with both hands or with the right hand supporting the left one. The host will then pour the wine or spirits. As the drinking continues, all the guests are offered a glass, and when they finish the wine or spirits they give the empty glass to another person. During the evening everyone ensures he exchanges glasses with every other guest. Two things one shouldn't do are to add alcohol to a glass that is already filled or to fill one's own glass. The same is true in Japan.

Pub etiquette   Letter *53*

FROM CANADA ABOUT THE **U.K.**

I've read that when in England one should always buy "rounds" in pubs, even at lunch, meaning that you buy for the whole group you are with. That must mean that everyone consumes a lot of alcohol. I'm not used to drinking much and am worried how I'll manage.

Relax. It's true that the tradition is to take turns buying for the group you came in with, but there's certainly no law to say that what you consume must be the locally brewed "killer" beer or whisky. It's perfectly acceptable to order soft drinks or low-alcohol beer instead. The purpose of the exercise is not to drink each other under the table but literally to give and take, and as such it's not good to stay outside the round. If offered a drink, it's regarded as bad manners to say that you only fancy a tomato juice and you'll buy it yourself, thank you. And once you're "in" the round you don't have to accept another drink if you haven't finished the first one. Buying rounds is all about reciprocity, and it's not good for your relationships with the British or Australians if you're seen as either antisocial or plain mean with money. It's much better to buy one round too many yourself than to risk being thought tight-fisted.

And don't worry if one lunchtime or evening everyone doesn't have the opportunity to buy the others a drink. British people have an automatic drinks counter programmed into their brains, so they'll remember the next time you go to the pub whose round it should be. The only problem is that businesswomen might find it hard to be allowed to buy their round because of Britishmen's chivalry or chauvinism (the alternative you choose depends on your point of view). If this is a regular occurrence, reciprocate later by buying a small present—a plant for the office or a box of chocolates to be shared by the department.

LETTERS 54–56

Drinking alcohol always carries the risk of drunkenness. Indeed, this may be the whole point of the exercise!

Nomunication   Letter *54*

FROM TURKEY ABOUT **JAPAN**

A colleague recently back from Japan talked about nomunication, *but I don't understand fully what it means. It's something to do with drinking, isn't it?*

It is indeed. *Nomunication* comes from a combination of the Japanese verb *nomu*, to drink, and the English word *communication*, and it refers to the process of socializing and communicating when drinking. Japanese companies often organize *nomikai* (drinking parties) for their employees a few times a year. These are regarded not only as opportunities for drunken revelry but also as important occasions for building "team spirit." The process of drinking is actually more important than what you drink, so you can stick to tea if you want as long as you continue to pour sake, beer, or whiskey into the glasses of your Japanese colleagues. These parties also give employees a chance to communicate with the boss, who may otherwise be a distant and unapproachable figure. Work issues that cannot be raised in the very formal atmosphere of the office may be freely discussed here, and managers have a chance to find out what's really on their employees' minds.

The sober truth   Letter *55*

FROM THE U.S. ABOUT **RUSSIA**

I've been talking to a colleague who just came back from Russia, and he's been telling me about the amount of drinking that goes on there—and I don't mean Coca-Cola! How on earth does business ever get done if everyone's drunk all the time?

Most Russians are certainly not puritanical when it comes to alcohol, and it plays an important part in their social life in the same way that it does for businessmen in Poland, Japan, China, and South Korea. Sharing a few drinks may well help to build bridges between people, but having said that, it is certainly not compulsory to get blind drunk at every meeting!

Russians are hospitable folk and may well invite their Western guest out to dinner, and at every restaurant a bottle of vodka will almost certainly be on the table. After opening the bottle, the custom is that it will be finished (in part because many bottles don't have resealable caps). Vodka is poured into tiny glasses and drunk in one go, not sipped. At dinner there will always be toasts and speeches (you may want to prepare one for such an occasion), and if you don't want to over-indulge, drink only during the toasts. Otherwise, drink the fruit juice or water that will also be available. And make sure you eat, otherwise you certainly will get drunk.

A Russian friend said to me recently that at parties and dinners it is often the Western businessperson rather than the Russian who gets drunk, simply because the constant availability of all this alcohol is too much for his or her judgment. Another interpretation is that most visitors simply aren't used to the local vodka. However, it is ultimately up to foreign visitors, not the Russian hosts, to moderate their intake and to ensure that their judgment and their ability to function efficiently the next day at work are not affected.

| Drink until you drop | Letter 56 |

FROM ITALY ABOUT **CHINA**

I'll be going to China for the first time soon with a group of colleagues, and I'm reading a number of books about the country. In one book it says that a good host in China will try to get his guest drunk. In Italy we regard drunkenness as the ultimate in bad manners.

There is always the possibility of "culture clash" with such different attitudes to the same phenomenon. In your own country, and indeed in the wine-drinking cultures of the Mediterranean and South America in general, it is unusual to see open drunkenness in the streets or restaurants, and as you say, getting even mildly drunk is seen as the behavior of boors.

In China, guests are often invited out for meals or banquets. These are important social occasions, and they are usually incomplete without beer, rice wine, or spirits. Generally, the more everyone drinks, the more friendly and open they become as shyness diminishes. The same applies in Japan and South Korea, as well as the Sweden-Finland-Russia "beer and vodka belt," where alcohol helps these naturally rather reserved people communicate with each other. However, if you feel you can be friendly and open *without* alcohol, so much the better. Just make sure you leave a little of whatever you're drinking at the bottom of your cup or glass as an indication that you don't want any more.

LETTERS 57–58

Laws and traditions regulating the sale or intake of alcohol vary from country to country. It's good to be aware of just how different these may be to those you know at home.

Still Puritans? Letter 57

FROM FRANCE ABOUT THE **U.S.**

I'm going to work in the U.S. soon and have heard that there are extremely strict rules regarding drinking there. Is that true?

The U.S. is a big place, and different states and companies have different rules. In general, the attitude to drinking alcohol (including wine and beer) during working hours is certainly more negative than in France, where a glass or two of wine at lunchtime is the norm rather than the exception. You will find the rules just as strict if you travel north to Scandinavia, rather than west to the U.S., and if you venture to Muslim countries, or countries with large Muslim populations, it may be impossible to buy wine or alcoholic drinks at all. There are also differences in the opinions of physicians from different countries about what is regarded as acceptable intakes of alcohol, and Europeans applying for jobs in the U.S. who admit to drinking a little over a bottle of wine a day (not unusual in many Southern European countries) have been rejected on health grounds.

I must add that both McDonald's restaurants in France and restaurants in Disneyland Paris serve wine, but this isn't the case back home in the U.S. I suppose it's a case of "When in Rome . . . "

Why not wine? Letter 58

FROM SPAIN ABOUT **SAUDI ARABIA**

I'll be traveling to Saudi Arabia soon to meet our local representative. I know that here in Spain he enjoyed our local wines and wondered if I should take him a bottle.

That's not a good idea. The Saudi kingdom, with an almost 100 percent Muslim population, strictly prohibits alcohol. Although your representative enjoyed your excellent Spanish wines when in Spain, he certainly wouldn't want you to get in trouble by smuggling it into the country. Nor would he want to risk breaking the law himself, or risk his fellow countrymen finding out that he had broken one of the rules of their religion. The same would apply if we were talking about any Muslim nation, like Indonesia or Pakistan, but this applies particularly to Saudi Arabia, which has the strictest anti-alcohol laws in the world. Foreigners who are found guilty of running illegal alcohol operations face imprisonment and flogging under strict Islamic laws, and for Saudis themselves the punishments can be even more stringent.

IN A NUTSHELL: *Drink*

GLOBAL BUSINESS STANDARD

Drink if you must, but stop before you start to lose control. It is a wise person who knows his or her limits.

GLOBAL WARNINGS

Alcoholism is a sickness with a high personal and corporate cost. People living and working alone in a foreign culture with unfamiliar drinking traditions and (perhaps) cheap and available alcohol are particularly at risk.

If you are female, don't drink much (even if you could drink every man in the party under the table). Women who drink more than a sip or two will be judged more harshly than men. It may also be inappropriate for them to offer a toast.

Their religion forbids Muslims, Sikhs, Hindus, and Buddhists from drinking alcohol, but some believers may not interpret these laws strictly.

- **Argentina:** It is among the top wine producers (and consumers) in the world. (See Letter 56.)
- **Australia:** Australians produce their own wines and beer. Going out to a bar or "pub" for drinks with colleagues or guests is common. The tradition typically includes each person paying for a round of drinks for everyone in the group. (See Letter 53.)
- **Austria:** Austria produces its own wines and beers. Austrians are the second biggest beer consumers in the world (after the Czech Republic).
- **Belgium:** This little country produces its own beers—over 300 different kinds! (See Letter 52.)
- **Brazil:** Alcohol (wine or beer) is commonly served at both lunch and dinner, but public drunkenness is uncommon. (See Letter 56.)
- **Canada:** Wine is popular with the French Canadian community. (See Letter 53.)
- **China:** Getting drunk together (for men) is seen as creating a bond and as a step toward getting to know each other better. At a banquet, if the Chinese host proposes a toast, the guest should reciprocate. (See Letters 55 and 56.)

- **Denmark:** Social drinking in pubs (*krogar*) is popular after work and on weekends. Danes are big beer drinkers. At meals, wait until everyone has said *skål* before drinking.
- **Finland:** Lots of beer is drunk in saunas, and vodka is drunk with meals. (See Letters 56 and 57.)
- **France:** Drunks are rarely seen in public, even though much alcohol is consumed. Drunkenness is strongly disapproved of. Wine is often drunk at lunchtime. The French have the second highest wine consumption (per head) in the world. (See Letter 57.)
- **Germany:** Toasting is an important aspect of business dining in Germany. Don't start drinking without a toast. When raising a glass for the first drink, say *Prost*. Everyone must reply. Germany produces its own (mainly white) wines, beer, and schnapps. Germans are the third biggest beer consumers in world.
- **Hong Kong:** See China.
- **India:** The majority of Muslims, Hindus, and Buddhists do not drink for religious reasons. (See Letter 57.)
- **Indonesia:** See India. (See Letters 57 and 58.)
- **Italy:** Drunks are rarely seen in public here, even though much alcohol is consumed. Wine is often drunk at lunchtime. Drunkenness is strongly disapproved of. Italy has the highest rate of wine consumption (per head) in the world. (See Letter 56.)
- **Japan:** Getting drunk together (for men) is seen as creating a bond and as a step toward getting to know each other better. You should always fill your companions' glasses, never your own. (See Letters 52, 54, 55, and 56.)
- **Mexico:** Visitors should be aware that high altitudes (in Mexico City, for example) can exaggerate the effects of alcohol.
- **Netherlands:** The Dutch produce their own beers.
- **Norway:** There are strict (unwritten) rules about not drinking during the working day. (See Letter 57.)
- **Poland:** Getting drunk together (for men) is seen as creating a bond and as a step toward getting to know each other better. (See Letter 55.)
- **Russia:** Getting drunk together (for men) is seen as creating a bond and as a step toward getting to know each other better. Toasts are

usually long and heartfelt. If you are host or a special guest, prepare a toast in advance. Vodka is often an accompaniment to food. (See Letters 55 and 56.)

- **Saudi Arabia:** Alcohol is strictly forbidden for religious reasons. (See Letters 57 and 58.)
- **South Africa:** Drinking with colleagues and guests at both lunch and after work is quite common. Bars are mainly male preserves. Wines and beers are locally produced.
- **South Korea:** Most drinking takes place after work and during meals. Getting drunk together (for men) is seen as creating a bond and as a step toward getting to know each other better. (See Letters 52, 55, and 56.)
- **Spain:** Drunks are rarely seen in public here even though much alcohol is consumed. Drunkenness is strongly disapproved of. Wine is often drunk at lunchtime and in the evenings. (See Letters 56 and 58.)
- **Sweden:** There are strict rules about not drinking during the working day. There are also strict rules governing toasting in more formal gatherings where they drink *snaps* (vodka). Don't drink until the host has said *skål*. (See Letters 56 and 57.)
- **Switzerland:** Drunkenness is strongly disapproved of. After the toast has been proposed, look at your host, raise your glass, and say "To your health" (or you may say *prost* in the German-speaking region, *santé* in the French-speaking region, or *salute* in the Italian-speaking region). Drink after you have responded to the toast and have touched glasses with everyone present. Switzerland has the fourth highest consumption (per head) of wine in world.
- **Taiwan:** See China.
- **Thailand:** Beer or rice whisky is drunk, but drinking is generally less heavy than in South Korea and Japan.
- **Turkey:** Although a Muslim country, the sale and consumption of alcohol is not forbidden. However, it's not easy to find outside large cities. (See Letter 57.)
- **UK:** Buying "rounds" in pubs is seen as a way of being sociable. This country spends the second highest total amount on alcoholic drinks after Ireland. (See Letter 53.)

- **US:** The U.S. is a large-scale producer of wines and beers. There are restrictive laws governing alcohol purchase and consumption. You have to be over twenty-one to buy alcohol. (See Letters 55 and 57.)
- **Venezuela:** Beer is popular. Rum, produced in the region, is widely drunk. (See Letter 56.)

Mealtimes

When we are going to eat together with people from another culture, we tend to be nervous that somehow we're going to get things wrong. We fear that at that all-important dinner we will use the steak knife for the fish, suffer a bad case of hiccups or drink out of the finger bowl. This insecurity probably has its roots in childhood; when children get to a certain age mealtimes can become fraught as they are drilled in the rules of good behavior with comments like, "Elbows off the table," "Only your right hand to pass things with please," and "Don't stick the chopsticks up in the rice like that." Parents all over the world make their children's lives a misery for the very good reason that they want their offspring to develop good table manners.

When you are abroad, the rules of good table manners change. You can solve some of the problems you have with questions like, "What is that funny little fork for?" or "What should I do with my glass?" People usually like to be asked for advice, and if they are sensitive they will understand that as a foreigner you cannot be expected to know the finer points of an alien system of table manners.

That doesn't mean you will escape difficult situations. I remember eating in the large open-plan dining room of a large Swedish pharmaceutical company one lunchtime when a group of Japanese visitors came in. As guests, they sat at a special table with waitress service, and because it was the appropriate season, they were served a local delicacy: crayfish, boiled and served whole. I was amazed, not because visitors had been served this local delicacy, but that their hosts hadn't realized how difficult it would be for their uninitiated guests to eat mini-lobsters wearing complete body armor while at least a hundred curious employees observed their every move. From the visitors' point of view, this must have been at best embarrassing and at worst painful for, even when boiled and stone dead, crayfish can still draw blood as unwary diners wrestle with their razor-sharp claws.

If you are charitable, you can see this eagerness to share the best of your local cuisine with foreigners as a sign of justifiable pride in your culture and a generous wish for others to experience it too. Yet sometimes, when I'm feeling cynical, I can't help but feel there is an element of conscious or unconscious sadism involved, especially if the guest can't speak the local language and ask exactly what, for example, the local delicacy *tête de veau vinaigrette* (calf's head in a vinegar dressing) contains.

But there are other more subtle ways of getting things wrong. If you are French or Italian and used to discussing everything from art to politics over your dinner, you may find the South Korean and Japanese habit of eating in silence unnerving, and they might find your constant flow of words distracts from an appreciation of the food. These same French and Italian businesspeople may also find their U.S. American counterpart's way of trying to close a deal over the first course of a meal inappropriate and rude.

And *when* do you start your meal? If your guests are used to having a snack at 4:00 or 5:00 P.M. and not dining until 10:00 or 11:00 P.M., as in Spain and Brazil, they aren't going to have much of an appetite for dinner at 7:00 or 8:00 P.M. or even earlier, which is the custom in Germany and Scandinavia. And what about smoking? Is it accepted that diners smoke at table (yes in Thailand) and will they mind if you ask them to stop (yes again)?

But despite the possible pitfalls and the fear we all have of making fools of ourselves, the experience of eating and drinking together marks a step forward in a relationship. For mealtimes are about much more than table manners, and sharing a meal is not just about eating and drinking. So don't judge the success of the meal by how good or bad the food was or by how many times you dropped your chopsticks. Consider instead whether you and your dining partner have shared a joke or a companionable silence or discovered a mutual passion for tango or tennis. If so, you have used the occasion to get to know each other better and, it's been time well spent.

LETTER 59

How to get your food into your mouth is not usually something you have to think deeply about. However, it's always difficult managing implements you are not familiar with.

Choosing chopsticks   Letter *59*

FROM SOUTH AFRICA ABOUT **HONG KONG AND CHINA**

I'll be traveling to Hong Kong and China for the first time and am not confident about my use of chopsticks. Do I really have to learn?

If your stay was limited to Hong Kong, you could probably manage without learning to use chopsticks, as a fork will almost certainly be provided upon request. However, because you are traveling on to China, you should probably probably buy a pair of chopsticks and start practicing at home, because alternative implements may not be available there and it's better to make your first mistakes in front of a friendly audience! Remember that Chinese food is served on a number of dishes from which you help yourself. Use the serving spoon if there is one, and if there isn't watch what your fellow diners do. If you see them turning their chopsticks around and using the blunt ends to pick up food from the communal plate, do the same. If you are going to Japan, you may not to be happy to hear that their chopsticks are round and even harder to use that the angular Chinese variety.

LETTERS 60–62

Good and bad table manners vary, of course, from culture to culture.

Embarrassing noise   Letter 60

FROM CHINA ABOUT **EUROPE**

I'd just like to warn other Chinese about a mistake I made on my first trip to Europe. I'd mastered the cutlery and was prepared for the food, but I made a real mistake with the soup. I drank it as we do in China and didn't try to be silent. I soon realized that everyone in the restaurant was looking at me, and that people regarded the sounds I was making as bad-mannered. It was very embarrassing.

It's always a shock to realize that things that are accepted at home are regarded negatively abroad. In Europe and North America, one is not expected to make any noise when eating or drinking. I must admit that I find it very difficult in China, Hong Kong, or Taiwan *not* to make a noise when drinking soup, because the flat-bottomed china spoons make it almost impossible to drink quietly. In the West, soupspoons are usually a different shape from other spoons (round instead of oval), and you tip the soup into your mouth silently rather than suck it up.

But the whole question of soup-drinking is a strange one. In the U.K., we are taught from childhood to move the spoon away from the body while eating soup, although when eating puddings and desserts we move the spoon towards us. Most other Europeans think us very peculiar, and when I think about it, I'm really not surprised!

Table talk   Letter 61

FROM SWEDEN ABOUT **FRANCE**

I'll be going on a trip to France, and I've heard a lot about the long lunches there. Is it true that you shouldn't talk business then?

It's very difficult to generalize, but usually meals in countries where people take their food seriously are not good times for discussing business—and in France, and also in Italy and Spain, they take food *very* seriously. If you are taken out to a restaurant for lunch in any of these countries, it will be a little later than you eat in Sweden, where foreigners are surprised to find you eating lunch already at 11:30 A.M. Expect lunch to take up to a couple of hours, rather than the 45 minutes you are used to, and to have between three and seven courses. It will probably include wine, and if you're not used to this in the middle of the day take it easy, or you'll find yourself nodding off to sleep in the afternoon.

During the meal itself you shouldn't talk business, and keep off the subjects of families and children too, as these are regarded as personal areas. You can talk about politics, history, literature, even sports—and food, of course. Take your lead from your French contact. He or she may well get around to talking business by the coffee stage, but don't push it.

Remember that manners are more formal there than in some other countries and that appearances count, so if you're male don't take off your jacket or tie during the meal, and do remember to allow women and more senior colleagues to go through the doorway ahead of you. If you are the guest, it is a good idea to write a short thank you note (in good French if possible) to your host at the end of your trip.

Foreign formalities   Letter 62

FROM FRANCE ABOUT **CHINA**

Next month I will be visiting China for the first time and know I will be attending a formal banquet. What will that involve?

Banquets are a well-established part of business life in China, Taiwan, and Hong Kong and have their own rules of protocol. If you are part of a team, make sure that the most senior member enters the dining room first. You will be seated at a round table (or multiple tables if there are a lot of you) where the host and principal guest face each other, and other guests are seated in descending order of rank. Because of this, take any inquiries about the exact nature of your job, how many subordinates you have, and so on seriously; they need to know this for their seating plan. It's good manners to wait until you're told where to sit, and to wait until the host and principal guest are seated.

The Chinese host will usually start by proposing a toast, and the principal guest should respond in kind. The Chinese take their food seriously and there will be a lot of little bowls to sample, so pace yourself. Because there are usually so many to choose from, it's comparatively easy to avoid the ones you don't like, but remember, if you make a gallant effort and finish all the sea cucumber on your plate, you'll be sure to be served more. So if you discover it isn't your favorite dish, leave a little.

I hope you have been doing some intensive chopstick practice, but remember that it's fine to use the spoon provided to eat your soup and the meat or vegetables it contains. Try to sample a little of everything. When you are served rice, it's perfectly acceptable to raise your bowl to your mouth and "shovel" it in, but leave a little in your bowl as an indication that you've had enough. When you've finished, place your chopsticks side by side on the table or on the chopstick rest rather than on top of the bowl.

LETTERS 63–64

When we eat can also differ widely from place to place.

Under starter's orders . . .   Letter 63

FROM ARGENTINA ABOUT **GERMANY**

I'd like to warn others of a mistake I made on a business trip to Germany. In my country restaurants don't even open for dinner until 9:00 P.M., and I'm not used to eating before 10:00 P.M. So when I received an invitation to a restaurant for dinner at 8:00 P.M., I wrongly assumed that people would not start eating immediately. I turned up at 8:30 P.M. to find the other guests halfway through their first course.

There are major differences between cultures regarding when different meals are eaten. In Latin America and the countries around the Mediterranean, people are used to starting dinner at around 10:00 P.M., or even later, while in Germany, Austria, the U.K., and Scandinavia they've usually finished long since, especially during the week. Recently a colleague told me that she was invited to "lunch" at 4:00 P.M. on her last visit to Poland, whereas many large companies in Sweden have a lunch break starting at 11:15 A.M., so you can see there is no set time for a particular meal.

There's also a difference in how punctual you need to be when arriving for a meal, especially in the evening. In Germany, people say what they mean, and an invitation for 8:00 P.M. means that's when you're expected. In the U.K., you may be invited "at 8:00 for 8:30," which means that you can turn up anytime during that half hour, but that the meal itself will start shortly after 8:30. In Argentina, it's not bad manners to arrive half an hour late; in fact, there it's rather rude to arrive "on the dot," which accounts for your late arrival in Germany.

. . . and they're off!   Letter 64

FROM ITALY ABOUT **JAPAN**

> *I'm involved with product presentations for salespeople from other countries. All groups follow the same program, which usually finishes with dinner and entertainment in a restaurant. Several Japanese groups have surprised me by suddenly getting up and leaving, whether dessert has been served or not. Why is this?*

I imagine this is a misunderstanding based on problems in communication, as most Japanese avoid being impolite. The sign that triggers their leaving can be that the senior manager gets up, and then everyone else must follow his example. But more likely is that they speak to each other and say, for example, *ikimashoo* or *ikoo*—"We're going now."

That they leave before dessert can be explained by the fact that desserts are not common in Japan, and neither is a pause between courses, so perhaps they thought the meal was over. At home, the Japanese may have a snack at work at about 7:00 P.M., then the group's ready to go out and have a beer together. They'll usually have dinner at home at around 10:00 or 11:00 P.M. One thing you can do the next time is phone the restaurant in advance and make sure that the food is served quickly and efficiently. Make sure too that the person with the highest status is served first, that he or she has the best position at the table, and that this person receives the most attention. To help matters, you could also draw up a detailed program that lists specific times for different activities so your guests will know what to expect.

One last point: this program, and the menu, should be written in both English and Japanese. Although it is taught in schools in Japan, the general standard of English is not very high (though much higher than most English-speakers' knowledge of Japanese). Your guests may be embarrassed to admit that they don't understand spoken or written instructions, so to be on the safe side, get things translated. Perhaps an interpreter would be a useful guest to have at dinner too.

LETTERS 65–66

Tipping can be a sensitive issue, especially if people are unaware of local rules. Some English friends of mine drinking in a New York bar discovered this when they did not tip the waitress (barmaid in British English) at one tough place they were at. The waitress stood up on the counter and shouted at them!

No tipping?   Letter 65

FROM BRAZIL ABOUT **JAPAN**

I've heard that you shouldn't tip anyone in Japan. Is that true?

That's right. Tipping in restaurants and hotels isn't customary in Japan because employees pride themselves on giving the best possible service as part of the job. In China too, tipping is not widespread and may be regarded by some Communist hardliners as rather insulting. In most cities, 15 percent of the total restaurant bill will be automatically added as a service charge, but having said that, a tip offered discreetly for excellent service will seldom be refused.

Most countries have their own customs governing tipping. In Germany, for example, a service charge is included in the bill at restaurants by law, but a tip is still expected for good service. But what is different there is that you don't leave the tip on the table as you do, say, in the U.K. or the U.S. Instead, you add it to the bill and tell the waiter or waitress to keep the difference.

In other countries, employers may pay very low wages to service personnel who rely on tips to make up their wages. In the U.S., taxi drivers and waiters, to take two examples, expect tips of between 15 and 20 percent, although rates vary from region to region. Finally, in other cultures, such as India, you may tip for a service *before* you receive it. Both sorts of tipping, for services already provided and services that are to be provided in the future, are included in the special term *baksheesh*.

Going Dutch   Letter 66

FROM SPAIN ABOUT THE **NETHERLANDS**

I'll be visiting the Netherlands soon and have a question regarding eating out. If I'm invited out for dinner, is it true that I should offer to pay for my own meal?

It is true that in the Netherlands friends eating out may well "go Dutch," which means splitting the bill between them. This is also common in the U.S., the U.K., and Sweden. However, if you are invited out by a business acquaintance, it is usually understood that he or she will pay the bill. If you're not quite sure of what to do, it's probably a good idea to offer to pay your share just to be on the safe side. In Southern European, Middle Eastern, and Latin American cultures, where people compete to pay the bill and welcome the chance it gives them to display generosity, this emphasis on equality can be interpreted as meanness, whereas it actually reflects the Dutch people's sense of fairness. In their minds, and in the minds of "bill splitters" from other cultures, it ensures that nobody is put under an obligation.

IN A NUTSHELL: *Mealtimes*

GLOBAL BUSINESS STANDARDS

Usually the person who has issued the invitation pays for everyone (but see Russia).

Some business acquaintances in countries with a strong tradition of hospitality may insist on always paying the bill (especially if you are a woman). If you wish to pay for the meal, speak to the manager of the restaurant when making reservations and arrange for the bill to be sent to you.

EUROPEAN STANDARDS

Knives and forks are held in right and left hands, respectively, and stay there throughout the meal.

A service charge is usually included in the bill, but a small additional amount may be left for really good service. (See Letter 60.)

MUSLIM STANDARD

Avoid using the "unclean" left hand when eating or passing someone food or any other article.

GLOBAL WARNING

Whether to discuss business during mealtimes is a tricky point. You can introduce business tactfully toward the end of the meal. If your dining partner joins in enthusiastically, fine. If not, drop the subject until you are back at the office.

- **Argentina:** Evening meals are eaten later than is usual in the U.S., Northern Europe, and Asia. Breakfast meetings are a rarity. (See Letters 63 and 66.)
- **Australia:** Tea may be either "afternoon tea," a light meal at 4:00 or 5:00 P.M., or "high tea," a more substantial meal at the end of the working day. It is common for friends to split the bill. In business, the host pays.
- **Austria:** Breakfast meetings are rare. People arrive punctually for meals rather than "fashionably late." Evening meals are earlier than in many other countries (approximately 6:00 to 8:00 P.M.). *Guten Appetit* is said at beginning of every midday and evening meal. (See Letter 63.)
- **Belgium:** Keep your hands on the table, not under it, during the meal. Business lunches are more common than dinners.
- **Brazil:** Evening meals are eaten later than is usual in the U.S., Northern Europe, and Asia. (See Letters 63, 65, and 66.)
- **Canada:** Most business entertaining is done over lunch, and sometimes over breakfast. It is less popular to engage in after-hours entertainment because it might interfere with private or family time. Evening meals are earlier than in many other countries (approximately 6:00 to 8:00 P.M.).
- **China:** Formal banquets are an accepted way of entertaining visitors. Diners often choose and share from several smaller dishes served simultaneously. Chopsticks are universally used. It is acceptable to make slurping noise when drinking soup. Tipping is not customary. If you use a toothpick, cover your mouth with your with hand. (See Letters 59, 60, 62, and 65.)
- **Denmark:** Work starts early, so breakfast meetings are acceptable. It is common for friends to split the bill. In business, the host pays.
- **Finland:** See Denmark. (See Letter 63.)
- **France:** Long lunches are taken seriously and considered as a way of getting to know each other. *Bon appetit* is said at beginning of every midday and evening meal. (See Letter 61.)
- **Germany:** (See Letters 63 and 65.)
- **Hong Kong:** See China.

- **India:** Diners often choose and share from several smaller dishes served simultaneously. Forks and spoons are the most usual cutlery (knife and fork in Western restaurants). At informal meals, people may eat with fingers only.
- **Indonesia:** Evening entertaining is more popular than lunches. Forks and spoons are usually used. If you use a toothpick, cover your mouth with your hand.
- **Italy:** Evening meals are eaten later than is common in the U.S., Northern Europe, or Asia. Use your fork and knife to eat fruit and cheese, which are common desserts. (See Letters 61, 63, 64, and 66.)
- **Japan:** Tipping is not customary. Western-style cutlery is not common. (See Letters 59, 64, and 65.)
- **Mexico:** Evening meals are eaten later than is common in the U.S., Northern Europe, or Asia. (See Letters 63 and 66.)
- **Netherlands:** It is common for friends to split the bill. In business, the host pays. (See Letter 66.)
- **Norway:** It is common for friends to split the bill. In business, the host pays. There is very limited nightlife outside big hotels. (See Letter 63.)
- **Poland:** Breakfast meetings are rare. Lunch can be as late as 4:00 or 5:00 P.M. (See Letter 63.)
- **Russia:** Meals are important for building relationships and give time for conversation. Even if invited out by a Russian contact, demonstrate a desire to pay for the meal (they can be expensive). Most business-related meals take place in the evenings and are often accompanied by alcohol and visits to bars or nightclubs.
- **Saudi Arabia:** When inviting Saudis, be sure to ask several times if they would like to join you, as they consider it polite to decline the offer at least once before accepting. People are likely to arrive for meals half an hour to forty-five minutes after the stated time. (See Letter 66.)
- **South Africa:** Tea may be either "afternoon tea," a light meal at 4:00 or 5:00 P.M., or "high tea," a more substantial meal at the end of the working day.

- **South Korea:** Evening meals are earlier than in many other countries (approximately 6:00 to 8:00 P.M.). Avoid holding your rice bowl near your mouth and scooping food into your mouth with your chopsticks. While this is acceptable in other parts of Asia, it is considered impolite in South Korea.
- **Spain:** Evening meals are eaten very late. Breakfast meetings are a rarity. (See Letters 61, 63, and 66.)
- **Sweden:** Breakfast meetings are acceptable. It is common for friends to split the bill. In business, the host pays. (See Letters 60, 61, 63, and 66.)
- **Switzerland:** When cheese, fruit, and sandwiches are served, in most cases you should use cutlery, even if you are accustomed to eating the offered food with your fingers in your home country.
- **Taiwan:** See China.
- **Thailand:** Thais typically eat with a fork and a spoon. Food is often shared from plates set in the middle of the table. Avoid helping yourself to the last bit of food in a serving dish. If it is offered to you, it is best to refuse it the first time, then accept it if asked again.
- **Turkey:** Turks may smoke between courses and use toothpicks. If you use a toothpick, cover your mouth with your hand. (See Letters 63 and 66.)
- **UK:** Tea may be either "afternoon tea," a light meal at 4:00 or 5:00 P.M., or "high tea," a more substantial meal at the end of the working day. It is common for friends to split the bill. In business, the host pays. Drink soup by moving the spoon away from your body. (See Letters 60, 63, and 66.)
- **US:** Snacking (eating small amounts at irregular times) is a national custom. People often eat lunch at their desks. It is common for friends to split the bill. In business, the host pays. Evening meals are earlier than in many other countries (approximately 6:00 to 8:00 P.M.). Business is often discussed during meals. It is important to leave a tip of between 15 and 20 percent. (See Letters 65 and 66.)
- **Venezuela:** Evening meals are eaten later than is common in the U.S., Northern Europe, or Asia. Three-hour lunches are not uncommon. (See Letters 63 and 66.)

PART II

Understanding Each Other

CHAPTER 4

Communication and Language

English has become the *lingua franca* of the business world, and people from Amsterdam to Zanzibar use it every day as a "tool of the trade." They also spend a lot of time and money trying to eliminate their language mistakes, not realizing that the fewer they make the more dangerous the errors are likely to become, because people aren't expecting them. Furthermore, just because someone has mastered the grammar and vocabulary of a language and pronounces it better than some native speakers does not mean he or she *uses* it in the same way.

Communication is not only about what the words mean in the dictionary, it's also about how you string them together. There is, after all, a certain difference between "Do that job tomorrow," "I'd appreciate it if you did that job tomorrow," and "Do that job tomorrow or I'll have your guts for garters," even if all three phrases are designed to achieve the same end. Those of us who are native English speakers have a responsibility not to use expressions that are likely to confuse non-native speakers (e.g., "Have you cottoned on, or do I have to spell that out to you?"). We also have to ensure that when "born" English speakers encounter a communication style that seems brusque, unfriendly, or arrogant in someone whose native language is not English, they will not assume that this is a true reflection of this person's personality or intention. It may well be that the speaker hasn't mastered the many nuances of words and body language that a native speaker interprets without even thinking about it. So in an unfamiliar culture, newcomers may find themselves wondering if the downcast eyes that accompany a statement are a sign of modesty or dishonesty.

Recently I ran an intercultural simulation, one part of which involved a group of ten British participants "learning" to be members of a fictitious culture. This made-up culture valued touch, and as part of the exercise participants were encouraged to touch each other at every opportunity, especially when communicating with each other. The simulation was a nightmare for everyone involved. The older male members of the group in particular found it extremely difficult to touch their colleagues at all. It wasn't surprising. Their physical contact with non-family members over the last forty years had been limited to a handshake with customers and a quick elbow in the ribs from strangers on a crowded subway, so to learn to communicate with colleagues in a tactile way that is the norm for millions of people in Latin America or Africa was just too much of a challenge.

Communication is about your facial expression, gestures, and actions. This was brought home to me a few years ago when a young family moved in to the next farm. My Swedish husband was born and brought up on a farm located on an island off the Swedish coast, and the new family had moved there from an outlying island and had two young children, as we did.

The four kids started to play together one day and were having a wonderful time when it started to rain. I went out and asked them, in Swedish, if they wanted to come into the house to play. The two new children looked at me and said nothing, then suddenly turned tail and ran as fast as they could in the direction of their home.

I couldn't make any sense of this, but when I went in and told my husband what had happened he showed no surprise. Without looking up from his newspaper he said, "They've gone home to ask their mother if they can come in." I was amazed. How did he know? He'd never even met them. But sure enough, in a couple of minutes there was a knock at the door and there they stood. Thinking about it, there were two things that surprised me. The first was that the two children hadn't said a word when I'd asked them a question, and the second was that my husband had understood the whole situation without even having seen what had happened.

The explanation was, of course, that he and the two children shared the same cultural roots. He had grown up, as they had, in a community where everyone knew everyone else; a homogenous community where people understood what their neighbors would do before they did it. If you grow up in a society like this you don't need to spell things out. Communication takes place without words because the situation is familiar and is governed by a set of unwritten rules that everyone understands.

If, on the other hand, you look at a country with an entirely different profile, like the U.S., for example, a relatively new country where enormous numbers of people immigrated from other cultures, communication patterns developed quite differently. With high levels of mobility as thousands of people headed west across the continent, individuals were forced to get to know one another quickly and establish their own rules as they went along. It's clear that in such a situation good communication skills were vital, because you couldn't expect the people you met to share your background or assumptions, so your communications with your peers had to be clear, unambiguous, and explicit. This explains why today many people in the U.S. have a very different communication style than the natives of the small island off the west coast of Sweden—and many other places where people have known each other all their lives.

◆ MORAL

The way we communicate, and what we do or do not say, may be entirely mystifying to people from other cultures, even though we believe we have made ourselves perfectly clear.

What to Say and How to Say It

Even those of us who pride ourselves on being direct don't always say what we mean. If English speakers were to phone a colleague's secretary and ask "Is David in?" we would be surprised if she answered, "Yes" and put the phone down. We assume she would answer the question we *didn't* ask, "May I speak to David?"

Different cultures have different attitudes to directness. I remember a time several years ago when I was in England and having problems with my car. I drove to a garage, parked the car in front, and went inside to report the problem. There was a long line, and as I waited a truck driver came in and addressed the woman waiting behind me in a broad Newcastle accent, "Thanks for moving your car, pet. The other wife just walked away and blocked me in."

In fact, "the other wife" was me. I hadn't seen the truck arrive behind me, and by leaving my car where I did had managed to block his exit. We're talking here about a Newcastle-upon-Tyne truck driver, with tattoos, beer belly, and shaven head, wearing a T-shirt with a picture of a man, not unlike himself, strangling a big snake. But because of the way he had been brought up, this poor guy could not bring himself to speak to me directly and tell me I was blocking his exit, but had to speak to the woman behind me to give him a pretext to tell the world of my stupidity. I mean, it wasn't as if he looked like he was afraid of conflict or had spent his formative years at Eton with Prince William learning how to conduct himself correctly in court circles. But somewhere in his cultural softwiring he'd learned that in certain situations, and addressing a certain type of person (e.g., a middle-aged woman, as opposed to a young man), he should use an indirect communication style.

Your own personal communication style will be affected by many factors. Obviously, the culture you come from plays a large part, as does your own native language. Even climate may have a role to play in how we express ourselves. One interesting (although not entirely serious) observation on this theme was made by the English writer Ford Madox Ford who wrote, "You cannot be dumb [silent] when you live with a person, unless you are an inhabitant of the North of England or the State of Maine." As someone with roots in the North of England I don't know if I can agree wholeheartedly with his conclusion that the colder the climate, the more taciturn the people. However, he's not alone in his conclusion: in both Italy and France the people of the south regard those in the cooler north as reserved and antisocial.

Other considerations affect both what we say and how we say it. For example, the CEO of a large corporation might mutter to a few friends over a drink at the club, "Well, guys, we really made a balls up of the last year's sales, didn't we?" However, he probably wouldn't make the same comment at the annual general meeting (although it might wake up the shareholders). He is more likely to say, "Due to circumstances beyond our control, our sales performance in the last year was disappointing." No matter where we come from, we all know that how we speak depends on the audience we are speaking to.

And speaking of audiences, if you gave a presentation and asked for questions, would you be pleased or worried if there weren't any? Would you take the silence to mean that you had made your point so clearly that everyone understood everything or as a warning sign that trouble was brewing? Would you assume that the audience had found your talk so boring they'd all dropped off to sleep? Or would expect questions to emerge later during the informality of the coffee break? It depends, among other things, on whether the audience was comfortable with silence and whether they came from a culture where asking questions in public is about losing face. Or perhaps they all came from the State of Maine or the North of England. . . .

LETTERS 67–68

Many of us ask questions if we don't understand something. However, in some cultures this is not a step to be taken lightly.

Asking questions   Letter 67

FROM THE U.S. ABOUT **MEXICO**

The company is introducing a complicated new process in one of its workshops in Mexico. We know it's difficult, and we have a training and support package we can offer if needed. I strongly suspect that they're having problems down there, but we haven't received a single request for advice or support. Why not?

As you know the process is a complicated one, why don't you provide the support package automatically instead of waiting for a request?

Admitting you need help can be a difficult thing to do no matter what culture you come from. Questions of prestige and fear of losing face can mean that people are unwilling to expose themselves to possible criticism. Also, if in your culture you have learned that good employees know all the answers, you may well hesitate to tell your bosses that you don't! This problem can be compounded if headquarters is located abroad, especially in a country that is bigger or richer than your own; this can make national sensitivities even worse.

He asked what?   Letter 68

FROM CANADA ABOUT **CHINA**

I enjoyed my trip to China, but I was very surprised by some questions business acquaintances I hardly knew asked me. Two questions they asked me during a meal were how much my watch cost and how old my wife was. (I'm just glad she wasn't there to hear it!)

It's odd what different cultures regard as acceptable questions. In France and many other European countries, they regard the North American exchange of personal information (Do you have any children? What do you do in your free time?) as rather intrusive, though the French will quite happily discuss matters of religion, which are regarded as taboo by, for example, many people from the Middle East. Canadians and North Americans, of course, simply see such inquiries as a friendly way of building a relationship, and they expect to answer the same questions themselves. At the same time, North Americans usually find questions about money and age too personal to ask business acquaintances. However, for many Chinese, whether in China or elsewhere in Asia, and for people in the Middle East these questions form part of ordinary conversation and are just one way of getting to know you better. Indeed, such questions are seen as a natural way to show you're interested in your new acquaintance. People in countries as far apart as China, India, and Mexico might even think it rather unfriendly if people they met did *not* show any interest in their personal concerns.

LETTERS 69-70

The way people communicate with each other at work is affected by the structure of the organization they work for and by the expectations of fellow employees.

Communication stop   Letter 69

FROM SWEDEN ABOUT **GERMANY**

> *I work for a multinational company and am involved in a project that requires a lot of technical input. I contacted a German colleague I'd met at a conference for a little help. When I spoke to him on the phone he was quite pleased to help us, but the next day my manager got an e-mail from the German guy's boss saying that my colleague was too busy to help me.*

I think the problem here is that you didn't use the "correct" channels of communication, according to the German company, anyway. In Germany, and indeed in the majority of European and American companies, the manager wants to be informed of what his or her department members are doing, as it's an important part of his or her role to co-ordinate their efforts. What you should have done first was to contact the manager and ask if you could approach your German colleague for some assistance. Not doing so might be interpreted by his or her manager as very rude, and even a bit underhanded.

I understand that you come from a country, Sweden, where it's the norm to delegate an enormous amount of power to non-managerial staff and give them a high degree of independence, especially if they are technical specialists. However, this is certainly not the case in most countries, which tend to be much more hierarchical. Indeed, most managers from the U.K. to the United Arab Emirates, by way of the U.S., would want to be informed of such an approach to a subordinate.

I suggest your manager make a formal request to his German counterpart asking if you may contact the specialist. You should include a
description of the kind of questions to be tackled, and a description of the
benefits your project will make to the company. And be *very* polite. After
all, you are asking the manager for a favor—to be allowed to use the valuable time of one of the department's members.

Communication breakdown   Letter 70

FROM NEW ZEALAND ABOUT **FRANCE**

*We're having real problems with our French subsidiary. We want a
couple of departments in the French head office to collaborate in
preparing a program for some visiting customers who want to see
production operations. Naturally, this will involve consultation with
the factory staff to see what is practicable. However, arrangements
seem to be at a standstill. We can't understand what the problem
can be.*

What you have asked your French managers to do is to communicate
in ways they may not be used to. First, you are asking your mangers to
operate across departmental boundaries; hence, it's not clear who is
responsible for what. Second, they are being asked to communicate across
hierarchical boundaries, because the managers will not be able to arrange
a trip to see production facilities without some collaboration and discussion with the factory personnel.

The French, as well as Latin American and Southern European business cultures, tend to have very clear hierarchies where each person's
responsibilities are spelled out. The same applies to cultures with a Confucian heritage like Japan, China, and South Korea, where respect is
awarded to age, education, and rank in the company. The French also have
rather compartmentalized communication patterns, and information is
not freely shared as a matter of course, but tends to remain the property of
those higher up the ladder. "Knowledge is power" is the name of the
game, and one likely to hinder interdepartmental collaboration. Your cul-

ture (which is more tolerant of uncertainty) is more like that of the Scandinavians, the British, and Irish in your belief in a free flow of information, but many other cultures find this difficult to deal with. You are more likely to get a positive result if you give *one* of the managers responsibility for arranging the visit, and instruct him or her to involve the factory in the plans.

LETTERS 71–72

You may like to have things out in the open, or prefer to leave them unsaid.

A major error   Letter *71*

FROM MEXICO ABOUT **GERMANY**

We have a new German manager who is making himself extremely unpopular here. He has introduced a new quality control system that is complicated and takes time to learn. Inevitably mistakes are made. However, when he finds an error, he seems to delight in pointing this out to the person involved in front of everyone. Several people are already thinking of handing in their notices.

Your new manager is certainly not trying to offend people intentionally. In his own direct way, a way shared by U.S. Americans who also believe that it is better to "tell it like it is," he might even be trying to help by identifying the problem. He obviously does not understand that Mexicans regard this very direct approach as fault-finding, confrontational, and aggressive. Mexicans, like most Central and South Americans and East Asians, are skilled at avoiding confrontations and situations that involve a loss of face, but this is still something your new manager has to learn. Until he does, try not to take his criticism personally.

No no   Letter 72

FROM THE U.S. ABOUT **INDONESIA**

I found it very difficult working in Indonesia because I couldn't get a straight answer to a straight question, and this often led to misunderstandings. As far as I could see, they often said yes *when they meant* no. *Why?*

Most Indonesians find it hard to give a straightforward *no* to a request. If you ask for something to be done that is difficult or even impossible, your Indonesian colleague, instead of saying *no* or *sorry*, may say instead that he will try. Also, a promise to do something that keeps getting postponed can be another indirect way of refusing a request. There is no intention to deceive, but simply a wish to avoid situations leading to open disagreement or disappointment that would cause you to lose face. And bear in mind that people from cultures with this indirect communication style are perfectly well understood by each other. They are simply tuned in to "reading between the lines" in a way you are not.

This communication pattern is not confined to Indonesia. In countries as far away from Indonesia as Pakistan, India, and Japan the word *no* is regarded as impolite and is rarely heard in a business context. In Mexico and South America, too, politeness and diplomacy are valued as useful ways of avoiding conflict.

But bear in mind that speakers of English can be indirect sometimes too. If invited to a party they don't want to attend, the vast majority of English speakers will say they have a cold rather than admit that they're planning to spend the evening in front of the TV. This is just another variation on the "white lie" theme, and as such is remarkably similar to the indirect response you mentioned in your question.

LETTERS 73–75

It's easy to create the wrong impression if you choose an inappropriate communication style—and what is inappropriate is in the ear of the listener.

Aggressive   Letter 73

FROM SWEDEN ABOUT **FRANCE**

I find it extremely difficult to discuss business with the French. It is impossible to talk about things with them calmly and sensibly. They are very critical of any ideas that they have not originated themselves, but take any criticism of their own plans personally and get angry.

If you come from a country like Sweden, where open conflict is frowned on, you may find the French debating style very aggressive. For the French, a love of words is combined with a liking for verbal combat, and they are used to organizing their case logically and presenting their arguments with force and conviction, not necessarily because they believe in them, but because they consider that it is through argument and counter-argument that you will eventually arrive at the truth or the best solution to a problem. And if you don't, the debate has been an enjoyable chance to flex your intellectual muscles anyway!

However, the bad feelings that may result from such spectacular clashes will usually quickly be forgotten, which is also hard for people from more low-key cultures to understand. Of course, the French are not alone in their love of discussion. Greeks, Israelis, Argentineans, and Poles all enjoy a good debate too, and North Americans and Australians are no shrinking violets when it comes to putting their points forward. For the French and Australians in particular, debate is a way of taking the measure of a new acquaintance.

In your particular case, at a meeting with the French you should emphasize the most important points of your argument and repeat them patiently. Don't get tied up with details or try to score debating points. Instead, focus on the most important points you want to achieve and keep the meeting focused on them. Be very well prepared, and if in a corner, be ready to use a weapon to which the French have no defense—silence.

Patronizing Pommie   Letter 74

FROM AUSTRALIA ABOUT THE **U.K.**

We have a new boss from the U.K. with one of the most affected upper-class English accents I have ever heard. Every time he opens

*his mouth I can just see him at the Queen's garden party in a tuxedo
and top hat. I just can't take him seriously, and I wonder how he
expects to communicate with the other guys in the company.*

For historical reasons an upper-class English accent in Australia is
associated with money and power, and the use and misuse of both. Australia is a proud new multiethnic country and many Aussies find remind-
ers of their colonial past, that includes the accent of the former ruling
class, embarrassing and even painful.

But it's true that this particular type of British accent (RP, which is
short for Received Pronunciation) is linked to a certain powerful social
group in a way that different U.S. regional accents are not. It also continues to be an accent that dominates the boardrooms of many companies.
Even in England itself people with strong regional accents may associate
RP with snobbery and privilege, which is why younger members of the
upper classes try to tone it down a bit. But give your boss a chance. It
would be unfair to judge how well he's likely to do his job on the basis of
his vowel sounds!

Just making conversation   Letter 75

FROM BRITAIN ABOUT JAPAN

*I met several Japanese businesspeople who visited Britain recently, and
I tried to be pleasant and help them relax. I told a few jokes that
seemed to go down well, but I later heard that they hadn't been
appreciated. Yet at the time everyone laughed!*

Your mistake was to treat your visitors as if they were from your own
country. I'm sure this was done from the best of motives, but it is a mistake to assume that every culture shares the same kind of humor. Just
because your Japanese visitors laughed didn't necessarily mean that they
found your joke funny—people from different cultures tend to laugh at
different things. Research about what people of different nationalities find
funny concluded that the Irish, British, Australians, and New Zealanders
thought that jokes involving word play were funniest. Canadians and U.S.

Americans preferred jokes where there was a sense of superiority—either because a person looked stupid or was made to look stupid by another person. Many European countries, like France, Denmark, and Belgium, liked rather surreal jokes and jokes about serious topics like death and illness.

You don't say whether you told your jokes during a business meeting or after work in the pub. However, in many countries humor is confined to non-work situations, and joking in an important meeting, for example, is seen as a sign that you are not treating the subject (or the individual) with respect. This would certainly apply to Germany and Finland as well as Japan, where humor when business matters were being discussed would be regarded as inappropriate. And of course it might well be that your visitors didn't understand your English but did not want to lose face by showing it, because even if you are fluent in a foreign language, jokes are always the last things you understand.

Finally, you need to know that people from East Asian countries as widely apart as Japan, South Korea, and Thailand may laugh if embarrassed or nervous as well as when they're happy.

LETTERS 76–77

Rudeness may be what the listener hears, rather than what the speaker intends.

Rude, or just informal?   Letter 76

FROM DENMARK ABOUT **DENMARK**

In Denmark we tend to communicate in an informal way and consequently leave out titles like "Mr." or "Dr." We also like to communicate directly rather than "beating about the bush." But I know this isn't the case in other cultures and wondered just how rude we are perceived to be.

It depends where you're going and who you're meeting. In Northern Europe, Australia, and the U.S., communication styles are quite relaxed and informal, and people take pride in talking to both manual workers and top managers in more or less the same way. They also tend to be rather pragmatic in their understanding of what language is for—generally it's to get things done. So they say clearly what they mean so the message comes over loud and clear. This group won't regard your informal and direct style as at all rude.

In other cultures, however, what you say may be secondary to how you say it, and the British, along with the Arabs and people from many Asian cultures, put a lot of weight on how the message is delivered. Words are regarded as an important way of establishing and building relationships, not simply a tool for getting things done. If your "tone" is wrong and you are perceived as rude, people from these cultures can take offense, and, for example, not using the right titles for an individual can be regarded as a sign of disrespect.

As a general rule, it's better to err on the side of formality when communicating with people of other nationalities, even if you've worked together for quite some time. Words define your relationship with an individual, and if you want to ensure that the relationship is one of mutual respect, your communication style must reflect that.

Let me finish!　　　　　　　　　　　　　　　Letter 77

FROM SOUTH AFRICA ABOUT **ITALY**

I travel often in Italy and in other Mediterranean countries, and I find it very irritating to be constantly interrupted. What can I do to stop this?

The short answer is—not a lot. What you as a South African would call a rude interruption, nationals from Southern European countries may regard as perfectly acceptable. They may instead see an interruption as an expression of interest and involvement in what the speaker is saying and in his or her ideas. In short, in countries such as Italy, if you wait for a pause in the conversation in order to present your own point of view, you'll never open your mouth! You'll find that the nationals of these countries interrupt each other too, so don't take it personally. This is because silence does not have an important role in the communication patterns of most Latin countries. Indeed, the tempo of conversation may simply be too fast to allow for a pause between speakers.

If you are interrupted in the middle of a presentation, don't show annoyance but say that you'll deal with the points raised at the end of your talk; don't let yourself be thrown off track. If the interruption occurs in the middle of an informal meeting, accept that this is regarded as a legitimate way of raising relevant points and practice your debating skills.

LETTERS 78–79

When to remain silent is a decision we make almost unconsciously when operating in our own culture. But in another culture this decision may be interpreted in a way we don't expect.

Struck dumb   Letter *78*

FROM POLAND ABOUT **SOUTH KOREA**

During my recent trips to South Korea I have built up a good relationship with an engineer of about my own age who works in my own area of expertise. He speaks good English, and we have had a number of informal meetings where we've made tentative decisions about some technical developments. However, when his boss is present he hardly ever opens his mouth, even though this manager has to use an interpreter and does not have a technical background.

It is quite usual in South Korea, and neighboring Japan, that a younger employee will be quiet in front of older managers as a sign of respect. It would be regarded as immodest to display his superior knowledge of English or the technical matter at hand in front of his boss. This manager will not be directly involved in the technical side of things, but will want to know a little about you personally and see you "in action" so he can come to some conclusion about whether you and the company you represent are likely to make good working partners.

Small talk versus silence	Letter 79

FROM FINLAND ABOUT THE **U.K.**

We hear a lot about the importance of "small talk" when doing business with the British. But if you don't have anything particular to say, why should you keep on talking? Surely it makes more sense to keep your mouth shut.

In cultures where conversation is an art form, as in France and Italy, a firmly shut mouth may be equated with a firmly shut mind. You may be regarded as rude if you are not prepared to make an effort to get to know your counterparts on a personal rather than simply on a business level. However, you are not the only one to find this need for "small talk" difficult. In addition to Finns, Swedes and Norwegians also have a problem with it. In your cultures silence is accepted as a part of conversation in a way it is not in many others (although the Japanese are more like you in their acceptance of silence). To many Europeans and Americans, general social conversation is a prelude to more serious discussions and is regarded as a way of getting to know your colleague before you get down to brass tacks.

If you are stuck about what to talk about, non-controversial topics are best to start with. In 1758, Samuel Johnson wrote, "It is commonly observed that when two Englishmen meet, their first talk is of the weather." Some things just don't change, and not only the English find this subject a useful "icebreaker" with strangers. Other useful subjects are the journey to the meeting, sports, and questions about your visitor's hometown or area, but the real secret is to relax and allow yourself to show you are interested in your partner and what he or she has to say. Feel free to ask questions, as long as they don't get *too* personal. People usually enjoy talking about themselves. Neither should you be afraid to talk about yourself and your own interests. Conversation is like dancing the tango (surprisingly, perhaps, this is very popular in Finland) in that it needs practice. It also requires sensitivity to what your "partner" is feeling and anticipation of the next move.

LETTER 80

Giving presentations at home can be bad enough, but speaking to people of other cultures can be even harder.

Political correctness   Letter *80*

FROM AUSTRALIA ABOUT THE U.S.

I've just returned from the U.S. where I gave a number of lectures on a technical matter. During one of my talks I used the expression "to call a spade a spade." One of my listeners raised his hand and said that he found the expression offensive—he had taken it as a racist comment! Is this political correctness run wild?

To put it bluntly, yes it is. The expression "to call a spade a spade" simply means to describe something truthfully and honestly. However, in the U.S. *spade* is a derogatory term for a black person; it comes from the expression "as black as the ace of spades." Your listener obviously confused the two.

When you speak in public on any subject, it is simple good manners to ensure that what you say does not unintentionally offend any particular group, hurt their feelings, or show them disrespect, especially if this group has been given a hard time by society at large over the years: women, black people, homosexuals, and handicapped people are some groups that spring to mind. It's obvious that people belonging to these groups are just as deserving of consideration and courtesy as the traditional top dogs—white heterosexual able-bodied males.

However, this respect for the dignity of others should not stop you from getting your own message across. The term *political correctness* has unfortunately come to be associated with a "holier than thou" attitude, and some North Americans use it to beat less politically correct fellow citizens over the head. Luckily, it is primarily a North American phenomenon, but one that the rest of us should be aware of when we have contact with Canadians or U.S. Americans.

IN A NUTSHELL: *What to say and how to say it*

GLOBAL BUSINESS STANDARDS

Good small talk topics:

Weather is always safe, although boring, especially in countries that don't have a lot!

Sports are usually safe too, unless the city or country has suffered a spectacular defeat in the national sport recently.

The art and cultural history of the country is usually safe (but watch out for any historical discussion that can lead to a political debate).

GLOBAL WARNINGS

No swearing in your own or any other language.

Keep humor to a minimum until you are sure your partners/guests laugh at the same things as you.

Don't comment negatively about another culture—especially on religion, politics, or sexual matters. (Occasionally requests for information on the first two may be interpreted favorably, but be careful.)

- **Argentina:** People like to express opinions and love to debate. Voices may be louder than elsewhere in South America. (See Letters 70, 71, 72, 73, 77, and 79.)
- **Australia:** People enjoy talking and debating. There is an informal style of communication that is not based on hierarchy. (See Letters 73, 74, 75, 76, and 80.)
- **Austria:** Communication within companies is inhibited by departmental and hierarchical boundaries. There is a direct yet formal communication style. May be an adversarial approach to debate among peers. (See Letter 69.)
- **Belgium:** Communication within companies is inhibited by departmental and hierarchical boundaries. French speakers' adversarial style in discussions may appear very negative or aggressive. Flemish speakers are more low-key. (See Letters 69 and 75.)
- **Brazil:** Relatively personal questions (in more reserved cultures) about income, age, and so on are acceptable. Emotions are expressed openly. (See Letters 70, 71, 72, 77, and 79.)
- **Canada:** There are different communication styles depending on whether you are in English- or French-speaking Canada. (See U.K. and France.) (See Letters 68, 73, 75, and 80.)
- **China:** Personal questions about income, age, and so on are acceptable. Ordinary conversations can be loud and may sound unintentionally rude or angry. (See Letters 68, 70, and 71.)
- **Denmark:** Informal communication style is the norm. (See Letters 70, 75, and 76.)
- **Finland:** Small talk is not usual. Silence is accepted. The verbal style is very quiet and restrained. (See Letters 70, 75, and 76.)
- **France:** Communication within companies is inhibited by departmental and hierarchical boundaries. Adversarial style in discussions may appear to outsiders to be very negative or aggressive. (See Letters 68, 69, 70, 73, and 75.)
- **Germany:** Communication within companies may be inhibited by departmental and hierarchical boundaries. There is a direct yet formal communication style. Adversarial style in discussions may appear very negative or aggressive. Negative messages are given directly; tact is not a priority. (See Letters 69, 71, and 75.)

- **Hong Kong:** Personal questions about income, age, and so on are acceptable. Ordinary conversations can be loud, and may sound unintentionally rude or angry. (See Letters 68, 70, and 71.)
- **India:** Personal questions about income, age, and so on are acceptable. In these "high context" cultures a straight *no* is regarded as rude. Explanations and communication styles may be indirect. (See Letters 68 and 72.)
- **Indonesia:** Quiet, calm polite conversation style is the norm. This is also appreciated in others. (See Letters 68, 71, and 72.)
- **Italy:** Overlapping conversational style is the norm. Interruptions are not regarded negatively. Emotions are expressed openly. (See Letters 69, 70, 77, and 79.)
- **Japan:** Deference to senior and older colleagues (when present) may inhibit Japanese from communicating. Self-consciousness about their English may be another inhibiting factor. There is an oblique and indirect communication style and modesty is important. A straight *no* is regarded as rude. (See Letters 70, 71, 72, 75, 78, and 79.)
- **Mexico:** There is an indirect communication style. Direct confrontation is avoided. It's important to "save face." (See Letters 67, 68, 70, 71, 72, 77, and 79.)
- **Netherlands:** People have a rather blunt and straightforward speaking style and are quite informal.
- **Norway:** There is an informal and direct communication style. Silence is an accepted part of communication. (See Letters 70, 76, and 79.)
- **Poland:** People enjoy debate and discussions. Politeness and formality are quite important. (See Letter 73.)
- **Russia:** The first response to any question is usually *no*, but persistence is often rewarded. It is important for Russians not to lose face in discussions. They may show disagreement or anger quite openly.
- **Saudi Arabia:** Ordinary conversations can be loud and may sound unintentionally rude or angry to outsiders. Emotions are expressed openly. (See Letters 68 and 76.)
- **South Africa:** Lots of sports analogies (from rugby, cricket, etc.) used. Different ethnic groups use different communication styles. (See Letter 77.)

- **South Korea:** When getting to know you, people may ask personal questions, but they are not intending to be rude. (See Letters 71, 75, and 78.)
- **Spain:** A straight *no* is regarded as rude. Explanations and communication styles may be indirect. (See Letters 69, 70, 77, and 79.)
- **Sweden:** Communication across hierarchical boundaries is common. Written communication in English may sound brusque, even rude, because of first language interference. Silence is an accepted part of communication. (See Letters 69, 70, 73, 76, and 79.)
- **Switzerland:** Humor has little place in business. German speakers will not make small talk, but French and Italian speakers will.
- **Taiwan:** See China.
- **Thailand:** There is a very tactful communication style, and heated debates are not popular. (See Letters 71 and 75.)
- **Turkey:** People may be reluctant to say *no*. It is more important to be polite than to be accurate or clear. (See Letters 69 and 70.)
- **UK:** Small talk is an important social skill. Humor is used widely to defuse tension and to create positive social contacts. People are judged according to how they use language. An oblique style, including understatement or irony, may be used. (See Letters 69, 70, 74, 75, 76, and 79.)
- **US:** Political correctness (and good manners) means that you should be very careful how you express yourself. This applies to all references to gender, age, race, religion, or sexual orientation. Communication is generally direct and explicit. (See Letters 67, 68, 69, 71, 72, 73, 75, 76, and 80.)
- **Venezuela:** People like to debate but rarely admit they are wrong or do not know something. (See Letters 70, 71, 72, 77, and 79.)

A Global Language?

There are over 400 million speakers of English as a first language in the world, with about the same number of people using it as a second language. However, over 700 million people speak one of the many dialects of Chinese. The world also contains almost 300 million Spanish speakers, and about 180 million speakers of Hindi and Arabic, respectively. (And undoubtedly included in these figures are a good few thousand gifted people who speak *all* these languages.)

However, English speakers can take comfort from statistics that say 75 percent of the world's mail, telexes, and cables are in English, that it is the medium for 80 percent of the information stored on the world's computers, and that it is the language of over half the world's technical and scientific periodicals. In fact, it can be said with justice that English is on the way to becoming the first truly global language.

The need for a language in which people from Siberia to Santiago can communicate directly with each other has long been acknowledged, and the establishment of artificial languages such as Esperanto has tried unsuccessfully to fulfill this need. Now, due to a series of accidents of history, it looks as if English is likely to step into the breach. But if a language is "global," it is no longer the exclusive property of its native speakers. Indeed, it is claimed that there is a European variety of English, sometimes called *Euro-English*, which is already evolving, and some people believe that it will eventually become the European language of business. It even has an official name: English as a lingua franca in Europe (ELFE). This version of English regards as acceptable some "mistakes" that most teachers of the language spend their careers trying to eradicate. For example, "He go to work every day at 8:00 o'clock" would be accepted as correct, as the meaning of the sentence remains clear.

Some academics believe that this modified version of English, which would turn increasingly to continental Europe rather than to the U.S. or the U.K. for its standards of correctness and appropriateness, is the future. Whether that is true remains to be seen, but whatever happens, the message is clear: English is a useful tool for international communication, but it is no longer the exclusive property of people who speak it as a first language.

And what about this privileged group: Those of us who by an accident of birth have learned to speak the global language of business and industry without effort? Can we just rest on our laurels secure in the knowledge that our customers, suppliers, and even our employers will communicate with us in *our* native language, rather than in *theirs*?

That might be a mistake. I know of at least one international company of management consultants that will not employ anyone who does not speak at least one foreign language fluently. The reason given is that each language gives you a new perspective on the world, and if you are going to work with people not from your own culture you need to be able to shift away from your "native" perceptions from time to time, because language affects how you think.

LETTERS 81–82

It's inevitable that when speaking English as a foreign language you will make mistakes, and these mistakes can take many forms.

Rude writers   Letter *81*

FROM SPAIN ABOUT **SWEDEN**

In the office where I work we have often had visitors from Sweden, and we've been very impressed both by their English and by their pleasant and friendly manners. However, we have received some letters from these very same people lately and have been amazed by the poor standard of their English and by the tone of the letters, which we find rather arrogant.

You'll be wiser to trust your first impressions. There's a major difference between how we speak and how we write, and whether we're using our native language or someone else's. For example, Swedish children learn English from about the age of eight and quickly become fluent and accurate speakers, but there isn't the same emphasis on written skills (the reverse is true in Japan and South Korea, where writing is prioritized).

When they write in their own language, Swedes are often very informal and rather blunt; this reflects their egalitarian approach to their fellow citizens. When they transpose this style into written English they can unintentionally sound very rude, especially as there isn't a Swedish equivalent for *please* as there is, for example, in Spanish (*por favor*).

It is often difficult to establish the right "tone" in written communication when body language and tone of voice are missing from the communication equation. I have noticed when people from French-, Arabic-, and Spanish-speaking counties write to me, although the grammar and vocabulary may be less than perfect, the tone is extremely polite and rather more formal than letters and e-mails from the U.S. or the U.K. This is because the writers are imitating the more formal and courteous written styles of their own languages and transposing them to English.

Misunderstandings such as you describe, which arise from the tone of a letter or written material, are often the result of "first language interference" and can be hard to identify and correct. It's easier if you make the wrong impression during a face-to-face encounter, because then you get immediate feedback from your listener's body language or facial expression.

The moral is that when writing in any language you should be more formal than when you're speaking, and most importantly, ensure that the tone of the letter is polite and friendly. This is hard to do in a foreign language, but it is even more important than getting the grammar or vocabulary right. If you feel that you cannot judge the tone of your letter yourself, try to get a native speaker to read it before sending it off to ensure that you're not going to offend anyone by appearing less charming than you actually are!

Thin skin   Letter 82

FROM THE NETHERLANDS ABOUT **FRANCE**

I made a mistake the other day when a French visitor used a wrong word when he was speaking English. He told a group of us when we arrived at this office to "Please sit down, and I'll enjoy you in a minute." We Dutch laughed a little about this, and thought he would too, for we know him well and have always worked well together. However, he was extremely offended. We are sorry for our tactlessness but also surprised at his sensitivity.

His reaction is not hard to account for. There is a lot of prestige involved in how well you speak a foreign language, and if the corporate language is English but it isn't your native language, you can feel threatened if you are concerned that your English isn't up to standard. And when people feel threatened, they can become both defensive and aggressive. Speaking a foreign language means that, like it or not, you have to give a public display of how well you command one of the most important tools of your profession, and that can be a nerve-wracking experience.

The standard of English in the Netherlands and in Northern Europe is extremely high, and this fact may have made your French colleague's reaction worse. Until relatively recently the French have not taken English-language learning seriously (although they have not been as bad as the British and Americans about learning foreign languages). He may have been able to accept a native speaker's superiority, but to have another non-native speaker laughing at his errors was humiliating.

LETTERS 83–84

There are many countries with more than one national lan guage and most nations have linguistic minorities. To forget these facts is to show an unacceptable degree of ignorance of the culture you are dealing with.

One country—two languages   Letter 83

FROM BRAZIL ABOUT **CANADA**

I'll be going to Quebec soon but speak only English. How important is it to be able to speak French as well?

I'd take at least a few lessons in French if you intend to do a lot of business in Canada, for this is one country where English is not regarded simply as an efficient tool for international business communication. Instead, it's regarded by some of its French-speaking citizens as a symbol of the oppression by the English-speaking majority of the French-speaking minority.

Canada is divided into ten different provinces, and they have both French and English as their official languages. Today you will find both languages on maps, tourist brochures, and product labels. Historically there has been friction between the French-speaking Québécois and the English-speaking people who have surrounded them for centuries. The Québécois have seen French speakers in other provinces become assimilated into the English-speaking culture, and they take great pains to preserve their language and culture so the same thing doesn't happen to them. So if Quebec is your destination I suggest learning as much French as possible before departure, both as a goodwill gesture and as a survival measure in case you meet some of the Québécois who can't or won't speak English. But be warned: The French they speak in Canada is not the same as that spoken in France, and even some of the English you hear in Québec may be unfamiliar, as many French words have been incorporated into the English they speak there.

One country—several languages   Letter *84*

FROM AUSTRALIA ABOUT **BELGIUM**

I will probably be traveling to Belgium in the near future. I speak elementary French and my native language is English. Will that be enough?

A lot depends on where in Belgium you are going, for despite its small size and population of around 10 million, there are two completely different languages spoken. In Flanders, the northern part of the country, the people speak Flemish, which is a variation of Dutch, and all employers in Flanders are required by law to use Flemish in the workplace.

In Wallonia, the southern part of the country, they speak French, as do many of the inhabitants of Brussels. For Belgians, which language they speak is very much a part of their national identity. The situation in the country is made even more complicated because many Walloons cannot speak Flemish and some Flemish people are reluctant to speak French!

However, in the capital about a quarter of the residents are non-Belgian, so there English is increasingly accepted. Be grateful that English is your native language, because it can be regarded as a sort of "neutral territory" outside the political and historical issues that otherwise make the language question in Belgium such a hot potato.

LETTERS 85–86

There are many different "Englishes," two of which are described here.

British versus U.S. English   Letter *85*

FROM FRANCE ABOUT THE U.S.

I've recently come back from the U.S. where I attended a conference. One lecture dealt with different human resources issues, and I was surprised to hear the term attrition *used in this context. The only time I've heard it before is in* war of attrition, *meaning a war involving total destruction of the enemy. When I got home I checked in my English dictionary and found* attrition *means "the state of wearing away." I'm none the wiser!*

I'm not surprised. This is an excellent example of what George Bernard Shaw meant when he wrote "England and America are two countries separated by the same language." I imagine you learned British English rather than American, and there is a little area where the two don't correspond. Don't be alarmed: *Attrition* doesn't refer to a particularly drastic (and permanent) way of getting rid of unwanted staff! It's a human resources term describing the process by which people leave their jobs at a company when they move to another position, retire, decide to study, and so on and are not replaced. The term for the same phenomenon in England is *natural wastage* (which most Americans think sounds like some sort of sewerage system).

Don't blame your dictionary. Apart from the British-English and American-English differences, the English language is in a constant state of change and dictionaries cannot possibly keep up with all developments.

"International English" for presentations   Letter 86

FROM THE U.S. ABOUT **THE REST OF THE WORLD**

I'm used to giving presentations in the U.S., but I will soon be going abroad for the first time. I'll be presenting information in a number of different countries where I guess most people do not speak English as their first language. Are there any changes I should make to my presentations to adapt them?

Speaking to non-native English speakers certainly requires extra thought, although in certain parts of Asia, for example, Singapore and Hong Kong, which are former British colonies, people may speak English as a first language.

To give a clear message speak slowly and clearly and pause often. In addition, use a tape recorder or ask someone not from your own hometown to establish whether you have a strong accent and if you do, try to tone it down. It's important to be confident and believe in what you are presenting, but make sure you don't come over as too loud (aggressive) or too relaxed (causal). In the more restrained cultures of Eastern Asia or Northern Europe you could appear to be trying to dominate your audience.

To give non-English native speakers a chance to absorb the key facts, repeat your main points in different ways. Try not to use sports metaphors. Violent metaphors are also inappropriate, especially in cultures that value gentle and controlled behavior, so don't use phrases like "bite the bullet," "twist your arm," or "ride roughshod over someone."

If you want your listeners to understand you, avoid the latest buzzwords, idioms, and slang. The use of initials and abbreviations can also be confusing, so use the full form instead. Two more things: don't use even the mildest swear words, and be careful in your use of humor.

It would also be wise to avoid using hand gestures to illustrate a point as they may not be interpreted the same way internationally. One example would be the way a Mexican speaker brought a presentation to a speedy halt in the U.K. by indicating the number two by two raised fingers with the back of his hand facing the audience. He had inadvertently told his British audience to f*** off. (For more obscene gestures, see Letter 93.)

What you *should* do is to make sure that you take plenty of visual material, as this can remove the need for words, and clarify points for people whose native language is not English. Another idea is to distribute written information (in English or the home language) before the meeting so participants have time to read it and translate it if necessary. Remember that it is hard work listening to a foreign language, so keep your presentation shorter than you would at home and make sure you have lots of breaks. This also gives people the chance to ask you questions, something they may not wish to do in front of a large audience if their English is shaky, or if they feel such questions would entail a loss of face by revealing they haven't followed everything you have said.

And a final word of advice: If you don't already speak a foreign language, start to learn one. It will give you an insight into what your Asian colleagues are up against.

LETTER 87

Native speakers of English have an enormous business advantage, but they should not misuse it, or they will cause resentment.

Sensitive speakers sought   Letter *87*

FROM MEXICO ABOUT THE **U.K.**, THE **U.S., AUSTRALIA,** ETC.

Why can't native English-speakers show a little more sensitivity in their dealings with non-English speakers? They often use their superiority in the language to dominate meetings, and if there are two or more present they speak far too fast and use words and expressions we are not familiar with.

Your question is a useful reminder to everyone who has English as his or her first language. People who speak no foreign languages themselves, and this includes many British and American people, often forget what a strain it is listening to a foreign tongue, and when speaking to foreigners they make no concessions when it comes to their choice of words. Not only that, they forget that their listeners may have learned to speak British RP (Received Pronunciation) or Network Standard American English at school and are not used to strong regional accents. Ironically, it's when non-native speakers speak really good English that the worst problems arise, for it's then that Aussies, Kiwis, or Brits forget they're talking to a foreigner and speak in exactly the same way they would to someone from back home, while their poor listeners struggle to keep up.

One of the most important things for native speakers to remember is to listen. Don't treat a person's silence as a sign for you to continue to speak, but wait. Your colleague has to formulate his or her ideas in a foreign language, and that takes time.

LETTERS 88–89

As long as there are different languages there will inevitably be problems with translation.

Language mistake   **Letter 88**

FROM SOUTH KOREA ABOUT **BRAZIL**

My company employed an agency to translate our material for the Brazilian market. We'd already sent away the material when we discovered that it had been written in Spanish and not Portuguese. Our Brazilian agents have told us that it's useless and they require new material. Are the languages really so different?

As well as being the language of Brazil, Portuguese is widely spoken in Venezuelan cities, and elsewhere in South America that Spanish isn't the primary language. It was lucky that your agents spotted the mistake before the material was printed, for national language forms a vital part of national identity, and not respecting this is asking for trouble. Spanish and Portuguese are closely related languages but they are far from being identical, and Brazilians dislike foreigners who do not appreciate this fact. I can imagine that a similar assumption about the inter-changeability of Swedish, Norwegian, and Danish or the different Chinese languages would cause the same sort of resentment. You really have no choice but to recall the Spanish version and provide a Portuguese version as quickly as possible. If you are interested in doing business in Brazil it would be wise to show an interest in, and a certain background knowledge of, the country so you avoid "putting your foot in it" again. You can consult appropriate books, and the Internet is a great source of useful information.

Interpreters   Letter 89

FROM MEXICO ABOUT **JAPAN**

I'm going to be traveling to Japan with a small group of other managers. We don't speak Japanese and were wondering if we should take an interpreter with us, which would be very expensive, or if we can ask the Japanese firm if they can arrange one for us.

It depends on how much money is at stake. If you're hoping to build a solid long-term relationship that is going to earn your company a fat profit, then it's worth thinking about developing a working relationship with a fluent Japanese speaker (preferably a native speaker) who is bicultural as well as bilingual and knows what your company does.

You can hire an interpreter from an agency in Japan, but then you'd have to make sure you allowed sufficient time in Japan to get to know each other before you met your potential partners. She (most Japanese translators are female) needs to know in advance what ground the talks are going to cover so she can prepare herself. She also needs to become familiar with the communication style of the person or people she's translating for. One more thing: if you do decide to hire an interpreter in Japan, book her well in advance as there are not many Japanese-Spanish translators, and you may have to accept a Japanese-English substitute.

Asking the Japanese company to provide an interpreter may not be a good idea, because even though you can be quite sure she will translate the Japanese side's message correctly (she will probably know their business very well), there's no guarantee your message is going to be expressed as you intended. For example, she may not want to take on the responsibility of delivering a message from you that will not please her fellow citizens. They may not have heard the expression "Don't shoot the messenger," but many interpreters are only too familiar with the meaning behind it.

To minimize the possibilities of misunderstandings, have a written summary of the points you are going to make at the meeting translated and distributed *before* the meeting, and get a written summary of the proceedings translated into Japanese shortly *after* the meeting.

IN A NUTSHELL: *A Global Language?*

GLOBAL BUSINESS STANDARDS

For native English speakers: learn at least one foreign language as well as you can.

    For non-native English speakers: learn English as well as you can.

    For everyone: learn a few words of the language of any country you visit and of any foreign visitor you are going to meet.

- **Argentina:** The official language is Spanish, but it is influenced somewhat by Italian. (See Letters 81 and 88.)
- **Australia:** The language is influenced by both British and American English, but it has a distinctive accent and a special Aussie vocabulary. (See Letter 87.)

- **Austria:** German is spoken with a distinctive accent.
- **Belgium:** Official languages are Flemish (similar to Dutch), French, and German. The language spoken is closely tied to a person's ethnicity, and group loyalty is strong. (See Letters 81 and 84.)
- **Brazil:** Portuguese is spoken here—not Spanish like the most of the rest of South America. (See Letters 81 and 88.)
- **Canada:** There are two official languages: English and French. The language spoken is closely tied to a person's ethnicity, and group loyalty is strong. (See Letters 81, 83, and 87.)
- **China:** The official spoken language is Mandarin, a language based on tones. It is also the only form of written language. In some provinces people speak one of four major dialects, but these aren't understood by speakers of the other dialects. (See Letter 86.)
- **Denmark:** Danish is almost indistinguishable to Norwegian in written form. Norwegians, Danes, and Swedes can often understand each other.
- **Finland:** The language is similar to Hungarian (!). In some areas Finns also speak Swedish.
- **France:** You are judged according to how well you speak French, and your command of the language is seen as an indicator of your education and intelligence. There is a big difference between using the familiar *tu* (informal) and the more formal *vous*. (See Letters 81 and 82.)
- **Germany:** There is a big difference between using the familiar *Du* and the formal *Sie*.
- **Hong Kong:** English, Cantonese, and Mandarin are widely spoken. (See Letter 86.)
- **India:** There are eighteen official languages and about as many dialects distributed geographically (e.g., Hindi, Punjabi, and Gujarati, and Urdu, which is spoken mostly by Muslim minority). English is widely spoken by educated people. Many people are bilingual or multilingual.
- **Indonesia:** There are more than 300 ethnic languages. Bahasa Indonesia, the major unifying language, is adapted from Bhasa Melayu (Malay). (See Letter 86.)

- **Italy:** About 60 percent of Italians speak a dialect, which may be impossible for other Italians to understand. The vast majority also speaks standard Italian.
- **Japan:** Spoken Japanese and Chinese are quite different. Basic literacy requires mastery of three alphabets, one of which is derived from Chinese and contains about two thousand characters. (See Letters 86 and 89.)
- **Mexico:** Spanish is spoken by 98 percent of the population. (See Letters 81 and 87.)
- **Netherlands:** Dutch is spoken. It is almost identical to Flemish, which is spoken in Belgium. It is also the ancestor of South Africa's Afrikaans. The Dutch are some of the best speakers of English as a foreign language in the world. (See Letter 82.)
- **Norway:** There are two distinct and rival versions of Norwegian. Norwegian is almost indistinguishable to Danish in written form. Norwegians, Danes, and Swedes can often understand each other.
- **Poland:** Polish is a Slavic language, but unlike Russian, it uses the Latin script.
- **Russia:** Russian uses the Cyrillic alphabet. Words are pronounced as they are spelled. Russian is spoken by most people, but Russia is made up of about a hundred ethnic groups, many with their own languages.
- **Saudi Arabia:** Arabic is the official language of the country and is widely spoken in the whole region. (See Letter 81.)
- **South Africa:** There are eleven official languages. English, Afrikaans (related to Dutch), and Zulu are the main ones.
- **South Korea:** Compared to Chinese and Japanese, the alphabet is easy to learn. Foreign (English) words are readily integrated into Korean. There is much pressure on young Koreans to learn English. (See Letters 86 and 88.)
- **Spain:** The Castilian dialect is the accepted standard. There are also three regional languages. Catalan (as well as Castilian) is spoken widely in Barcelona, Spain's second-largest city. There are some differences from the Spanish of Latin America. (See Letter 81.)

- **Sweden:** A sharp intake of breath can mean *yes*. Norwegians, Danes, and Swedes can often understand each other. (See Letter 81.)
- **Switzerland:** There are four official languages and most Swiss speak at least two fluently. The result of the most recent census shows the breakdown of first language speakers as follows: (Swiss) German 63.9%, French 19.5%, Italian 6.6%, Romansh 0.5%, others 9.5%.
- **Taiwan:** Mandarin is the official language, but 70 percent of the population speaks Southern Fujianese, often called Taiwanese. They do not use the modernized Chinese script currently used in China.
- **Thailand:** Like Chinese, Thai is a tonal language. The written script is based on ancient Indian languages. Fellow Thais usually understand regional and ethnic dialects. (See Letter 86.)
- **Turkey:** Turkey is an oral culture. What is said and heard is taken more seriously than what is written.
- **UK:** Differences between British and American English may lead to misunderstandings. (See Letters 81, 85, 86, and 87.)
- **US:** Differences between British and American English may lead to misunderstandings. Spanish is widely spoken by Latin American immigrants in southern states and California. (See Letters 81, 85, 86, and 87.)
- **Venezuela:** Spanish is spoken. There is a distinctive Venezuelan accent, and some specifically Venezuelan vocabulary exists. In major cities Portuguese is quite common. (See Letters 81 and 88.)

Body Language

Some research estimates that up to 90 percent of a message comes from body language, which doesn't leave a lot left over for words. As someone who spends a lot of time teaching people to speak a foreign language, I find this is rather a depressing statistic. People spend all that time and effort to learn the grammar and vocabulary of another language when all they really need is to learn to read each other's facial expressions and gestures! Of course, it's not as simple as that. Try explaining how a car works or blood circulates using only body language, and you'll realize pretty quickly that words have an important part in the communication process.

Yet in face-to-face communication, words themselves give us only a part of the picture. When it comes to interpreting feelings and moods, body language is often a more reliable indicator. We have all heard people say one thing when the evidence of our senses, or our reading of the speaker's body language, tells us another story. "I'm so glad to see you" spoken between clenched teeth conveys a different message to the words taken on their own.

Even relatively primitive machines like lie detectors can read body language, while dogs have been trained to recognize the infinitely small signals in their owners that precede an epileptic attack. As humans we recognize some common physical signals in people from other cultures, like a smile of happiness or an expression of rage.

Even so, there are significant differences in body language that are culture-dependent. For example, the amount of eye contact regarded as appropriate in different situations even in the *same* culture can vary enormously. Not meeting someone's eyes in a business meeting in the U.S. can mean you're hiding something, while on the subway a glance that lasts a fraction of a second too long at a fellow passenger can be interpreted as a challenge.

Touching is another area where there are wide cultural differences. In Latin American and much of Africa and the Middle East, for example, a friendly conversation between members of the same gender involves frequent physical contact in the form of a touch on the upper arm, a pat on the back, or an arm around the shoulders. The more physically reserved Japanese or British, however, will feel uncomfortable in this situation and may "freeze" with embarrassment.

It's not surprising, then, that when you're in a foreign culture you make mistakes by translating physical signs into your own native body "language." And because we don't carry around the *Dictionary of International Body Language* (because it doesn't exist), we will probably unconsciously interpret the signals of people from other cultures according to our own standards. But this is risky, because most interpretations are made unconsciously and possible misinterpretations are harder to correct; for example, the customer who gets close enough to you to breathe in your face would probably be considered by a North American or North European as making some sort of sexual advance or threat. For a fellow Arab he is simply being friendly.

There are few other areas where so little (a glance, a smile, a shrug) can be misinterpreted so dramatically by so many. If there is any section in this book where the words "Don't jump to conclusions" are warranted, this is it.

LETTERS 90–92

Learning to interpret another culture's physical signals is just as important as learning to interpret its language—and it is just as easy to make mistakes.

Nodding   Letter *90*

FROM THE U.S. ABOUT **TURKEY**

I've heard from U.S. American colleagues who have visited Turkey that it was very difficult for Turks to accept no for an answer. Can this be a language problem, or do you think it depends on cultural differences?

A misreading of a simple headshake can lie at the bottom of this confusion. Turks do not shake their heads from side to side to say *no* as Americans and most Europeans do. Instead, they usually toss their head backwards and raise their eyebrows at the same time. For Turks, the side-to-side headshake is a signal that someone doesn't understand something and requires further explanation. The head toss to mean *no* is also common in Greece and Bulgaria, and in Arab countries, where it might be accompanied by a click of the tongue.

Holding hands   Letter *91*

FROM GERMANY ABOUT **THAILAND**

> *I've heard from some people who have visited Thailand that they've often seen men wandering about hand in hand. This strikes me as very odd. I'm going there soon and wouldn't know how to react if another man tried to hold my hand!*

Isn't it strange how attitudes to physical contact are so very different depending on which country you're in? In Europe and North America, many people find same-sex couples holding hands strange or even offensive, but regard men and women holding hands as perfectly acceptable. In other lands, especially strictly Muslim countries like Saudi Arabia, Pakistan, and Indonesia, the reverse is true. All physical contact between the opposite sexes (even between husbands and wives) in public is taboo, whereas people of the same sex holding hands is regarded as a simple gesture of friendship.

But it isn't only in Thailand and in Muslim countries that patterns of physical contact differ from those of Northern Europe or North America. It's quite common, for example, in Peru and other Latin countries to see same-sex friends walking along and chatting arm-in-arm. But I wouldn't worry if I were you: if you're going on a short business trip you're not likely to get to know someone well enough for either hand-holding or arm-linking.

Eye contact   Letter *92*

FROM THE U.S. ABOUT **JAPAN**

> *I'll be going to Japan soon and have heard that it's rude to look someone directly in the eye. Is this really true? I don't want to be regarded as discourteous.*

In the U.S. and in most parts of Europe, failure to make frequent eye contact on meeting, and indeed throughout a conversation, can be interpreted as showing you have something to hide and that you're "shifty." In the U.S., directness is highly valued and a direct look is regarded as a reflection of honesty. In Greece, many Latin American, and Arab countries, speakers will maintain even more intensive eye contact while delivering a message, which to non-natives can appear intimidating. There, looking away can be interpreted as a sign of dislike.

In Japan, however, intense eye contact would be regarded as staring and could be interpreted as a lack of respect. Eye contact is avoided there much of the time, and the listener looks at the collar of the speaker and looks down when speaking. The same applies in Vietnam, although in another East Asian country, South Korea, direct eye contact is acceptable and is regarded as a sign of trustworthiness.

I heard a funny story from a man who attended a course on cross-cultural awareness during which he and his colleagues learned about the differences I've described. Afterwards they went to an important meeting in Japan. There all the Americans who had been on the course gazed at their Japanese counterparts' ties, while the Japanese, who had also been on a cross-cultural awareness course and learned about Western customs, gazed straight into the U.S. Americans' eyes. It's getting to be a pretty small world!

LETTERS 93–94

We don't usually intend to offend our cross-cultural partners. But if we do, we may have to learn some new gestures in order to do it!

Offensive gestures   Letter 93

FROM FINLAND ABOUT **MEXICO**

In the 1990s I worked in Iran checking selected vehicles. Every time an Iranian technician checked something, I asked him in sign language if it was okay. The signal I used was the famous "thumbs up." I later learned that the sign I was giving was obscene—the equivalent to the famous raised middle finger! I'm going to Mexico soon and want to know if there are signs there that I should avoid.

This area is very confusing. In Mexico you should avoid making a circle with your index finger and thumb. In Finland and most of Europe that means *okay*, but unfortunately in Mexico, Brazil, and Germany it is highly obscene. The thumbs-up sign is the correct way to show that all's well (although, as you found out, this is obscene in the Middle East). And on the subject of offensive signs, I've mentioned elsewhere that the raised two fingers sign, with the palm of the hand facing inwards is highly obscene in the U.K., South Africa, and Russia, while pointing your finger at anyone is regarded as very rude throughout the Middle East and East Asia. If you want to beckon someone in these countries, keep your palm down and waggle your hand or fingers. You may think it would make sense in the face of all these conflicting standards to keep your hands in your pockets when you spoke to people, but unfortunately that is interpreted negatively just about everywhere.

Physical taboos   Letter 94

FROM SPAIN ABOUT **INDIA**

What should I not do on my first visit to India? I've heard there are numerous physical taboos and I'm terrified I'll do something awful.

India is a country with a lot of experience with foreign business people, and I doubt you'll manage to shock anyone even if you do unwittingly break some rules. However, there are a few unwritten rules governing physical gestures and actions that you should observe. The left hand is regarded as unclean, so you shouldn't use it for eating or passing things. (This fact applies, by the way, to all Muslim countries too.) Indians don't appreciate physical contact with strangers, so backslapping and bear hugs are not recommended. It's particularly bad mannered to touch or point at anyone with your feet or sit with the soles of your shoes exposed; Indians, as well as people from as far away as Syria and Thailand, find this offensive.

Finally, both Muslims and Hindus frown on any physical contact between the sexes in public, so it's a good idea for a man to nod or bow on being introduced to an Indian woman instead of offering his hand.

LETTER 95

Not getting the response you expect can be a confusing experience.

No response Letter *95*

FROM ARGENTINA ABOUT **FINLAND**

I'm visiting Finland and feel I'm getting nowhere with the Finns. I get no response when I make presentations and find it impossible to guess what they think. Are they the world's best poker players?

The Finns are not alone in being facially impassive or in having the sort of subtle body language that only fellow nationals can understand. This is true of Scandinavians as a whole, and the British are also experts at keeping "a stiff upper lip" when the situation arises. Many people find the Dutch hard to "read," and the Japanese and Chinese regard it as a virtue to be able to hide their feelings. It's not that they don't use body language— everyone does—it's just not the table-banging, shoulder-shrugging sort. If you want to do business with these undemonstrative types, you will have to learn to observe how they communicate with each other and not to expect immediate or extravagant reactions to your ideas. You may find that they respond better to you if you tone down your own way of expressing yourself and keep things low-key and understated.

LETTER 96

How close we like to get to each other varies enormously. Even if you are expecting different standards, the first "eyeball-to-eyeball" meeting can be a shock.

Space "bubble" Letter 96

FROM THE U.K. ABOUT **BRAZIL**

> *On our recent first visit to Brazil our Brazilian counterparts were very friendly, but we noticed that when speaking they'd come closer and closer and we British ended up backing away. The Brazilians saw this, and in the end we could all joke together about how they chased us round the office. I suppose we just had different ideas about what was appropriate body space.*

Yes, that's right. When first visiting a country (and if your schedule permits), it's time well spent if you can find somewhere to watch ordinary people meeting and greeting each other and conducting normal conversations. Then you can get an idea of the kinds of gestures they make, how loudly or quietly they speak to each other, and how expressive their faces are. It's just as important to observe what they make of your own body language. In your case it was lucky your Brazilian colleagues didn't interpret your need for more space as being standoffish. In many Western European countries and in North America we expect to stand a couple of feet apart when talking. In other countries, for example, in Latin America, North Africa, sub-Saharan Africa, and the Middle East, people stand extremely close and may keep in physical contact by touching hands, arms, or shoulders throughout the conversation. As you say, they're simply being friendly.

Other nationalities go to great lengths to avoid touching each other. In the U.K. and U.S. people signal that they might be on a collision course by saying *Excuse me* or *Pardon me*, and then if the worst happens and they actually touch a stranger or even an acquaintance (and assuming the earth does not open up and swallow them as a result), they apologize. The Swedes and Finns often don't say anything, but when faced with the problem of getting around a stranger in a confined space, they will adopt strange limbo-like poses to sidle around without making physical contact, while at the same time trying to pretend the person isn't there—it's quite a feat! The Germans and South Koreans will also avoid eye contact, but they won't turn a hair if they bump into someone and wouldn't dream of apologizing. They didn't do it on purpose, after all.

IN A NUTSHELL: *Body Language*

GLOBAL BUSINESS STANDARDS

The closer the relationship, the closer people get physically (within their cultural parameters).

Don't touch any part of the body of the opposite sex (apart from a handshake, with the right hand, which is acceptable in most non-Muslim countries).

GLOBAL WARNINGS

Offensive and insulting gestures:

Most places: a raised middle finger.

Mexico, Brazil, and Germany: the finger and thumb forming an *O*.

The U.K., South Africa, and Russia: two fingers forming the *V* for Victory sign, but with the thumb facing inwards.

Australia and the Middle East: a raised thumb.

- **Argentina:** People stand closer than in most Western European and North American cultures. People make regular physical contact when talking to each other. (See Letters 92 and 96.)
- **Australia:** There is little physical contact between business acquaintances.
- **Austria:** Smiling is not a "must" in business communication; it is reserved for friends. (See Letter 91.)
- **Belgium:** See Austria.
- **Brazil:** People stand closer than in most Western European and North American cultures. (See Letters 92, 93, and 96.)
- **Canada:** Standing about an arm's length between two speakers is considered appropriate. (See Letters 91 and 96.)

- **China:** Subtle, undemonstrative body language is the norm. There is little intentional body contact between strangers, but close friends, especially girls and women, often walk arm in arm. People don't show emotions freely in public. (See Letters 93 and 95.)
- **Denmark:** Subtle, undemonstrative body language is the norm. (See Letter 95.)
- **Finland:** Subtle, undemonstrative body language is the norm. Faces can remain almost impassive. (See Letters 91, 93, 95, and 96.)
- **France:** Smiling is not a "must" in business communication; it is reserved for friends. Male and female friends may kiss each other on the cheek.
- **Germany:** Smiling is not a "must" in business communication; it is reserved for friends. There is limited physical contact when people communicate. (See Letters 91, 93, and 96.)
- **Hong Kong:** See China.
- **India:** Touching between strangers (except for shaking hands) is not generally acceptable. The left hand is regarded as unclean. It is not accepted to touch anyone with your foot. A side-to-side head sway means *yes*. (See Letter 94.)
- **Indonesia:** Don't touch people's heads, and don't touch people with your feet. It is not common to show emotions freely in public (See Letters 91, 93, and 94.)
- **Italy:** Body language is demonstrative and hands play an important part. There is a lot of physical contact between speakers.
- **Japan:** Subtle, undemonstrative body language is the norm. People stand farthest apart of all cultures and don't touch anyone anywhere at all if they can help it. The handshake is an exception. There is little direct eye contact. (See Letters 92, 93, and 95.)
- **Mexico:** People stand closer than in the U.S., Canada, and Western European cultures. (See Letters 93 and 96.)
- **Netherlands:** Subtle, undemonstrative body language is the norm. People leave a wide space between each other when they talk. (See Letters 95 and 96.)
- **Norway:** There is little physical contact between people when communicating. People prefer undemonstrative body language. (See Letters 91 and 95.)

- **Poland:** An older man may kiss a woman's hand when being introduced. Male friends may kiss each other on the cheek.
- **Russia:** People stand much closer than is usual in the West. Greetings with friends can be quite physical, with vigorous handshakes, hugs, and kisses. (See Letter 93.)
- **Saudi Arabia:** People stand closer than in Western European and North American cultures. There is a lot of physical contact between members of the same sex. Men holding hands is regarded as a sign of friendship. (See Letters 90, 91, 92, 94, and 96.)
- **South Africa:** Men greet each other in quite physical ways, for example, strong handshakes and backslapping. Black South Africans, more reserved initially, will later become more physical, and hugs and long handshakes are signs of friendship. (See Letter 93.)
- **South Korea:** Staring or intense eye contact may be regarded as hostile or bad manners. (See Letters 92, 93, and 96.)
- **Spain:** Lots of physical contact accompanies communication with people they know. (See Letter 94.)
- **Sweden:** Undemonstrative body language and rather impassive faces are the norm. There is little physical contact during communication. (See Letters 91, 95, and 96.)
- **Switzerland:** There is little physical contact between people when they are communicating. Undemonstrative body language is the norm. (See Letter 91.)
- **Taiwan:** There is little intentional body contact between strangers and even between friends. (See China.)
- **Thailand:** There is very limited physical contact between individuals. It is taboo to touch someone's head or to touch people with your feet. They don't show emotions freely in public. (See Letters 91 and 94.)
- **Turkey:** People stand closer than in most Western European and North American cultures. To indicate *no*, people will usually toss their heads backwards, raising their eyebrows at the same time. The individual's "comfort zone" is smaller than in European countries. People of the same gender touch regularly. (See Letters 90 and 94.)

- **UK:** There is relatively little physical contact in public. People don't show emotions freely in public. The V sign with the palm inward is an obscene sign. (See Letters 91, 93, 95, and 96.)
- **US:** Americans stand eighteen to twenty-four inches apart when speaking. This is more than in the Middle East and Southern Europe but less than in Asia. For most North Americans, about an arm's length between two speakers is considered appropriate. (See Letters 91, 92, and 96.)
- **Venezuela:** Constant eye contact, frequent touching, and lots of gestures commonly accompany communication. People are physically demonstrative. (See Letters 92 and 96.)

CHAPTER 5

Time

Once upon a time, many years ago, in a large wooded country in Northern Europe, a powerful and prosperous company had its headquarters. Naturally the company had a mighty leader (let's call him *ML* for short), a very important man, and many less important people called *managers*.

One day one of the big managers (we'll call him *BM* for short) decided to hold a meeting with a lot of his less important managers and even some non-managers too (they are called *workers*). He also invited ML to come to tell everyone about how well the company was doing.

Anyway, the day dawned and those invited assembled in a big room to hear how BM's staff were about to launch an exciting new development in a country far away that would make the whole company rich beyond its wildest dreams.

The seconds ticked away. It was time to start, but ML wasn't there. Another sixty seconds, and still he had not arrived. Three more minutes ticked away as people looked uneasily at each other. After five minutes BM stood up. "Lock the doors," he said. People looked at each other. Had their ears deceived them? "Lock the doors," he repeated, and added, "The time for waiting is past. We will start now." And they did.

After three more minutes ML arrived. His attendants tried the door but they couldn't get in. Their faces were red, and ML's face was a delicate shade of purple. But there was no help for it; they had to go all the way back to their offices and miss the fun!

Inside the locked doors everyone was very happy that BM had stood up for his principles, because everyone knows that being punctual is a sign of respect for other people, and that people who are regularly late for appointments sooner (or possibly later) will end up in a Very Bad Place Indeed.

Of course this all happened a long time ago and both ML and BM have gone their separate ways. But whenever people in the powerful and prosperous company in the north are tempted to make just one more phone call or finish an important piece of work before going to their meeting, they remember the story of ML and BM, and they put down their receivers and switch off their PCs and hurry down the corridor to their appointments.

Anybody not born and brought up in one of the relatively small number of clock-obsessed cultures (led by the Nordic countries, Germany, Switzerland, and Austria, and followed by among others the U.K., the U.S., Australia, New Zealand, and Singapore) is going to find the above "fairy tale" impossible to believe. However, I know that the main points of the story are true. The CEO of a large Swedish multinational corporation was locked out of an important meeting by a manager because he came late. And equally surprising, perhaps, was that the manager didn't lose his job and was generally admired for his actions.

There are two main ways of looking at this story:

- You regard the manager who locked the door as a power-mad petty dictator with a bizarre set of priorities, focused on rules and details, and lacking in respect for his senior. After all, what's a few minutes in the scheme of things?
- You applaud a man who by his actions said the same rules apply to everyone, and that the rule of punctuality is an indicator of your respect for your fellow men and women. Wasting someone's time is not only rude, but it is a sign of inefficiency, or worse, arrogance.

The alternative you choose indicates which culture you come from. It also gives an indication of your own individual perception of time, because we don't all conform to "our" cultural stereotypes when it comes to punctuality. Of course, many Germans and Swedes always arrive late at meetings, just as the only person I know who has never been late for *any-thing* is a Spaniard (who obviously doesn't share the *mañana* mentality that is supposed to characterize many Latin cultures).

Punctuality is about prioritizing clock time above other things, whether that means leaving a discussion unfinished, a task uncompleted, or a colleague ungreeted. People who follow clock time believe they are being efficient, but is that always the case? Many cultures, like Turkey, India, and most of Latin America and the Middle East, believe that time is an endless rolling cycle in which many things can be done at once. They also believe that time *includes* what you want it to and should not be used to *exclude* activities that do not happen to fit into neat bite-sized pieces.

The area of intercultural contact where problems and misunderstandings are most likely to arise is how we regard time. How we divide it up, the practical and symbolic value we place on it, and what it's *for* are all questions that divide cultures, but because it's easier to define differences in the way we present business cards or hold our cutlery, it's an area that is often ignored.

Whichever group you fall into (the clock watchers or the more relaxed types who believe that time is elastic and will always stretch sufficiently to allow them to do what is important), you will have to spend some time trying to understand the other group if you don't want to drive your counterparts crazy. Why not arrange a meeting to discuss the subject? Just make sure you arrive on time!

◆ MORAL

We grow up with attitudes and beliefs about time that we rarely question. When we go abroad it's important to re-examine them.

Calendars and Holidays

It's important to know as much as possible about the calendars and holidays of any country you're likely to do business with. The first reason is obvious: You don't want to spend a couple of days flying to the opposite side of the globe only to find that shops and offices all shut the moment you get off the plane. The second reason is that if you know what your counterparts celebrate, you will learn what is considered important in their culture, and that knowledge can only help strengthen any future relationship.

The Chinese calendar, for example, is still used for determining festivals, and the Chinese New Year is the main holiday of the year for more than one quarter of the world's population, yet it exists alongside the Gregorian (Western) calendar in the People's Republic of China. Similarly, the Muslim states around the Arabian Gulf use the Western calendar in addition to the Hijrah calendar (which is based on the date of Muhammad's emigration to Medina). In Russia, the Orthodox Church still follows the Julian calendar, not the Gregorian one, which means that Russians celebrate Christmas Day (if they celebrate it at all) on January 7, and oddly enough, the Bolshevik revolution, which started on October 25 in 1917, is currently celebrated on November 7.

There are three main kinds of national holidays: there are the ones based on religion or a set of beliefs, the ones that commemorate a historical event, and the ones that reflect the seasons. (Of course, a few holidays don't fit into any of these categories, including international holidays like Labor Day and International Women's Day, which are observed more or less enthusiastically from country to country.)

Festivals of the major world religions or belief systems—Christianity, Islam, Buddhism, Hinduism, and Judaism—can be included in the religious group. Not all *holidays* (a word whose origins lie, appropriately enough, in *holy days*) are celebrations, but may be occasions for contemplation, prayer, or fasting, and deserve to be treated with the utmost respect by believers and non-believers alike.

The second category celebrates historical events that have played a part in shaping the national identity. These holidays are often expressions of national pride and identity, and visitors should treat these celebrations seriously: not to do so is asking to be labeled as an arrogant and ignorant foreigner. Examples of the third kind of holiday, based on the changing seasons, include the Japanese cherry blossom festival, harvest festivals in Spain and Germany, the Swedish Midsummer holiday, and the Chinese Mid-Autumn or Moon festival, when family members get together to celebrate the changing seasons.

LETTER 97

The Western calendar is not the only way of calculating the date, but it is the most common in international business contexts.

Check your Chinese calendar   Letter 97

FROM SPAIN ABOUT **CHINA**

I was doing business in China a while back, but when we were close to signing an agreement, my Chinese partner suggested that we wait until the Chinese New Year as the Snake was more auspicious for our business. I really wanted to get on with the deal and found the reason for the delay ridiculous. However, I kept my feelings to myself and agreed to wait, and the business went very well. But I've never really understood the connection between the New Year and the Snake.

You did well to be patient and show respect for the beliefs of your partner. In China, and countries with a large ethnic Chinese population, many millions take Chinese astrology very seriously, and people may consult an astrologer before making important business decisions.

According to legend, twelve animals came to bid Lord Buddha farewell before he left the Earth. They were the rat, ox, tiger, rabbit, dragon, snake, horse, sheep, monkey, rooster, dog, and boar. Very briefly, the Chinese believe that each of these animals "rules" a particular lunar year (which begins with the Chinese or Lunar New Year in January or February) and influences what happens in that year. They also believe that the individual is strongly influenced by the nature of the animal that ruled his or her year of birth. You may be asked your date of birth by people you meet there so that they can work out which animal sign you were born under, for Chinese astrology continues to have a strong influence, even after 4,500 years.

The Snake governed most of the year 2001, and your business partner had obviously had a horoscope drawn up that said this was an auspicious year for your business. Whether you believe in Chinese astrology or not, it gives a fascinating way of viewing ourselves and our world. You will find firms in China with international contacts that observe the Western calendar, but the ancient festivals of the Chinese calendar are still observed enthusiastically by the local population.

LETTERS 98–100

Writing the date should be simple, but that is not necessarily the case.

Writing the date   Letter *98*

FROM THE U.S. ABOUT **EUROPE**

Is there any foolproof way for Europeans and Americans to avoid misunderstandings when writing the date? As you know, we have different conventions here in the U.S. to the ones you have in Europe.

This can indeed be a problem. Even within Europe there are different systems. In Eastern Europe, including Hungary and Poland, they write the year, month, and then the day (as do the French Canadians). The Swiss and Italians write the dates like U.S. Americans do—month, day, and then year; this is also the Latin American standard. Inevitably, though, there are exceptions, and Brazilians and Argentineans, as well as most Europeans, the Russians, and Australians, start with the day followed by the month and then the year. The result is, of course, that if your next meeting is set for 8.9.04, half of your group is likely to turn up a month late.

There have been attempts to solve this problem, but like many great ideas, the solution has created new and improved problems. There is an international standard, with the catchy title *ISO 8601*, that decrees that the date should be written year, month, and day. The problem is that if you are writing to people not aware of the standard, and you arrange a meeting for 050604, you give your readers the interesting opportunity not only to turn up in the wrong month but also the wrong year, as they may well assume that the last figure refers to the year. Dear, oh dear.

The only way to eliminate the chance of mistakes is to write out the month, even if you abbreviate it. It does not matter then if you start with the day or the month, as everyone can see that 2 Jan 2005 and Jan. 2, 2005 refer to the same day. That way you can be sure that you and your colleagues all turn up for your meeting at the same time on the same day.

Holidays, nationality, and religion   Letter 99

FROM CHINA ABOUT **AUSTRALIA**

Last year before I paid a short visit to Australia I checked carefully that my visit wouldn't coincide with any public holidays there. However, when I arrived I found that I couldn't meet some of my potential customers because it was Yom Kippur, a Jewish holiday. I found this very confusing.

It's important to remember that in many countries there are significant religious minorities: Muslims in the U.S., for example, or in the case you describe, Jews in Australia. It's risky to make assumptions about someone's religion based on the country he or she comes from. If you are doing business with people from a religious minority you will have to observe their religious holidays, even if in the rest of the country it's "business as usual."

Working over weekends   Letter 100

FROM THE U.S. ABOUT **BELGIUM**

I work for a large U.S.-owned multinational with a growing presence in Belgium. To get us all pulling in the same direction work-wise and to help colleagues get to know each other better, I've organized a "kick off" meeting at a conference center for a whole division. It will start on Friday afternoon and end on Sunday morning. In other words, participants will be required to spend two nights at the hotel. The weekend will be a mixture of work sessions and lighter social activities. I'd expected one or two people to be unable to attend, but have been surprised to find the majority of employees, including managers, unwilling to come.

In Belgium and many Southern European countries, the extended family is still an important institution and the weekend is a time for spending time with them or with friends. This does not imply any lack of commitment to the company, just a belief that there is more to life than work. You'd have more luck with your proposal in Sweden, Norway, and Denmark, where the demands of the extended family are rather weaker, though even here your suggestion would probably be less than popular. In Europe generally there is more of an emphasis on the work-life balance than in the U.S. and especially in a country like Belgium, where traditionally work and home life are kept separate, this appropriation of a weekend is regarded as an imposition. And as for the managers, stepping outside their traditional roles and socializing with subordinates on an equal basis may be an uncomfortable experience. I'd think again about the best way of achieving your objectives.

IN A NUTSHELL: *Calendars and Holidays*

MAJOR RELIGIOUS HOLIDAYS

Religious holidays play a part in most countries' calendars. The list below shows the major holidays of different religions. Remember, though, that most countries will have religious minorities whose holidays should also be respected. Among countries sharing the same religion (e.g., Christianity and Buddhism) there may be different variants (e.g., Protestantism and Catholicism, and northern, eastern, and southern forms of Buddhism). They may also have entirely different festivals. An asterisk (*) denotes that the dates for the holiday change from year to year.

Buddhist (Bu): Different holidays depending on whether it is
  Southern Buddhism (in Southeast Asia): New Year festival*; Vesakha, usually in May*; Kathina, October or November*
  Eastern Buddhism (in China, Korea, and Japan): Birth of Buddha*; Birth of Kuan Yin, usually in March*; Obon, usually in August*
  Northern Buddhism (in western China and northern India): Modlam Chenmo*, Guru Rinpoche's birthday*, Lhabab Duchen*

Christian (Ch): Christmas Day, December 25; Easter*;
  Whitsun*; Ascension Day*

Orthodox Christianity (ChO): Eastern Orthodox Christmas, January 7; Easter*

Hindu (Hi): Holi*, Diwali*

Jain (Ja): Diwali night*, Nirvana celebration*, New Year*

Jewish (Je): Rosh Hashanah*, Yom Kippur*, Hanukkah*, Pesach (Passover)*

Muslim (Mu): Ramadan*, Eid al-Fitr*

Sikh (Si): Baisakhi, April 13th; Diwali*

Shinto (Sh): Bean throwing festival in February, Star festival in July, Bon festival in August*

Taoist (Ta): Lao Tzu's birthday*, Chinese New Year*, Zhong Yuan (Ghost Day)*

The following holidays are secular and observed to a greater or lesser degree around the world: the first two are observed by many millions of people, the latter two less widely.

New Year's Day, January 1

Lunar New Year (date varies from year to year)

International Women's Day, March 8

International Labor Day, May 1

GLOBAL BUSINESS STANDARDS

The Western calendar is usually used for business purposes.

In some areas of commerce and industry, especially in Europe, week numbers may be used to express the date (e.g., "delivery is expected in week 12"). Week numbers are also found in the programs of an increasing number of handheld PCs and electronic organizers.

The following lists some of the most important *non-religious* dates in each country's calendar, but be sure to check for others when you plan your journey. The abbreviations indicate the *major religion of each country* (the abbreviations are listed in the preceding Major Religious Holidays box).

- **Argentina:** (Ch) Anniversary of the 1810 Revolution, May 25; Flag Day, June 20; Independence Day, July 9; Day of the Races, October 12. (See Letter 98.)
- **Australia:** (Ch) Australia Day, January 26; Anzac Day, April 25; Queen's Birthday, June 9. (See Letters 98 and 99.)
- **Austria:** (Ch) National Day, October 26.
- **Belgium:** (Ch) National Holiday, July 21. (See Letter 100.)
- **Brazil:** (Ch) Carnival, 41 days before Easter; Tiradentes Day, April 21; Independence Day, September 7; Patron Saint Day, October 12; Proclamation of the Republic, November 15. (See Letter 98.)
- **Canada:** (Ch) Canada Day, July 1; Thanksgiving Day, second Monday of October. (See Letter 98.)
- **China:** (Bu, Ta, but officially atheist) National Day, October 1 and 2. (See Letter 97.)
- **Denmark:** (Ch) Constitution Day, June 5. (See Letter 100.)
- **Finland:** (Ch) Midsummer's Eve, June 21; Midsummer's Day, June 22; National Day, December 6.
- **France:** (Ch) Victory Day, May 8; Bastille Day, July 14; Armistice Day, November 11. (See Letter 100.)

- **Germany:** (Ch) Fasching/Carneval days before Ash Wednesday; Day of German Unity, October 3.
- **Hong Kong:** (Ch)(Bu) (Ta) National Day, October 1 and 2. (See Letter 97.)
- **India:** (Hi, Mo, Si, Ch, Ja) Republic Day, January 26; Independence Day, August 15; Mahatma Gandhi's birthday, October 2.
- **Indonesia:** (Mo) Independence Day, August 17.
- **Italy:** (Ch) Women's Pride Day, March 8; Republic Day, June 2. Note that patron saints' days can shut down whole cities. (See Letters 98 and 100.)
- **Japan:** (Bu, Sh) Adult's Day, January 15; Golden Week, April 29 to May 5; Respect the Aged Day, September 15; Emperor's Birthday, December 23.
- **Mexico:** (Ch) Constitution Day, February 5; Battle of Puebla Day, May 5; Declaration of Independence Day, September 15; Independence Day, September 16; Day of the Races, October 12; Anniversary of the Mexican Revolution, November 20. (See Letter 98.)
- **Netherlands:** (Ch) Queen's Day, April 30; Liberation Day, May 5.
- **Norway:** (Ch) National Day, May 17. (See Letter 100.)
- **Poland:** (Ch) Constitution Day, May 3; Independence Day, November 11. (See Letter 98.)
- **Russia:** (ChO, Mo, Je) Victory Day, May 9; Declaration of Independence, June 12; November Revolution, November 7. (See Letter 98.)
- **Saudi Arabia:** (Mo) The Western calendar is used for business, and the Hijrah calendar for religious holidays.
- **South Africa:** (Ch) Human Rights Day, March 21; Freedom Day, April 27; Youth Day, June 16; National Women's Day, August 9; Heritage Day, September 24; Day of Reconciliation, December 16.
- **South Korea:** (Bu) Independence Movement Day, March 1; Arbor Day, April 5; Children's Day, May 5; Memorial Day, June 6; Constitution Day, July 17; Liberation Day, August 15; National Foundation Day, October 3.
- **Spain:** (Ch) Carnival, February or early March; Hispanic Day, October 12. Note that patron saints' days can shut down whole cities. (See Letter 100.)

- **Sweden:** (Ch) Midsummer Eve, approximately June 21; Lucia, December 13. (See Letter 100.)
- **Switzerland:** (Ch) National Day, August 1. (See Letter 98.)
- **Taiwan:** (Bu, Ta, Ch) See China. Also National Day, October 10; President Chiang Kai-Shek's Birthday, October 31. (See Letter 97.)
- **Thailand:** (Bu) Chakri Memorial Day, April 6; Coronation Day, May 5; Queen's birthday, August 12; King's Birthday, December 5.
- **Turkey:** (Mo) National Sovereignty and Children's Day, April 23; Ataturk Commemoration and Youth & Sports Day, May 19; Victory Day, August 30; Republic Day, October 29. (See Letter 100.)
- **UK:** (Ch) Early and Late May Bank holidays, first and last Mondays in May; late Summer Bank Holiday, last Monday in August; Boxing Day, December 26.
- **US:** (Ch, Je, Mo) Martin Luther King Junior Day, third Monday in January; Washington's Birthday/Presidents' Day, third Monday in February; Memorial Day, last Monday in May; Independence Day, July 4; Labor Day, first Monday in September; Columbus Day, second Monday in October; Veterans' Day, November 11; Thanksgiving, fourth Thursday in November. (See Letter 98.)
- **Venezuela:** (Ch) Carnival (two days), March 3; Mov. Precursor de la Independencia, April 19; Battle of Carabobo, June 24; Birth of the Libertador (Bolivar Day), July 24. (See Letter 98.)

The Working Day

A friend from South Africa told me that the first thing she does when she gets home from work is to take off her wristwatch. When she mentioned this I was almost shocked. I am so used to wearing a watch that I only take it off in bed, and not always then. When I thought about this I realized that for good or ill, I had carried over the "clock consciousness" that was so important in my working life to my non-working life. But where does work begin and end? Our working days are punctuated by other things like eating, sleeping, talking to our friends, and even praying (if we are religious Muslims).

External factors play a part too. If the temperature regularly goes over eighty-five degrees Fahrenheit in the early afternoon, it makes sense to take a siesta and work later in the evening instead. The hours we work are also influenced by our gender, which may even determine if we are allowed to work outside the home at all. In Saudi Arabia, the kinds of jobs open to women are strictly limited, while until 2000 there was a law on the French statute books that forbade women (except in nursing) to work nightshifts.

And speaking of statutes, of course unions and social legislation have had their part to play in limiting the working day and indeed the working week. Taking France again as an example, the government decided in 2000 that its citizens should work a maximum of thirty-five hours a week. Though a lot of French people work longer hours than this, the working day for many French people ends at 4:00 instead of 5:00 P.M. In Britain, on the other hand, the "long hours culture," which the government has done nothing to hinder, means that the average person there works the longest hours in Europe, 43.6 hours per week in 2002.

There is a strong element of tradition in how we divide up the day. A Swedish mechanic I know who was sent to a French workshop to solve a technical problem was surprised by a couple of things when he got there. The first was that the lunch break started an hour and three-quarters later than the 11:15 A.M. that he was used to. And then at the stroke of 1:00 P.M. the lights were switched off in the workshop, while he was halfway through a difficult job, and everyone went to a nearby restaurant for lunch. But at 4:00 P.M., which was technically the end of the working day, and when at home the Swede would have been getting his coat on, everyone ignored the clock and stayed to get things finished. There was no hurry to get home, but being late for the midday meal would have been a cardinal sin.

LETTERS 101–102

"The early bird catches the worm" is a saying familiar in many parts of the English-speaking world. However, it is not necessarily one that translates well to other cultures.

Too early?   Letter *101*

FROM FINLAND ABOUT **SOUTH KOREA**

I realized I had made a big mistake on my last visit to South Korea when I asked the manager I wanted to meet if I could see him at 8:30 A.M. This would be quite natural in Finland, but I could see from his reaction that this was certainly not the custom there.

In South Korea, the usual time for business is from 9:00 A.M. to 5:00 P.M., as it is in many other countries. In fact, the Nordic countries are exceptional in their early starts at the office, despite these same countries being pitch black on winter mornings until after 9:00 A.M. The flextime system is widespread there, and it's not unusual for white-collar Finnish workers to be at their desks at 7:30 A.M. or even earlier.

In other cultures, where entertaining customers or spending free time with colleagues in the evenings is the norm, late nights of socializing (with or without the use of alcohol) can mean that early starts may not be popular. So Italian, Mexican, and Russian managers might be just as unprepared for an early meeting as the South Korean manager. (In fact, in Russia, avoid planning any meetings on Monday mornings.) But this may not be the only reason for the manager's reaction to the suggestion for an early meeting. In some Asian and South American countries it is the boss's privilege to arrive late at the office in the mornings, and the bigger the boss you are, the later you can arrive. Asking for such an early meeting here may be interpreted as showing a lack of respect for his status.

Breakfast meetings   Letter *102*

FROM THE U.S. ABOUT **FRANCE**

I'll be in France for a few days next month and have an extremely packed schedule. I was wondering if it would be possible to organize breakfast meetings to meet my new French subordinates so I can make the most of my time there. Do you think my suggestion is likely to shock them?

Reexamine your schedule and try to find another way to solve your problem. French people, like Russians, Latin Americans, and people from the Middle East and the countries around the Mediterranean, don't like to be rushed, especially by foreigners or people they don't know. However, they have a great respect for authority, so they would probably turn up, but it would be an unpopular move for many reasons. It would be seen as making demands on private family time, which the French are loath to sacrifice to business. It would also (perhaps equally importantly) be seen as a demand for them to sacrifice a mealtime too—even if that meal consists only of croissants and café au lait. In a country that takes food as seriously as the French this would be seen as a barbaric move, and it would confirm their worst prejudices about U.S. Americans' obsession with the clock. It would be better to meet your new coworkers on your next visit than run the risk of getting off to a bad start.

LETTER 103

We all do other things during the "working day" apart from work.

Prayers at work   Letter *103*

FROM ARGENTINA ABOUT **INDONESIA**

I know that Indonesia is a Muslim country and have heard that Muslims are supposed to pray five times a day. How do they arrange this at work? Do they have time off from work for this?

You're right about the five times a day rule. Two occasions for prayer are at dawn and at night and are usually done at home. However, there are two or three times during the working day (there are local variations) when religious Muslims might pray: midday, mid-afternoon, and sunset. Midday prayers take about fifteen minutes and afternoon prayers about half that. Some workplaces in Indonesia have a separate room for prayers where employees can go. This is particularly important during Ramadan, the period of fasting, and on Fridays, the holy day of the week. On this day lunchtimes may be extended so that male employees can visit the mosque. It's important that any foreign firms with a presence in Indonesia observe these customs about providing places for people to pray. The rooms themselves don't have to be particularly well appointed or devoted solely to prayers, although it would obviously be insensitive to allow people to smoke there or for non-Muslims to eat their lunches in them. Not providing such a room could be seen as showing a lack of respect for your employees' religion and could cause the firm serious problems.

All of the above applies to any country where the established religion is Islam or there is a large Muslim minority, such as India.

LETTER 104

How exact can you be about how you are going to divide your day?

No planning possible   Letter *104*

FROM SWITZERLAND ABOUT **MEXICO**

I find it difficult to plan my time here in Mexico, because even though I know (very roughly) when a meeting will start, there is never an indication of when it will finish, so I can't make definite arrangements for the rest of the day. I find this very frustrating.

In many countries in South America, Southern Europe, the Middle East, and Russia it would be regarded as rather odd to set an exact time for a meeting to end. The reasoning would be, how could you possibly know in advance how long the meeting will take? It sounds as if you find this lack of precision rather inefficient, but I'm sure your Mexican colleagues find your preoccupation with exact timing rather inefficient too. I mean, if you and the people you're meeting with are near to finding the solution to a problem at 10:55, surely it's not a good idea to rush away simply for the sake of being on time for an 11:00 o'clock appointment, is it?

LETTERS 105–106

At the end of the day we usually go home. But when does the day end?

Leaving so early?   Letter *105*

FROM THE U.S. ABOUT **SWEDEN**

We recently had some visitors here from Sweden, and as we were chatting I was amazed to hear a quite senior manager say that he regularly left work early (about 4:00 p.m.) to pick his children up from the local day care center. Is it usual for family commitments to take precedence over work there?

It is the law in Sweden that parents of young children should be allowed to work 80 percent if they wish to. As a result of this law, many parents decide to work a six-hour day so they can go home comparatively early. This measure, along with the generous system of state-subsidized parental leave and day care centers, is designed to help mothers and fathers of small children combine parenthood and a career as smoothly as possible. There is an awareness in Sweden, Norway, and Denmark of the need for a work-life balance, as well as a realization that the country needs as many as possible of its well-trained workforce to work outside the home, even when the children are small, if the economy is to continue to prosper.

Swedes work hard and they are extremely conscious about using time in the most efficient way while they're in the office. It's also quite common for them to take work home with them in the evenings and weekends, so

I wouldn't say that they neglect their work for their families. Indeed, some people might say they needed to do that more often!

Working overtime   Letter *106*

FROM GERMANY ABOUT THE **U.S.**

> *We have a new American boss here who has made it clear that he expects us to work late when we have a lot to do. We can understand having to do this in a crisis, but this seems to be becoming a regular occurrence. We feel that it is his job to organize our workloads so that we can finish our work within normal working hours.*

Both the U.S. and German cultures are known for valuing hard work very highly. Indeed, in cultures with a more relaxed attitude they joke that both nationalities live to work rather than work to live. However, it sounds as if you and your boss have different ideas about what hard work means. For your boss, long hours are an important sign that you take your work seriously, but your priority is to work as efficiently as possible during office hours.

In Germany, most people set great store by their private life and keep it separate from their life at work. In the U.S. this is also the case, but work seems to consume more and more leisure time too. Personally, I find it healthy that there are people and cultures that resist the growing trend to be available for work twenty-four hours a day. In other European countries, South America, and the Middle East, people may also object to working overtime, because in these cultures people like to enjoy the moment and set a high value on time spent with family and friends.

However, there is also the fact that in a global economy international companies must provide "never-close" services for customers worldwide, so the old 9:00 to 5:00 mentality seems increasingly old-fashioned. The best solution would be to talk to your boss and see if there was some way he and your colleagues could work out the most effective way to use your time during the working day so you could avoid overtime work.

IN A NUTSHELL: *The Working Day*

- **Argentina:** People work later in the evenings, sometimes until 9:00 or 10:00 P.M. and eat even later. Business lunches are common, often between 1:00 and 3:00 P.M. (See Letters 101, 102, 104, and 106.)
- **Australia:** Colleagues may go for a drink together at the end of the working day, about 5:00 P.M. Australia has three time zones that have to be taken into account when planning meetings.
- **Austria:** Employees go home promptly at the end of the day, and overtime is not the norm.
- **Belgium:** Managers may arrive at the office later than their subordinates.
- **Brazil:** Breakfasts, lunches, and dinners are all popular occasions for business meetings. Managers may start later in mornings than subordinates. Business lunches can last two hours. People may work later in the evening, until 9:00 or 10:00 P.M. Modern companies are trying to abolish the siesta, but it's an uphill battle. (See Letters 101, 102, 104, and 106.)
- **Canada:** The business breakfast is less popular than the business lunch. It has six time zones, some of which correspond to those of the U.S., and this has to be taken into account when planning meetings.

- **China:** Despite its size, China has only one time zone. Businesses usually open at 8:00 A.M. Everyone stops for lunch and a nap between noon and 2:00 P.M. Business socializing (dinners, banquets) in the evening is important. (See Letter 101.)
- **Denmark:** There is an early start to the day, so an early lunch is quite common and people go home early too. It is difficult to arrange business meetings in July. (See Letter 105.)
- **Finland:** Most businesses open at 8:00 A.M. People go home early in the afternoon in summer (about 4:00 P.M.). It is difficult to arrange business meetings in July. (See Letter 101.)
- **France:** In accordance with a law passed in 2000, people work a 35-hour week. Breakfast meetings are not popular. Lunchtime starts at 12:30 or 1:00 P.M. Business lunches are very popular and can take two or more hours. The best times for meetings are about 11:00 A.M. or 3:30 P.M. Managers may work late in the evening, until 9:00 P.M. (See Letter 102.)
- **Germany:** Breakfast meetings are rare. Employees come to work early and most go home promptly at the end of the day. Overtime is not the norm. Some offices close early on Friday afternoons. People usually have at least four weeks of vacation in the summer. (See Letter 106.)
- **Hong Kong:** Many firms follow a six-day workweek, including Saturday. Afternoon naps, common in China, are less common here. (See Letter 101.)
- **India:** There is only one time zone, despite its size. Indian standard time is five hours ahead of Greenwich Mean Time. Indian executives usually prefer late morning or early afternoon appointments and don't work very late in the evenings. Usually there's only a one-hour lunch. Muslims pray five times a day. (See Letter 103.)
- **Indonesia:** There are three time zones, which must be taken into account when planning meetings. Muslims pray five times a day. (See Letter 103.)
- **Italy:** Lunch is the day's main meal, and usually starts about 1 .P.M. Most people go home between 6:00 and 7:00 P.M. Modern companies are trying to abolish the siesta, but it's an uphill battle, especially in the south. (See Letters 101, 102, 104, and 106.)

- **Japan:** The working day often extends to evening socializing, so early meetings are not very popular. Employees don't take all their vacation entitlement, so it's seldom that they are not at work. (See Letters 101 and 104.)
- **Mexico:** Modern companies are trying to abolish the siesta, but it's an uphill battle. (See Letters 101 and 104.)
- **Netherlands:** Lunch is usually the only meal where business is conducted, and it usually lasts just one hour.
- **Norway:** There is an early start to the day, and people finish early in the afternoon in the summer (about 4:00 P.M.). (See Letters 101 and 105.)
- **Poland:** Breakfast meetings are not common, even though firms open quite early. Firms may also be open on Saturday mornings.
- **Russia:** It has eleven time zones that need to be taken into account when planning meetings. Meetings usually don't start until 10:00 A.M. (and not until noon on Mondays). Lunch is usually one hour, from 1:00 to 2:00 or 2:00 to 3:00 P.M. Russians may stay at work after hours to socialize. Most business-related social meetings are held in the evenings. (See Letters 101, 102, and 104.)
- **Saudi Arabia:** Friday is holy day and no business is done. The working week is from Saturday to Wednesday, Thursday and Friday being free. Most people do not work on Thursday either. Because of summer heat, businesses often close between noon and 4:00 P.M. and open after dark. Muslims pray five times a day. (See Letters 102, 103, 104, and 106.)
- **South Africa:** Offices open between 8:00 and 8.30 A.M. and close about 5:00 P.M., with thirty to sixty minutes for lunch.
- **South Korea:** Socializing takes place mainly in the evenings, so early morning starts are not appreciated. (See Letter 101.)
- **Spain:** Long lunch breaks are the norm. Business socializing may require late evenings, so early morning starts are not appreciated by managers. Modern companies are trying to abolish the siesta, but it's an uphill battle. (See Letters 102, 104, and 106.)
- **Sweden:** Workdays start early, and working breakfasts are not unusual. Early lunches are common (from 11:15 A.M.). People finish early in the afternoon in summer (about 4:00 P.M.). People will

usually have at least four weeks of vacation in the summer. (See Letters 101 and 105.)

- **Switzerland:** People start work early (around 8:00 A.M.) and a one- or two-hour lunch around midday is the norm. (See Letter 104.)
- **Taiwan:** Many people take a nap at lunchtime. Business socializing is popular in the evenings (dinners and banquets). (See Letter 101.)
- **Thailand:** Traffic in Bangkok is extremely heavy and can cause delays to the start of morning meetings. Business dinners are extremely common, and socializing after working hours is important. (See Letter 101.)
- **Turkey:** Muslims pray five times a day. (See Letters 102, 103, and 104.)
- **UK:** Employees work the longest hours in Europe. The workday may well involve a pub lunch, and colleagues may go for a drink right after work.
- **US:** Employees may work through lunch and have a sandwich at their desks so as not to "waste time." Breakfast meetings from 7:00 A.M. onward are quite normal for the same reason. The six time zones have to be taken into account when planning meetings. (See Letters 102, 105, and 106.)
- **Venezuela:** Three-hour business lunches are not unusual, and people work well into the evening. (See Letters 101, 102, 104, and 106.)

Attitudes toward Time

In the U.K. and the U.S. you can now dial a local number for information about your mobile phone bill when you get home from work, and your call will be answered by someone in a call center thousands of miles away in Bangalore, India, by an operator working the night shift. The manager of this call center is quoted as saying enthusiastically, "Geography is history. Time is irrelevant."

Indeed, the latest time- and geography-defying technologies, including satellite communications and the development of the Internet, have meant that a multinational organization never sleeps. It has employees in different parts of the globe up and working twenty-four hours a day every day of the year.

But even if people start and finish work at exactly the same time and have the exact same length of time for a lunch break all over the globe, there will still remain important local differences in how they *use* their time. For when it comes to issues of, say, what you prioritize during your day, what you regard as an efficient way to work, or the time you give to social relations at work, there continue to be significant cultural differences.

And it's disturbing how quickly the words *right* and *wrong* or *good* and *bad* come into the picture when we start talking about these matters. It's as if the way we use time has a moral dimension, and as soon as *morality* comes into the picture, we should prepare ourselves for fireworks, because it's then that people's deepest cultural values come to the fore.

One question guaranteed to provoke a lot of soul searching is, "How do you balance your job with your family life?" Do you work every hour of the day to earn the money to give your family a comfortable lifestyle, or do you spend as much time with them as you can, even if that means the job suffers? Which choice should you make if you want to be both a responsible citizen and a good family member? How you answer depends on the culture you come from. The Japanese phenomenon of *karoshi* (death by overwork) is an extreme version of the "work above everything" philosophy, while cultures like the French and Mexican, which value who you *are* rather than what you *do*, will find an insistence on fifty-hour weeks and lunches at the desk too high a price to pay for success at work.

Another time-related question to which people have widely different responses is "to queue or not to queue?" The British and North Americans generally believe in the essential rightness and fairness of queuing and show open hostility to those who try to push to the front of lines. Queue-jumping is not merely regarded as bad-mannered—it is seen as reflecting an arrogant belief that the "jumper's" time is more important than that of others. However, this attitude is not shared by everyone. An Italian friend of mine gets very irritated by the orderly and slow-moving lines that form to and around the *smörgåsbord*, the Swedish buffet tables. She reckons that the Italian way of doing things (no queuing, and everyone going directly to the dishes they want as quickly as possible) would result in everyone being served in about half the time. But this belief in the fairness of standing in line affects how the British, North Americans, and

Scandinavians work. For them, working in the "correct" way means doing one thing at a time, while the next job waits its turn. (For more discussion about queuing, see Letter 35 in Chapter 2.)

If you want to avoid culture clashes in this most sensitive of areas, never use any of the following words to describe a group of people who look at time in a different way from you: *lazy, sluggish, work-shy,* or *disorganized,* or alternately: *inflexible, mechanical, robot-like,* or *inhuman.* Because, strangely enough, *they* may feel that at least one of these less-than-complimentary expressions describes *you!*

LETTERS 107–109

In your view, is being late the eighth deadly sin? If so, do not assume that your attitudes are shared by the rest of the world.

Deadline delays   Letter *107*

FROM GERMANY ABOUT **POLAND**

We have had enormous problems getting our Polish suppliers to deliver what they have promised on time. The word deadline *does not seem to mean anything to them, and contracts we have signed are treated only as guidelines. It's very difficult to work with such inefficient partners.*

In Germany delay equals failure, but there are few other countries that follow the calendar, and indeed the clock, so rigorously. But you need to realize that not sticking to deadlines is not the same as being inefficient. In Japan, for example, deadlines as such are not particularly popular, even though the Japanese have a reputation for being very efficient.

Your view of deadlines may be regarded by other cultures as reflecting a lack of flexibility. The infrastructure in Poland is not as developed as that of its neighbor Germany, and that may create problems for your Polish suppliers. It only needs a truck to break an axle on a bad road and your deadline becomes a fond memory. It's also true that Poles, Russians, and the citizens of other ex-Communist countries share a rather fatalistic attitude about problems and delays. They regard them as inevitable and may lack a sense of urgency in identifying and solving problems especially the further from the top of an organization you are. In a country where full employment in the still recent Communist era was a government pledge, and simply turning up for work guaranteed a (small) salary, it can take awhile to understand the idea of meeting deadlines. However, the advantage of coming from such a background is that Poles are used to dealing with unexpected situations and sudden changes and will rise to the challenge.

Finally, try to appreciate that the insistence on meeting deadlines that is so common in the U.S., the U.K., and Germany can be seen by the other partner as a form of bullying, or a sort of threat ("if you don't meet the deadline we will. . . . "), and even as a way for a rich powerful country to make people in the poorer country jump through hoops. Tough talking here can be counterproductive. Instead, try to be diplomatic when dealing with the whole question of timetables and deadlines, or you may lose such potentially profitable markets as India, Mexico, South America, and China, countries that traditionally don't set a lot of store by such things.

Sacred timetable	Letter *108*

FROM MEXICO ABOUT **SWEDEN**

My company ordered a delivery of goods from Sweden to be delivered in early June, but because of unexpected customer demand we will need it earlier. Our Swedish supplier knows this but refuses to change the delivery schedule. It seems that our order is in some sort of queue, and they cannot or will not interfere with this. This attitude seems to us completely lacking in flexibility and shows a lack of consideration for their customers as well.

Scandinavians, like Germans and U.S. Americans, are careful planners. They usually have efficient systems in place designed to give manufacturers control over their processes, and they may find acting without a ready plan hard to deal with. They don't like having to find impromptu solutions to problems and prefer to stop them from arising in the first place by careful preparation.

They also believe that the same rules should apply to everyone, and as they have a queuing system, your request to "jump the queue" makes them feel uneasy. That is because, like the British and U.S. Americans, Swedes equate waiting in line with fairness, for this ensures that every customer waits the same amount of time. Try to talk to them again and explain in detail the financial implications of a delay. And then follow up any calls with an e-mail to the production manager or the person highest up the chain of command. He or she will probably try to help you if possible, but only if this doesn't create problems for their other customers.

Punctuality first, friendship second   Letter *109*

FROM SPAIN ABOUT THE **U.S.**

Normally I have a good relationship with my American manager. We're about the same age, we work together well, and he's friendly and open. We often go out for lunch together and we've met each other's families. However, if I come just ten minutes late to work he acts like the big boss, as if I've committed some terrible crime. It's almost as if he suffers from some personality disorder!

I can see you find this behavior confusing, and indeed rather hurtful, but I'm sure your boss is not trying to be difficult. It's simply that U.S. Americans, Canadians, and Northern Europeans among others take punctuality very seriously and regard lateness as a sign of discourtesy. In this case, you obviously feel your manager has put his regard for the clock above his personal relationship with you. But for a U.S. American this is normal. It's a part of his or her belief system that everyone, irrespective of status, should follow the same rules, and those not doing so need to know that their behavior is unacceptable. For your manager, his liking for you has nothing to do with his upholding of company rules, for his personal life and business life are two different things. However, for people from the Middle East, Africa, and Central and South America, this is doubtless going to confirm their belief that North Americans and Northern Europeans are a cold-blooded set of workaholics with no sense of personal loyalty.

There's an old Protestant saying, "Cleanliness is next to Godliness," but I think that today in some countries with a Protestant heritage (the U.S., Germany, Switzerland, the Netherlands, the Nordic countries, and others) it should be replaced by "Punctuality is next to Godliness." For your American boss, being on time is a sign of respect both for the company and for your coworkers, and if you were to expect him to "bend the rules" because you were friends, he would see this as a threat to his integrity, and the chances are that you will lose his friendship. It would save a lot of trouble for you both if you managed to get to work a little earlier in the future.

LETTER 110

"More haste, less speed" is an old saying that has gone out of fashion in the West, but the sentiments are certainly understood and shared in other parts of the world.

Long term versus short term   Letter *110*

FROM THE U.S. ABOUT **JAPAN**

I work for a young, growing IT company. We're introducing a new product in Japan but can't get past first base with potential customers. When I give presentations I'm always asked about my company rather than our product. They want to know how many years we've been in business, the background of the executive management—anything but the technical performance. Our products are top quality and we have many satisfied customers. How can I get them to start looking forward and develop some sense of urgency?

You're asking a lot. Entering into a relationship with a new company is taking a big risk, and risk-taking is something that doesn't come easily to many Japanese, even though it is second nature to many U.S and

Canadian firms. The people you have talked to may well feel that you're going too fast. For the Japanese and for companies in China, Turkey, Saudi Arabia, and Germany, the reputation of any company they are to do business with is vital, and they are looking for a long-term relationship with a partner they can trust. In such countries, it is the relationship of mutual trust that precedes and underwrites an agreement, and a legal document is simply empty words if this relationship is not in place. In their eyes, a company's track record, its history, and traditions are seen as a good although not infallible guide to its future performance.

This must be frustrating for someone coming from a culture that focuses more on the present and the short-term future. Your impatience would be shared by others from countries that share your view of things, like Brazil, Ireland, and the Philippines (all countries, by the way, with quite a young population). However, don't show your impatience or try to rush things, as this would brand you as immature and arrogant. One way forward might be to find a reputable Japanese representative who would help you form the right relationships. You say that despite being a young company you have many satisfied customers. If among them is a large international company that the Japanese are likely to have heard of, try to emphasize this, as it will help enhance the reputation of your firm. And remember, it takes time to build relationships, and if you don't have the time to invest, perhaps Japan isn't the market for you.

LETTER 111

A productive use of time or simply inefficient? It all depends on your point of view.

No focus   Letter *111*

FROM CANADA ABOUT **MEXICO**

I work in marketing and I find doing business here in Mexico really hard going. I've gotten used to things never starting on time, but last week when I was finally allowed into the office of the manager I was to meet I was surprised to find four other people there, too, discussing (in Spanish) some issue completely unrelated to my business. He also had a couple of phone calls from his wife while I was there. And yet, when I could finally get a word in edgeways, he seemed genuinely interested in what I had to sell.

For people working in Mexico and Central and South America, it's perfectly possible to do more than one thing at a time, hence the presence of others in the office. Traditionally, people living in Latin countries and the Middle East like to carry out a number of tasks at the same time. They think it makes sense to deal with matters as they arise rather than set themselves a fixed and inflexible schedule. So all the activity in the manager's office during your visit was a result of his working simultaneously with several issues (and not all work-related ones either). But as you noticed, this lack of focus did not imply a lack of interest, so don't be disheartened.

LETTER 112

Power and status bring with them control over other people's time.

Time and status   Letter *112*

FROM THE U.K. ABOUT **BRAZIL**

I've just returned from a visit to Brazil where I was to meet an influential local factory owner about a supply contract. I'd made the appointment a month before and confirmed it on the phone with his secretary two days before we were due to meet. When I turned up I waited one and a half hours before he deigned to see me. By that time I was too angry to be as diplomatic as I should have been, and the meeting was not a success. In my opinion you simply can't sacrifice your self-respect for the sake of a contract!

I can understand your irritation. In Australia, Northern and Central Europe, Germany, Canada, and the U.S., wasting someone's precious time is seen as a sign of disrespect. And in these relatively egalitarian societies, people with power, managers, and politicians will often downplay their status and influence and usually try to be as punctual for meetings with subordinates as they are for superiors. There, good time management skills are a sign of efficiency.

Things aren't the same everywhere. In many South American and Mediterranean cultures, being "on the dot" for appointments is not regarded as a particular virtue. It makes more sense to finish what you're doing or to take care of an important situation that has arisen without warning. However, the biggest difference of attitude is in the status of the manager and how that status is displayed. To put it simply, bosses in cultures where hierarchies are important expect people to wait for them. The reasoning is that the more important the boss, the more important things he has to do, which makes him a busy man. If you don't have a comparable status, then your time cannot be as important as his. People from the U.K and the other "clock conscious" and more egalitarian cultures will interpret this as a "my time is more important than your time" attitude and find it extremely irritating.

Relax. There is simply no point in getting angry at this behavior; it is not meant as a personal sign of disrespect to you. On the contrary, it's just a fact of life that in many cultures people with power use their control over other people's time as a measure of their own status. And in certain societies (such as Latin America, South Europe, South Korea, India, and Pakistan) it is important that there is no doubt about one's status in the pecking order.

The next time you think such a situation might arise, go prepared with a couple of magazines or books, perhaps a bit of background reading on the country you're visiting, or on the company you are hoping to do business with. Chat with the secretary, write some letters, or phone some friends, as you learn that you too can take a flexible view of time.

IN A NUTSHELL: *Attitudes toward Time*

GLOBAL BUSINESS STANDARD

Be punctual as far as possible, whatever culture you find yourself in, but don't necessarily expect others to do the same.

- **Argentina:** Dealing with immediate issues takes precedence over planning. People are used to doing many things at the same time and to dealing with interruptions. They aim for immediate results. Relationships take priority over schedules. Clock-bound time management is not a priority. (See Letters 107, 109, 111, and 112.)
- **Australia:** They prefer to work on one thing at a time. There is an emphasis on short-term results. Punctuality is seen as a sign of courtesy. As a manager it's not enough to insist that your Australian employees arrive on time; you will have to give convincing evidence that their lateness is harming the organization. (See Letter 112.)
- **Austria:** They are prepared to work toward long-term future gains. They prefer to work on one thing at a time. Punctuality is very important. (See Letter 112.)
- **Belgium:** The need to have immediate results leads to emphasis on short-term goals. (See Letter 112.)
- **Brazil:** Working on many things at the same time is the norm. The need to have immediate results leads to emphasis on short-term results. Dealing with immediate issues takes precedence over planning. Relationships take priority over schedules. Appointments are often arranged at short notice. Punctuality is not especially prized. (See Letters 107, 109, 110, 111, and 112.)
- **Canada:** Punctuality is seen as important. There are differences in French-Canadian and Anglo-Canadian attitudes toward time. See France and U.K. (See Letters 109, 110, and 112.)
- **China:** People are prepared to work toward long-term future gains. There is a patient and unhurried management of time, and people may resist being held to timetables. Past precedents are important.

Relationships take priority over schedules. Punctuality is a sign of politeness. (See Letters 107 and 110.)

- **Denmark:** See Austria. (See Letters 108, 109, and 112.)
- **Finland:** See Austria. (See Letters 108, 109, and 112.)
- **France:** People are used to doing many things at the same time. They may start a task slowly and finish fast. Clock-bound time management is not a priority.
- **Germany:** They do one thing at a time and work at a steady pace. Planning—time limits, deadlines, and so on are extremely important. They favor long-term goals and benefits. Punctuality is very important. (See Letters 107, 108, 109, 110, and 112.)
- **Hong Kong:** Past precedents are important. They are prepared to work on many things at the same time, and to work toward long-term future gains. Relationships take priority over schedules.
- **India:** Managing time is not an urgent problem for most people. They may have a fatalistic attitude toward the future (what will be, will be) and prefer to do one thing at a time. Relationships take priority over schedules. The need to have immediate results leads to short-term planning. (See Letters 107 and 112.)
- **Indonesia:** People prefer to do many things at the same time. Limited effort is put into planning ahead. Clock-bound time management is not a priority.
- **Italy:** Dealing with immediate issues takes precedence over planning. People in northern areas are more clock-conscious than those in the south, but clock-bound time management is not a priority. (See Letter 112.)
- **Japan:** People are prepared to work toward long-term future gains. Making decisions can take a long time. Attention to detail results in efficient use of time (the just-in-time delivery system method originated here). Punctuality is important. (See Letters 107 and 110.)
- **Mexico:** People prefer to do many things at the same time. Relationships take priority over schedules. Punctuality is not a priority. (See Letters 107, 109, 111, and 112.)
- **Netherlands:** People prefer to work on one thing at a time. Time limits, deadlines, and so on are more important than business rela-

tionships. Punctuality is seen as a sign of courtesy. (See Letters 108, 109, and 112.)

- **Norway:** People prefer to work on one thing at a time and favor long-term goals and benefits. (See Letters 108, 109, and 112.)
- **Poland:** The need to have immediate results leads to short-term planning. They are used to working on many tasks at the same time. (See Letter 107.)
- **Russia:** It's currently difficult to make and fulfill long-term plans. Deadlines and schedules may not be taken seriously. Can work with many things at the same time. In business, patience is valued more highly than punctuality. (See Letter 107.)
- **Saudi Arabia:** People can work on many things at the same time. They may have a fatalistic attitude toward the future (what will be, will be). Clock time is valued less than social obligations. Punctuality is not a priority. (See Letters 109, 110, and 111.)
- **South Africa:** The bigger the company and more formal the structure, the more likely people are to keep to schedules. In smaller companies there is a much more relaxed view of schedules.
- **South Korea:** People are used to working on many things at the same time. Making decisions can take a long time. They are prepared to work towards long-term future gains. Relationships take priority over schedules. (See Letter 112.)
- **Spain:** (See Letters 109 and 112.)
- **Sweden:** Business usually takes a long-term view. Planning—time limits, deadlines, and so on—have high priority. Making decisions can take a long time. Punctuality is seen as a sign of courtesy. (See Letters 108, 109, and 112.)
- **Switzerland:** People do one thing at a time. They favor long-term goals and benefits. Punctuality is seen as a sign of courtesy. (See Letters 109 and 112.)
- **Taiwan:** People are used to working on many things at the same time and are prepared to work toward long-term future gains.
- **Thailand:** People are used to working on many things at the same time. Interest is in short-term results. Relationships take priority over schedules.

- **Turkey:** Dealing with immediate issues takes precedence over planning. People can work on many things at the same time. Relationships take priority over schedules. (See Letters 109, 110, and 112.)
- **UK:** People prefer to do one thing at a time. Time limits and deadlines are taken seriously. Making decisions can take a long time. Punctuality is regarded as a courtesy. (See Letters 107, 108, and 112.)
- **US:** People prefer to work on one thing at a time. However, they are getting used to working with more than one thing at a time as a result of "the networked economy." There is less interest in the past than the short-term future. Time is money. (See Letters 107, 108, 109, 110, and 112.)
- **Venezuela:** People are used to work being interrupted and to doing more than one thing at a time. They like to see immediate results and have a comparatively optimistic view of the future. Relationships take priority over schedules. Clock-bound time management is not a priority. (See Letters 107, 109, 111, and 112.)

PART III

Working Together

CHAPTER 6

Personal Profiles

We all know that our appearance has an enormous influence on how we are regarded by other people, at work and elsewhere. Magazines are full of advice on how we can lose weight, improve our complexions, and choose clothes to flatter us at that important job interview. However, there is little we can do about two biological truths that shape us physically, mentally, and perhaps even spiritually: our age and gender.

Of course, people do spend enormous amounts of money getting their wrinkles removed and their bottoms lifted simply because they don't want to *look* old. But basically, if we are lucky enough to live that long, we get old and eventually die and there's nothing we can do about it. We can't do much about our gender either, for even if sex-change operations are performed regularly now in the West, not even the cleverest surgeon would claim the results were perfect.

But what about ethnicity? It affects our appearance too, but whereas age and gender are quite easy to define, *ethnicity* is a vague, fuzzy word that has all sorts of other associations, mostly negative (think of *ethnic purity*, and worst of all *ethnic cleansing*). In fact, it is a generic word that includes religion, language, and race. Race is usually the only outward sign of ethnicity, and in large, multiracial cities it is an unreliable one at that. Yet even if we know that assumptions about people based on their appearance are often plain wrong, we still keep making them.

At a Swedish IT firm where I work, a manager told me this true story. A representative from a Japanese firm had come on a visit and was due to meet the manager responsible for the installation of the hardware that his firm had just delivered. As it happened, this manager was in a meeting when the visitor arrived, so the assistant manager went down to the reception area to meet him. As the two men were walking along the corridor the departmental manager appeared from the conference room where the meeting had just finished. Naturally the assistant manager introduced his boss, who was surprised that the Japanese visitor made no attempt either to shake hands or bow. In fact, he appeared to be looking for something as he glanced up and down the corridor. Obviously he couldn't find whatever it was, and driven to desperation, he finally stood on tiptoe and tried to look over the manager's head.

The problem was that the Japanese visitor had expected to meet a white Swedish middle-aged man and was faced, he finally realized, with a young brown-skinned Swedish woman wearing trousers and a sweater. His assumptions about what a manager should look like simply didn't match the reality that he encountered in that particular company. Basing his judgment on his experience back home in Japan, the visitor considered that the manager's age, gender, and race didn't correspond with her status, and thus he didn't know how to relate to her.

Over the last decade or so many international companies have found that similar mistakes in judgment have cost them money because they have not realized the full potential of their employees. They have also begun to see that a more diverse workforce can provide them with a competitive advantage, and they are making efforts to include in their workforce employees with widely different personal profiles—including people of different ages, genders, and ethnic backgrounds. Companies with diverse workforces are supposed to be more likely to have an inclusive, balanced view of people, processes, customer needs, and business methods in general. What is usually left unsaid is that although diversity is the best option, it is not at all easy—quite the reverse.

The process of trying to understand unfamiliar points of view, whether they come from the opposite sex, a different age group, or a new ethnic group, takes a lot of imagination and energy, and most of us don't have unlimited supplies of either. If, on the other hand, your team is made up of people like yourself, you can communicate in shorthand because you can take a lot of things for granted without discussion. It's not surprising, then, that many international companies talk happily about diversity in the workplace without actually doing anything to encourage it or utilizing the talents of "non-conforming" smaller groups already working in the company (whether they happen to be female, older than their colleagues, or from an ethnic minority).

But the world is changing and there is a growing realization that personal profiles that do not correspond to those already on the team, in the department, or on the board might be an asset rather than a handicap, and not only because different skin tones and hair colors provide a more interesting photo for the annual report. For even though employing people of different ages, genders, and diverse ethnic backgrounds is not an easy option, and indeed increases the risk of conflicts and delays, firms are starting to see that it's the right thing to do not only because it is fairer to the individual employee, but because it also contributes to their own long-term prosperity.

◆ **MORAL**

Including people with another cultural background, age, or gender in your group or team may force you to reexamine what you have previously taken for granted. This may make you uncomfortable, but it is a good thing.

Gender

Any discussion of gender in the workplace usually looks at how female working patterns differ from male (which are routinely regarded as the norm). In fact, in most cultures during most periods of history, women have worked outside the home in paid employment, often in domestic or agricultural roles, and later in nursing or teaching. However, they have rarely, if ever, done so on the same terms as men. And old habits die hard. For example, there used to be a law that forbade Frenchwomen to work night shifts, presumably to protect both their virtue and male jobs. Guess when it was repealed: 1900? 1920? 1950? Wrong, 2000.

Nowadays, even in countries where the majority of women work outside the home, where girls and boys receive the same kind of education and legislation ensures no overt discrimination, their average pay is less and their status in the workplace lower than their male counterpart's. How women are regarded in the workplace is a reflection of how they are regarded in the national culture in general and the specific corporate culture in particular.

I know of an IT support desk in Scandinavia staffed by highly trained young people working around the clock to provide computer assistance to engineering workshops throughout the world. Occasionally callers ask the women on the team when a male colleague will be there to deal with their problems, and the women answer (through gritted teeth) that the caller can either wait eight hours for Testosterone Ted to come on duty or entrust the problem to their own poor female wits (or words to that effect). The funny thing is that these queries do not necessarily come from countries where workingwomen are the exception—Japan or some of the North African states, for instance. They are equally likely to come from the Philippines, Australia, or Brazil, where women have been part of the workforce for many years. The attitudes are less affected by the position of women in society as a whole, and more by "industry culture." Engineering workshops worldwide are traditionally male-dominated, and however far equality has come outside, inside the workshop it is males who are the problem-solvers. So when some of these men have to ask for help and advice from a woman, they may be unsure how to react.

Occasionally governments and corporations try to take positive action to encourage women employees to work and make their lives easier if they do. Increasingly generous maternity leave in certain European countries is one example. In the U.S., some companies have introduced *Mommy tracks* with the aim of keeping women employees on the management ladder even after having children. But usually women put their careers on hold when their children are young, and it is not necessarily a good thing for the parents, the children, or even the corporation. So in certain Swedish companies male managers are actively encouraged to take parental leave, and the company guarantees that they will not lose out financially if they do so. Companies reckon that the experience of running a family will help these men become better managers with a deeper understanding of the everyday pressures on the men and women in their departments.

In cultures as far apart as the Netherlands and the United Arab Emirates, the trend is to have a higher percentage of women working outside the home (although in the UAE the increase is not large). But the move from home to workplace is just the first step. It's then that the big decisions have to be made about how women should work and how they should be treated.

LETTER 113

For women already in a minority in their workplaces at home, moving to a culture where they may be in an even smaller minority can be very trying.

Negative reaction?   Letter *113*

FROM DENMARK ABOUT **BRAZIL**

We are sending a small team to Brazil soon to finalize a contract. Our technical expert in this field is a woman, but we know that there are few if any women working in our area in Brazil and are not sure if the reaction to her presence there is likely to be negative.

The fact that your coworker is female and that there are few women in managerial positions in the country she is doing business in need not be a disadvantage. The situation in Brazil is not unique, and societies as far apart as South Africa and Japan have little experience with female managers. Even in cultures where women are an accepted part of the workforce, like the U.S. and Western Europe, there are still plenty of examples of male-dominated industries. However, the Brazilian team is not likely to judge her by the same standards they would a fellow national, and her status as technical expert is one likely to inspire respect. In fact, the unexpected can work to her advantage, and the men she meets may well not wish to confront or offend her, especially if she is middle-aged or older.

Your colleague should be prepared for occasional displays of male gallantry, whether that takes the form of compliments on her appearance, having doors opened for her, or having things fetched and carried for her that she is perfectly able to fetch and carry for herself. To most male and female Latin Americans this is simply a gender-related expression of good manners, and not to acknowledge gender in this way would be regarded by most as unpardonably rude.

Occasionally this rather "macho" view of the relations between the genders can take an unexpected turn. One petite female Brazilian truck assembly worker, when asked if she found the work physically tough, admitted that occasionally she did find some tasks required a lot of muscle, but her male coworkers on the line liked to think of themselves as gentlemen and were happy to give her a hand when she needed it. For both her and her colleagues it was important that her gender and her different physical make-up were accepted rather than ignored. As long as your female colleague is prepared for similar differences in working patterns and is not likely to overreact to them, there is no reason not to send her.

LETTER 114

A lot has been written on "female management style," but most does not take into account cultural differences, which are another factor in the managerial equation.

Bathroom blues   Letter *114*

FROM FRANCE ABOUT **SWEDEN**

The department on the same floor as mine has a female manager, and both departments share the same toilets. Some younger male employees, to save themselves walking the extra few yards to the men's toilets, had been using the women's and many women felt uncomfortable with this. My first reaction, as a male manager, was to identify the men in question and have a word with them. My female counterpart, however, had other ideas. One morning a woman in my department told me that the women's toilets now had tasteful posters of handsome young men on the walls, dried flowers in vases, and scented soap. No man has been to those toilets since.

Simple but effective! This shows you do not have to be confrontational to win your case or to get people to change their ways. You don't even have to use words. Generally speaking, women's management style is seen as less aggressive, and women are less likely to give orders than their male counterparts. But a high degree of conflict avoidance is also part of the Swedish management style, and it is impossible to be certain to what extent this manager's actions were the result of her gender and how much to her being Swedish. On occasion this lack of direct verbal communication may be interpreted as weakness by some individuals who come from very verbal cultures, like the U.S., Australia, and France, where everything is usually spelled out very explicitly, but this is a great example of a way this "softly, softly" approach has been successful.

LETTERS 115 – 116

The position of women in Muslim countries varies greatly. Some countries allow educated women to work in responsible positions outside the home, others don't.

Working women   Letter *115*

FROM THE NETHERLANDS ABOUT **SAUDI ARABIA** (1)

We're a small family company producing high-quality bathroom fittings and are in the running for a very large contract in Saudi Arabia. The question is, can we send a women there to close the deal? Our sales manager (one of the partners) is female, very experienced in working in Europe, and very successful. However, I know that the position of women in Saudi Arabia is not the same as in the West.

I'm afraid that you would not be doing your firm any favors if you sent a female sales manager to Saudi Arabia. Saudi women rarely work outside the home, except in strictly defined areas like kindergarten education and interior decoration, and it is unusual to find foreign businesswomen working there either. Saudis like to build relationships before they do business, and for religious reasons it would be very difficult for a man and a woman to get together to build a professional relationship over the gender divide.

Of course, this is not the case in all Muslim countries or in all cultures with a large Muslim minority. In more progressive countries like Lebanon, Jordan, Malaysia, and Turkey, educated women may work in the professions or in business, but working relationships with members of the opposite sex must be very formal to avoid attracting gossip or hostility—and that applies to non-Muslim women too. That means female business travelers to Muslim countries should wear modest clothing in subdued colors and, for example, make sure the office door stays open when working with a male colleague or customer. They also need to think very carefully about accepting any kind of social invitation, even if it's to a working lunch. If they work in a managerial position and would otherwise be traveling alone, if the budget allows they might consider traveling with a female secretary or translator, not only to provide the manager with secretarial services but also as living proof of her managerial status. She would also make a very useful chaperone.

Desperate measures	Letter *116*

FROM THE NETHERLANDS ABOUT **SAUDI ARABIA** (2)

> *After reading your reply we've arrived at a solution. The sales manager's husband also works for the company in the IT area, and we're going to send him to try to finalize the deal, with her as the accompanying wife. This way she can advise him from behind the scenes. We have little experience of Saudi Arabia and wonder if you have special advice for her before she goes.*

Clever solution! I'm sure they will enjoy their trip. Visitors to Saudi Arabia will find the level of personal security high and experience little hassle. Having said that, your female manager has to be aware of certain things, the most important being that her independence will be curtailed. It is, for example, against the law for a woman to take a taxi alone or with a man to whom she is not related.

Nearly all of the better-class restaurants have special sections for men only and another for families or parties containing women. If it is made known to your Saudi contacts in advance that your male representative is taking his wife, and they are used to Western ways, perhaps a family meal can be arranged where your female sales manager can also attend, although only in the capacity as spouse. She would need to adopt a very low profile during the meal—even looking directly at a man may be regarded as "forward"—but at least she would meet your Saudi customer. She should be aware that modest clothing is essential, especially in Jeddah, which is close to Mecca, the Muslim holy city. Here, Western women may well feel more comfortable if they buy one of the long, loose-fitting dresses or caftans that are sold locally and wear it over their "normal" clothes. It is also a good idea for women to carry a headscarf so that they can cover their heads if the need arises. Finally, even in situations where physical contact between the sexes would be the norm in the West, for example, welcoming a spouse at the airport, is not allowed in Saudi Arabia.

LETTERS 117–118

Light-hearted flirtation at work may be fun; sexual harassment never is. How flirtation and harassment are defined can differ widely from culture to culture.

Sex and the single girl   Letter *117*

FROM SWEDEN ABOUT **MEXICO**

> I'm a female manager in my early thirties and will be going soon to Mexico on business. I'm in a minority as a hardware specialist at home, but I know I will be even more of a rarity abroad, and in Mexico I shall be meeting only men. I've heard that single women there are "fair game" and sexual advances are common. Do you have any special advice for a single woman?

In Mexico there aren't many women at or near the top of large organizations. However, you shouldn't find any problems at work as long as your status is made clear before your visit and the nature of your trip is well defined. In fact, most visitors find that the business climate in Mexico is friendly and relaxed, but as a woman you would be wise to be pleasant while at the same time a little reserved with male colleagues who may not be used to working alongside women on equal terms. If you aren't familiar with the unwritten rules of flirtation (and coming from the Scandinavian countries you probably don't have much experience in this particular art), you may find it difficult to know how to cope in this situation. Flirtation is a skill that Latin youngsters of both genders pick up as they mature and that they enjoy using.

There's a fine line between gallantry and attempts at flirtation, and this line is often breached, but such attempts are not intended to be offensive but complimentary, and may even be expected and welcomed by the women concerned. The same applies to Southern European and other South American countries, where an acceptance of flirtatious behavior can exist quite happily alongside strict laws against sexual discrimination or bias in the workplace.

Use common sense if you want to avoid unwelcome advances. Avoid one-to-one dinner dates, for example, and if you want to get to know your Mexican counterparts better suggest lunch instead. If you do invite people for lunch, make sure that you arrange with the waiter to pay beforehand in case your guests try to beat you to it, because Mexican men may find it difficult to accept women picking up the bill. Don't hesitate to bring forth the photos of your own (or even someone else's) husband, boyfriend, or delightful children if you get onto personal topics. And although it's a very simple rule, and we all know it shouldn't be necessary, remember the more you dress like your grandma the less likely you are to be bothered by unwelcome male advances (as long as your grandma doesn't wear tight-fitting clothes, short skirts, shorts, or low-cut tops!).

Not my intention   Letter *118*

FROM FRANCE ABOUT THE **U.S.**

*I attended an after-work social event recently in the U.S. and
mentioned to a female colleague how nice she looked. Her response*

was, "So?" and a suspicious look. I felt really awkward—as though I'd been caught with my hand up her skirt.

It is a shame that your compliment was misinterpreted so completely. Such an attitude shows a narrow-minded belief that anyone saying something positive about a women's appearance must have sexual motives. Don't judge her too harshly. This is the result of generations of unfairness in the workplace, where the presence of women was sometimes barely tolerated and their contributions undervalued. Women have been victimized in the past and still feel justly that equality in the workplace has a long way to go. This feeling of injustice, combined with the habit of most U.S. Americans of expressing their feelings openly and directly, can account for what was to you her aggressive manner. People with a pragmatic attitude toward communication and a very direct communication style, as in the U.S., Germany, Scandinavia, and Australia, may be suspicious that compliments from someone of the opposite sex is a sneaky way of trying to get what they want (sex) and is not motivated simply by the wish to make someone feel good (why would they want to waste their time doing that, the pragmatic ones ask themselves).

This attitude can lead to the joyless political correctness of the U.S. and the Scandinavian countries, which results in a refusal to acknowledge any differences between the genders. This is something most people of both sexes in Southern Europe and Latin America, where the occasional compliment or flirtatious remark is regarded as perfectly harmless, would find hard to understand. However, be aware that many lawyers make a lot of money by pressing sexual harassment charges, so be careful not to lay yourself open to them.

IN A NUTSHELL: *Gender*

GLOBAL BUSINESS STANDARDS

No one country is a utopia for women. It is a mistake to assume yours is best in all respects, and it is very bad mannered to imply this is the case.

Foreign businesswomen, especially young ones, should wear ultra-modest clothing when on business trips. In some cultures, even bare arms may be regarded as provocative.

GLOBAL BUSINESS WARNINGS

Men who aren't used to working with women as equals or superiors may find it difficult to interpret whether women are being friendly or whether they are flirting. To be on the safe side, women abroad should be friendly and businesslike rather than friendly and personal with male colleagues (a fine line indeed!).

- **Argentina:** The traditional division of women at home and men at work is changing. More educated and middle-class women are entering the workforce. Many women work as domestic servants. Many women leave work once married, and most people have little experience with women managers. Some flirtation is accepted and regarded as normal in the workplace. (See Letters 113, 117, and 118.)
- **Australia:** The legislation prohibiting the discrimination on grounds of gender is tough. Women managers are frequently found. Open attitude to homosexuality. (See Letters 114 and 118.)
- **Austria:** Traditional prefeminist attitudes toward women and their roles are still prevalent, but Austrian women are making considerable advances in the workplace. Foreign women will be freely accepted as decision-makers.
- **Belgium:** The status of homemakers is high, but women are working increasingly outside the home. Foreign women will be accepted as decision-makers and will be treated with respect. (See Letter 113.)
- **Brazil:** The traditional division of women at home and men at work is changing. More educated and middle-class women are

entering the workforce, but most people have little experience with women managers. Some flirtation is accepted and regarded as normal in the workplace. (See Letters 113, 117, and 118.)

- **Canada:** Consciousness of sexual harassment is very high, and legislation prohibiting discrimination on grounds of gender is tough. Women managers are frequently found. Open attitude to homosexuality.
- **China:** There are few women at the top, and many older men find it difficult to accept women in the business environment. Businesswomen may be excluded from informal after-work socializing. Dating and premarital socializing is strictly regulated.
- **Denmark:** There is a high degree of equality in education and in the workplace. Flirtation as practiced in Southern Europe and South America is almost unknown. Women managers are frequently found. Open attitude to homosexuality. (See Letters 113 and 118.)
- **Finland:** Women are fully accepted as equal in society and the workplace. Flirtation as practiced in Southern Europe and South America is almost unknown. (See Letters 117 and 118.)
- **France:** Generous parental benefits encourage women to combine work and family. Gallantry is accepted as natural within and outside the workplace. Most women work. Women managers are frequently found. (See Letters 113, 114, 117, and 118.)
- **Germany:** Women are fully accepted as equal in society and the workplace. Women managers are frequently found. Open attitude to homosexuality. (See Letters 113 and 118.)
- **Hong Kong:** Women work frequently outside the home. Businesswomen may be excluded from important after-work socializing.
- **India:** Middle- and upper-class women are often very well educated and routinely enter the professions, but fewer are in the business environment. Dating and premarital socializing is strictly regulated. Modest clothing for women is a "must." Homosexuality is illegal in Islam. (See Letter 115.)
- **Indonesia:** Women in the workplace is the norm, but single women in business may have some difficulty without a "back up" male on her side. May be harder for Muslim women than Chinese

women to work. Modest clothing for women is a "must." Homosexuality is illegal in Islam. (See Letter 115.)

- **Italy:** Some flirtation is accepted and regarded as normal in the workplace, but cases of sexual harassment are starting to go to court. (See Letters 117 and 118.)
- **Japan:** There are very few women at the managerial level in Japanese companies. Businesswomen are usually excluded from important after-work socializing. Some foreign companies actively recruit Japanese women because they are considered well educated and competent. (See Letter 113.)
- **Mexico:** The traditional division of women at home and men at work is changing. More educated and middle-class women are entering the workforce. Many women work as domestic servants. Many women leave work once married, and most people have little experience with women managers. Some flirtation is accepted and regarded as normal in the workplace. (See Letters 117 and 118.)
- **Netherlands:** Many women stop working when they have children. The status of homemakers is high, but women are working increasingly outside the home. Foreign women are accepted as decision-makers and are treated with respect. Open attitude to homosexuality. (See Letters 113 and 116.)
- **Norway:** State child care and generous parental leave encourage women to combine work and family. Men are expected to help in the home. Flirtation as practiced in Southern Europe and South America is almost unknown. (See Letters 117 and 118.)
- **Poland:** Male gallantry to women is regarded as a sign of good manners. Female managers are a rarity.
- **Russia:** There are very few women managers. The business world is male-dominated, but women are in the professions. Visiting businesswomen may be patronized. Women are expected to take responsibility for all domestic work and the children.
- **Saudi Arabia:** The genders are kept strictly separate. Women are forbidden from working except in a few proscribed areas. Modest clothing for women is a "must." Homosexuality is illegal in Islam. (See Letters 115 and 116.)

- **South Africa:** Very few women, black or white, are at the managerial level. Women's roles are seen primarily as homemakers. Men aren't accustomed to dealing with women as equals. (See Letter 113.)
- **South Korea:** There are very few women at the managerial level. Men aren't accustomed to dealing with women as equals. Women's primary role is seen as homemaker. Married women also care for husband's parents when they are old.
- **Spain:** Class, educational success, and connections override prejudice against women employees. However, gallantry may become harassment. (See Letters 113, 117, and 118.)
- **Sweden:** Despite efforts by government and employers to encourage equality, there are still far fewer women than men in top management. However, state child care and generous parental leave encourage women to combine work and family. Flirtation as practiced in Southern Europe and South America is almost unknown. Men are expected to help in the home. Open attitude to homosexuality. (See Letters 114 and 118.)
- **Switzerland:** See Netherlands.
- **Taiwan:** See Hong Kong. Very modest clothing is required.
- **Thailand:** Thai women make up about half of the university population and are accepted in the business world. However, they are excluded from after-dinner socializing, which makes it hard for them to form important business relationships.
- **Turkey:** Modest clothing for women is a "must." Most people have little experience with women managers. Homosexuality is illegal in Islam. (See Letter 115.)
- **UK:** The consciousness of sexual harassment very high, and legislation prohibiting discrimination on grounds of gender is tough. Women managers are frequently found. Open attitude to homosexuality.
- **US:** See U.K. (See Letters 113, 114, and 118.)
- **Venezuela:** Most people have little experience with women managers. Some flirtation is accepted and regarded as normal in workplace. (See Letters 113, 117, and 118.)

Age

One of the consolations of getting older is that one gets wiser, or so the saying goes. So why is it that in the West *old* trips off the tongue so easily as a term of abuse, such as when people mutter "silly old fools" and "white heads" under their breath when older people drive slowly and cautiously, can't understand their cell phones, or dither in front of ATM machines? Perhaps we react like this because Western society depends on constant technology-based change, and the young adapt quickest to new developments. Or perhaps it's because youthfulness, beauty, and good health—all things the elderly don't often have—are so highly valued in the U.S. and in many other countries.

Japan is also a technology-driven culture, but there Respect the Aged Day is a national holiday when young people are encouraged to remember the contributions older people have made to their lives. But in the West, who would want to be "aged" even if it did bring respect with it? We want to be admired for the money we've made, our brains, or even our good looks—but not respected for our age or wisdom (and what an uncool word *that* is). Perhaps we don't go so far as to "hope we die before we get old," in the words of The Who, but we'd like to die before we start to *look* or *feel* old.

But in many Asian countries, like China, Japan, and South Korea, age is seen as an outward sign of wisdom and is accorded a high status. In the Confucian heritage everyone in the family has a role, and the roles with the highest status go to the oldest members of the family. This hierarchical system, with its network of duties and obligations and with the emphasis on unquestioning obedience to the head of the family, is carried over to the workplace. Up-to-date technological knowledge is valuable, of course, but less so than a general knowledge of the business as a whole, a thorough knowledge of the people who run it, and the ability to get the best out of them. The rashness of youth and the risk-taking that is part of it are seen as natural but not admirable, because they can disturb the harmony that is the hallmark of a smooth-running and efficient organization.

Age is not something we actively work toward, of course, it just happens. It's this inevitability that is so hard to accept if we come from cultures in Northern Europe, the U.S., or Canada, where we believe that we should exercise control over as much of our lives as possible.

In such cultures gestures of respect aren't always appreciated by the elderly. My father, in his eighties, was nonplussed the other day when a youngish woman on a bus in England offered him her seat. He's not really sure he is ready for that much respect. I sympathize with his unwillingness to be relegated to the status of "the old," a group regarded by many Western societies as a financial burden, and one seen as taking from society but giving nothing worthwhile in return. As a character in Anthony Powell's *A Dance to the Music of Time* said, "Growing old's like being increasingly penalized for a crime you haven't committed." In Western cultures, the punishment for this crime is the same as for other criminals—a place in an institution—but in this case it's a home for the elderly rather than a prison. In Asia, Africa, and South America such institutions are rare, and adult children take their responsibilities to look after their parents at home very seriously.

One Finnish manager I know moved to the city from the country many years ago, leaving his mother in her hometown. When I spoke to him recently he had been back there on a visit to her, to see her in her new nursing home. He was full of admiration for the staff, especially for a group of new workers. They were middle-aged female immigrants from Africa who had started to work there, and they were very popular with staff and patients alike. At first I was surprised—the cultural differences between African immigrants and old Finnish country folk would surely mean that they had very little in common. However, these immigrants came from cultures where elderly relatives were usually looked after at home and where the old were very much respected and valued. The African staff liked and were genuinely interested in their Finnish patients, and the old people flourished in their care.

LETTER 119

Parents and children may inhabit the same country but different worlds, for within a generation cultural patterns in a country can change dramatically.

Generation gap   Letter *119*

FROM THE U.K. ABOUT **RUSSIA**

We are a British company trying to get a foothold in Russia. We are considering entering into a partnership with a Russian company but have a real problem finding the right people to talk to. The more experienced managers don't seem to understand business, and the younger ones have no practical experience.

With the rapid decline of communist control in the 1980s, state-owned enterprises came to an end and were replaced by a market economy. Instead of a centrally run, politically steered system of control, companies had to start thinking in terms of pricing strategies, efficiency targets, and profit margins. Younger people, especially those educated abroad, may well be familiar with these concepts and the principles behind them, but to employees who were managers before the communist collapse, concepts like *service* and *profits* were foreign and may still be equated with servility and profiteering. The result is an enormous generation gap, where theoretical knowledge about the market economy is the (almost exclusive) property of the young, while practical experience of managing fellow Russians is the province of the middle-aged and elderly. Furthermore, each generation may be skeptical about the value of what the other knows.

This is a problem for many Western companies operating in the former communist bloc, and although there are many multinationals operating successfully in Poland, Hungary, and other Eastern European countries, getting these partnerships started has been far from painless. In

Russia the problems are compounded, as free enterprise and capitalism are relatively recent foreign imports and tend to be treated as scapegoats by the older generation for the hard times that many Russians have experienced since the collapse of communism. The only way forward is to find a Russian intermediary familiar with representatives from both generations, but this will not be an easy task.

LETTERS 120–121

Age is often a consideration when it comes to employment.

Don't ask Letter *120*

FROM INDIA ABOUT THE U.S.

We are going to be opening a subsidiary in the U.S. soon and will need to employ local staff. I heard interviewers aren't allowed to ask questions about age during job interviews there. Is that correct?

It certainly is. Companies in the U.S. are very anxious to avoid accusations of being "ageist." This may be because they realize that if they don't have a good age mix in the workplace their businesses will be turning their backs on an enormous amount of valuable wisdom and experience. But it is also because of the simple fact that discriminating against anyone on the grounds of age is illegal, and ignoring this fact could lead to an expensive lawsuit. Anti-ageism laws are being introduced in other countries too, and recent laws in Australia and Canada provide legal protection for older workers. Europe is moving in the same direction. A European Union law guaranteeing older workers basic rights coming into force in 2006 will prevent more experienced people from being discriminated against in the workplace.

However, if you really think that it is important to know someone's age before offering them a job, it is often possible to "read between the lines" of someone's resume to deduce, more or less, how old they are, and there is usually a face-to-face interview before you make your final choice.

Age a handicap?   Letter *121*

FROM SWEDEN ABOUT **TURKEY**

I have heard that there is a tremendous respect for older people in Muslim countries generally. I'm a male manager in my early thirties and about to take up a post in Turkey. Do you think my age will be a handicap?

It need not be a handicap, but it certainly won't help. The Muslim tradition tends to be strongly patriarchal, which means that the status of men is higher than women, and older men are more highly regarded in the family and the workplace than younger ones. In this, Muslim cultures are no different from those of East Asia, India, or non-Muslim Africa. In fact, you can say that the U.S., Canada, the U.K., and Northern Europe are the exceptions in their encouragement and ready acceptance of the "whiz kid" boss who may be intelligent and highly educated but, inevitably, does not have a lot of experience. The assumption in Turkey is that age brings both status and wisdom. This makes it hard, for example, for an older manager to report to a younger one, as this might cause the older employee to lose face.

However, as you are from Sweden, you will inevitably find yourself in the role of outsider in Turkey and will not be judged by local standards. Also, as you come from the home of the parent company, you will automatically have a high status, and as a manager you will be seen as having the weight of headquarters behind you. This does not mean, of course, that you can afford to ignore local traditions and values, so be particularly tactful when dealing with older employees. Make an effort to build good relationships with them, and listen to what they have to say, because they will have a lot of valuable information and insights that will be useful to you. By demonstrating respect for these older individuals, you will also indirectly be showing respect for the Turkish culture as a whole.

LETTERS 122–124

How respect is shown varies greatly. In Asian and African cultures respect for age is particularly marked.

Showing respect?   Letter *122*

FROM AUSTRALIA ABOUT **SOUTH KOREA**

I will be visiting a small South Korean firm next month and will be meeting the family who owns it. I know I'm supposed to show special respect to older people there and want to know how to go about doing it.

It's certainly important to observe hierarchy, for this social order is what holds society together and defines the position of the individual within it.

When meeting older people, address them by their title plus surname (e.g., Managing Director Kim or Madam Lee). Bow, unless they extend their hands first. The rules of conversation are mostly common sense and apply even in societies where old people do not have such an elevated status. In fact, when you were a child, your parents probably ran through similar rules before taking you to visit your grandparents.

Listen politely to whatever older people have to say, defer to them, don't contradict, don't ask difficult questions (although questions about health are acceptable), and don't speak too loudly. When eating, elders will be served first, and most Koreans will wait for them to begin and will not leave the table until they have finished. You shouldn't smoke in front of older guests unless invited to do so. Finally, if you are drinking in front of an older person, turn your head away as you drink to demonstrate respect.

Can't treat people like this   Letter *123*

FROM HUNGARY ABOUT **MULTINATIONALS**

A large U.S. American multinational took over our production plant six months ago and now it has started to lay off large numbers of

*workers, myself included. I have worked loyally for this company for
thirty-five years, and I am losing my job while young kids with less
than five years experience are staying.*

This is a sad but unfortunately common story repeated in many countries of the world. Most large multinationals, wherever their headquarters
are located, are ruthless about keeping costs down, and if this involves
cutting jobs, so be it. These are impersonal institutions and they don't
give any consideration to how long an individual has worked for the company (especially if there are new owners) or how much he or she has left
to contribute. The ties of mutual loyalty that may bind employer and
employee in a small family-run firm, or the political ideology that determined how organizations were run in totalitarian or communist states
(Poland and Russia, for example) do not apply here any longer. Instead,
the interests of efficiency and productivity are paramount, and measuring
performance by these yardsticks means that older people may be at a disadvantage. This is particularly hard to accept in cultures where traditions
of employer-employee loyalty have been or remain strong, such as Japan,
China, South Korea, and Latin America.

How old is he?   Letter *124*

FROM POLAND ABOUT **CHINA**

*I feel a bit stupid asking this, but how can you tell how old someone
is? A group of us will be going to China for the first time and we'll be
meeting a corresponding group of Chinese managers. We've heard
that it's important to give special respect to older people, but what if
they're all old? How will we be able to tell who is the most senior?*

Luckily there's a simple answer to this that doesn't involve counting
wrinkles. The most senior-ranking person will enter the room first in
China, and also in Japan, and will be introduced first, probably by the
interpreter. When you are seated, he (rarely she) will be seated in the middle of one side of the negotiating table. You will also notice that the other
members of the party defer to him, and that he is offered refreshments

first. He may not speak much himself, but make sure you speak to this person directly when addressing the group.

IN A NUTSHELL: *Age*

> ### GLOBAL BUSINESS STANDARD
>
> Special courtesy and consideration for older people are good manners everywhere. It is especially important that business-people from North America, Northern Europe, and Australia, where older people are often treated with scant respect, remember this.

- **Argentina:** The fact that it has a very young population and that a high value is placed on an attractive personal appearance may work against older employees (especially women). However, within the extended family the status of older members is high. (See Letter 123.)
- **Australia:** Legislation makes it illegal to discriminate against older employees. What you achieve rather than your position outside work is important. Status diminishes both inside family and in the workplace as people age. Youth is frequently valued above experience. Managers may be very young. (See Letters 120 and 122.)
- **Austria:** The European Union will make ageism in the workplace illegal in 2006. Legislation is partly the result of Europe having an aging population. (See Letter 120.)
- **Belgium:** See Austria. (See Letter 120.)
- **Brazil:** See Argentina. (See Letter 123.)
- **Canada:** See Australia. (See Letters 120 and 121.)
- **China:** Everyone in the family has a role, and the roles with the highest status go to the oldest (male) members of the family. This is reflected in the workplace, where managerial roles depend on seniority and the decisions of elders are obeyed. Age is seen as an

outward sign of wisdom and older people are treated with great respect. "Youthful" risk-taking and the desire for change are not encouraged. (See Letters 121, 123, and 124.)

- **Denmark:** See Austria. (See Letters 120 and 121.)
- **Finland:** See Austria. What you achieve rather than your position outside work is important. Status diminishes both inside the family and in the workplace as people age. Managers may be young. (See Letters 120 and 121.)
- **France:** See Austria. Educational qualifications may outweigh seniority when it comes to management positions. (See Letter 120.)
- **Germany:** See Austria. Educational qualifications may be just as important as seniority when it comes to management positions. (See Letter 120.)
- **Hong Kong:** See China. Third-highest life expectancy in world: 79.9 years. (See Letter 121.)
- **India:** In Muslim and Hindu traditions, elders have higher status in the extended family. India has a young population with many young graduates. Well-educated, bright young managers may attain high positions in high-tech industries. (See Letters 120 and 121.)
- **Indonesia:** Muslim tradition ensures that older men have high status within the family and at the workplace. Respect must be shown to older coworkers and managers; their right to decide is undisputed by the young. (See Letter 121.)
- **Italy:** See Austria. (See Letter 120.)
- **Japan:** See China. Highest life expectancy in the world: 81.5 years. (See Letters 121 and 123.)
- **Mexico:** See Argentina. (See Letter 123.)
- **Netherlands:** See Austria. (See Letter 120.)
- **Norway:** See Austria. (See Letters 120 and 121.)
- **Poland:** There is a significant generation gap, where theoretical knowledge about the market economy is the property of the young while the middle-aged and elderly have extensive practical experience of management in a socialist economy. (See Letters 119 and 123.)
- **Russia:** See Poland. (See Letters 119 and 123.)

- **Saudi Arabia:** See Indonesia. (See Letter 121.)
- **South Africa:** In black African cultural tradition, elders of both genders have high status. (See Letter 121.)
- **South Korea:** See China. (See Letters 121, 122, and 123.)
- **Spain:** See Austria. The Spanish population is relatively young when compared to some of the countries around it in Europe. (See Letter 120.)
- **Sweden:** The European Union will make ageism in the workplace illegal in 2006. Status diminishes both inside family and in the workplace as people age. Life expectancy is the second highest in the world: 80.1 years. Youth is frequently valued above experience. Managers may be very young. (See Letters 120 and 121.)
- **Switzerland:** See Austria.
- **Taiwan:** See China. (See Letter 121.)
- **Thailand:** See China. (See Letter 121.)
- **Turkey:** See Indonesia. (See Letter 121.)
- **UK:** See Austria. What you achieve rather than your position outside work is important. Status diminishes both inside family and in the workplace as people age. Youth is frequently valued above experience. Managers may be very young. (See Letters 119, 120, and 121.)
- **US:** See Australia. (See Letters 120, 121, and 123.)
- **Venezuela:** See Brazil. (See Letter 123.)

Ethnicity and Nationality

I don't like the word *ethnicity*. I think it sounds like a new form of ecologically correct energy: "Have you seen my new car? It runs on ethnicity." It is, in fact, a relatively new word, just over fifty years old, and is shorthand for a group of people's racial, religious, and linguistic identities. I guess *ethnicity* came into being in part because of the sinister associations of the word *race* (think race riots, race laws, racial superiority), but if we use this word, and many people use it unwillingly, we are in fact talking about the physical signs of ethnicity.

Clues to your ethnic and racial background can be found in your skin color, your stature, and a host of other physical features that can be a remarkably accurate indication of your ancestry. My husband comes from a large island off the west coast of Sweden, where his family farmed the same patch of ground for seven generations. One day when he was a teenager he was visiting friends in the north of the island, about ten miles away. The boys were playing together when an old woman walked past and asked the lads where they came from. My husband (an inventive teenager) said that he came from the next village, but she took a quick look at him and told him to save his breath. She could see by the shape of his head, the length of his neck, and the way he walked exactly where he came from, and proceeded to place him within a half mile of his own little farm at the other end of the island.

Now because of easier communications, intermarriage, and mass migration, a person's appearance no longer says as much about his or her geographical origins. It's not surprising that the word *race* has begun to sound a little old-fashioned, because appearance tells us less and less about the national and ethnic roots of an individual.

That doesn't stop it from being a problem, though. When I talk to second-generation immigrants, whether British people of Irish or Pakistani descent, or Germans with Polish or Turkish parents, the individuals who have experienced the most problems being accepted by their fellow Brits or Germans are those who don't look like the ethnic majority. This is strange, for in the cases I'm thinking of, these people's education, language patterns, and even sporting affinities have been identical with that of their white neighbors. The children of the ethnic Irish and German immigrants have been easily accepted into the new cultures, presumably because they blended into the background more easily. Most countries have legislation in place that is designed to stop racial discrimination, but the simple fact that such legislation is necessary says a lot about how individuals react to people who don't look the same as they do.

Religion is also an important part of the ethnic picture. Few people show outward signs of their religious affiliations; Hasidic Jewish men with *payos* (side curls) and untrimmed beards, Sikhs with turbans, and Muslim women in the West wearing *burkhas* are the exceptions rather than the rule. However, religious beliefs and traditions certainly affect us in whatever country we find ourselves. These differences might be easy to identify and accommodate, like different holidays and religious festivals, or they may put us at odds with the culture in which we live. For example, strict Catholic medical staff from Ireland who work in England refuse to perform abortions, which are perfectly legal in the U.K., and some traditional Jordanian Muslims living in Germany believe that "honor killings" of their female relations are a religious duty if the girls break Islamic law.

But sometimes your new colleague's ethnic background is not revealed until she opens her mouth, and you hear English spoken with a Nigerian accent or French with a Marseilles accent. How we speak, and indeed *what* we speak, reflect our ethnic identities.

Sometimes it's a mixture of all three elements of ethnicity—race, religion, and language—that divides people into groups, but given the human propensity for conflict, differences in just one of the three can provide people with the excuse to label the other group as "ignorant," "arrogant," "blasphemous," or just about any other unpleasant adjective you can think of. Millions of individuals have died because one or more of the elements of their ethnic identity have been found objectionable by people of another ethnicity. If one more ingredient, "nationality," is added to this already potent mixture, it can become truly explosive.

The relationship between ethnicity and nationality is an uneasy one. In large countries like the U.S., Russia, and China, nationality overrides deep ethnic divisions with varying degrees of success. Twenty years ago when I taught in the tiny nation of Singapore, teachers and students alike were required to swear before school every morning that we were part of "one united people, regardless of race, language, or religion." The government knew from experience that when people are happy with their own and their neighbors' ethnic and national identities, life goes on as usual. But if there is a conflict between the two, bloodshed may result. In the Second World War the fact that people were Germans did not save them from extermination if they also happened to be Jewish. It also led to the destruction of a nation—Yugoslavia—as the country tore itself into ethnic groups.

Our ethnic background and nationality are part of what makes us what we are. But they are not the only part. Wherever two people come

from, if they make the effort to get to know each other they will find there
is more that unites them than divides them.

LETTER 125

Most of us are proud of our nationality. However, nationalism is
something that can cause problems.

Nationality as a problem   Letter *125*

FROM THE U.S. ABOUT **MEXICO**

*I feel the people I am working with here are really negative toward
me because I'm a U.S. American. They don't actually say "Yankee, go
home," but it certainly feels like they'd like to. Is there any way to
overcome this sort of hostility?*

If you look at the relations between your countries from a historical
perspective, you will understand it's probably not you as a person who
elicits this hostile reaction but something in the history of your two countries that causes it. And sometimes a country doesn't actually need to *do*
anything to be unpopular. Being richer, bigger, or more powerful than
another nation is enough to make others envious until another nation
takes over the role. (The British, *the* world power in the nineteenth century, are still trying to come to terms with their new role as citizens of just
another medium-sized European nation.)

It's not a comfortable situation if you feel you are being required to
apologize for or defend your country when abroad. However, like it or
not, when you are there you are acting as both your country's and your
company's representative, so try to reflect the positive aspects of your culture while respecting local feelings. Try to avoid political and religious discussions, and try to keep cool and patient in the face of criticism even if
you do find it unjust. If things go too far and you feel yourself or your

country under some sort of verbal attack, keep calm, ask for a break, and explain that you don't want to continue the discussion.

Do a little research into the history, art, sports, or famous sights of the country so you have an alternative topic to switch to in social situations if things get sticky. Take the time to build personal relationships, so that those who may not have met any people from your country before, and who have acquired their knowledge of the U.S. from the media, get a positive impression of you and the nation you represent.

LETTERS 126–127

The relationship between nationality and ethnicity is not clear-cut any longer.

Joint identity   Letter *126*

FROM POLAND ABOUT **BRAZIL**

I have had increasing contact with Brazil and have been surprised to come across a couple of people with Japanese-sounding names. Is this common?

It's certainly not unusual. Brazil contains a wonderful mixture of different ethnic groups, including the largest community of Japanese outside Japan. Japanese immigrants started settling in Brazil in 1907 and are now found mainly in the cities of the south (with 75 percent of them in São Paulo).

But the Japanese are only one of many immigrant groups. Although most Brazilians of European descent have Portuguese ancestry, substantial German and Italian communities also exist. Some of these groups have retained their own language and culture, while at the same time speaking fluent Brazilian Portuguese and adopting a Brazilian lifestyle. With its African, Asian, European, and indigenous roots, Brazil must be one of the most racially mixed countries in the world.

"People of color"   Letter *127*

FROM SWEDEN ABOUT THE **U.S.**

I work in the HR department of a medium-sized multinational, and we have created a new employment policy that describes our commitment to diversity. When we got the document back from the U.S. American translators we saw the expression "people of color," which I have never seen before and find very odd.

The translator has not made a mistake. It is simply the most recent in a long line of terms used to describe people from non-European ethnic backgrounds. When I was a child in England my mother used the term *colored people*, which was then considered more polite than *black*. Later *black* became preferable (although I have always thought it a strange word to choose to describe skin that might be only the palest café au lait). In the U.S. this was followed by *African American*, which in turn has been superseded by *person of color*, a term that includes anyone who is not white. (This is, of course, another inaccurate word. E. M. Forster said it would be more accurate to call the Caucasian race "pinko-grey.")

Language like everything else has its fashions, but if the language isn't your own it is difficult to keep up with the latest trend, or in this case, the most politically correct version, and you are right to double-check on the appropriateness of the expression. So you can relax and use it in your HR policy knowing that your company is implying that it is up-to-date and diversity conscious. (Unfortunately, though, there are few companies where the reality lives up to the company "blurb.")

LETTER 128

While stereotypes about nationality or ethnic groups are dangerous, there may be broad similarities in the way members of the same cultures act in certain situations.

Ethnic and national rivalry   Letter *128*

FROM CANADA ABOUT **RUSSIA**

We are starting to work with some businesspeople from Russia and met them for the first time in Moscow. We were surprised, though, to learn that some of them were not Russians but introduced themselves as Moldovans and Chechens.

The full name for Russia is the Russian Federation, and it is an enormous multinational state made up of people from many "nations" or ethnic groups, many of which have distinctive languages and traditions. Nationality and religion are closely related in Russia, so Chechnya is mainly Muslim, whereas Moldova is Orthodox Christian. Nationality is, in fact, stated on each Russian citizen's identity card and is something that all Russians are very conscious of, so the people you met obviously thought of themselves as Moldovan or Chechen first and second (if at all) as Russian. It is important for foreigners to know that ethnic and local consciousness is increasing within the Russian Federation, with actual or potential conflict as a result.

LETTERS 129–130

Whether we are religious or not, we cannot avoid being influenced to a greater or lesser extent by the religion(s) of our native culture.

Religious requirements   Letter *129*

FROM THE U.K. ABOUT **INDIA**

We are about to open a production facility in Northern India. We want to encourage diversity in our company, including religious diversity. What kind of measures will we have to take to meet employees' different requirements?

India is a vast country with many ethnic and religious groups. Most of its population, however, is Hindu, so you may have to pay attention to the caste system. Discriminating against a person based on his or her caste or untouchability is legally forbidden, and the government also allows positive discrimination in favor of lower castes. In cities you can see different castes mingling with each other, but in some rural areas there is still discrimination, and sometimes there are violent clashes connected to caste tensions.

Problems can sometimes arise if, for example, someone from the "wrong" caste works in the kitchen preparing food (which would make it inedible to many other employees) or if you employ people from widely different castes to work closely together. And on the subject of food, it is extremely important that dietary laws are observed, so when McDonald's opened restaurants in India it sold mutton burgers (although undoubtedly gave them a more appealing name) rather than risk offending its Hindu and Muslim customers for whom beef and pork are forbidden. Consult with local companies there for details. Apart from that, you should also do your homework regarding local religious holidays and festivals.

India also contains a sizeable Muslim and Sikh population and a smaller Christian one. If you are employing Muslims, you should reserve a room with washing facilities nearby for prayer, and be prepared to allow flexible hours for mosque visits on Fridays. Naturally, you will allow religiously prescribed clothing to be worn at work—for example, the Sikh turban and the Muslim woman's headscarf.

An excuse for laziness   Letter *130*

FROM THE U.K. ABOUT **SPAIN**

We do a lot of business in various parts of Spain, but are always hearing that they can't do something because they're having a religious festival. The Spanish people I know aren't particularly religious and I feel that religion is often used as an excuse for laziness.

The U.K. today is a very secular society with low rates of churchgoing and observance of religious traditions. However, you should not assume that everyone else shares your views on the unimportance of religion. Certainly the days in Spain are gone when everyone attended Mass on Sundays, but the observance of holy days is still an important aspect of life. The same applies in Italy and Latin America, all prominently Catholic countries. And it is certainly not laziness to prioritize participation in a religious or communal celebration over work.

Even if you don't think of yourself as religious, religion affects the values of the society we live in, and we are all social animals. In Catholic countries, where people work hard but see work as a part of life rather than its most important constituent, people talk about Protestant North Americans or Northern Europeans as living to work rather than working to live, and that is not necessarily a compliment. Certainly the Protestant ethic with its belief in the virtue of hard work helped shape the economic success of the richest and most powerful nation in the world, the U.S. However, people in Catholic countries are likely to think that leisure time is just as important as money. So in addition to their thirty vacation days (the British get twenty), Spaniards enjoy fifteen days off for national holidays as well as local fiestas. I can understand that all this free time might be irritating to you in the U.K., but it is important you show a respect for local traditions if you are to establish a good working relationship with your Spanish partners.

IN A NUTSHELL: *Ethnicity and Nationality*

For notes on the religions of these countries, see the Nutshell listing in the section "Calendars and Holidays" in Chapter 5. For information on the languages spoken in these countries, see the section "A Global Language" in Chapter 4.

GLOBAL BUSINESS WARNING

Questions on international or inter-ethnic disputes, race, and religion are subjects *not* to discuss when chatting with people from other cultures, even if you know them well.

- **Argentina:** People of Spanish and Italian origin (also German, English, and Welsh) predominate among immigrant groups. In the north there is a larger indigenous presence. (See Letter 130.)
- **Australia:** A nation of immigrants, except for the native Australians (Aborigines), Australia has a multi-ethnic population, but those with European origins hold most power.
- **Austria:** Immigrants and "guest workers" from Eastern Europe might pose a big problem when the European Union forces all its member states, including Austria, to remove restrictions on foreign workers from other EU states (probably in 2010). Geographically, Austria is closest to these poorer countries and fears a tidal wave of immigration.
- **Belgium:** Flemish and French are the main ethnic (linguistic) groups. There is also a German-speaking minority. There are strict language laws to ensure political fairness.
- **Brazil:** This is a multi-ethnic country, with Portuguese, West African, and indigenous ancestry most common. (See Letters 126 and 130.)
- **Canada:** There is an English-speaking majority, a large powerful French-speaking minority, and a large Asian community. There are strict language laws to protect the status of the French language. (See Letter 130.)
- **China:** This is a multi-ethnic country, with many spoken Chinese dialects, although Mandarin Chinese has been adopted as the common language. There are attempts to integrate ethnic minorities (e.g., the Kazaks and Turkic peoples) into mainstream Chinese culture.
- **Denmark:** The country had a very homogenous population until relatively recently. The influx of political and economic refugees has led to some tension. (See Letter 130.)
- **Finland:** See Austria. The population is quite homogenous (although there is a well-established Swedish-speaking minority), and this may lead to an ignorance about, and suspicion of, non-white foreigners. (See Letter 130.)
- **France:** A multi-ethnic country (it had French colonies in North Africa), but ethnic tensions do arise between the immigrant population and other citizens from time to time.

- **Germany:** See Austria. Large numbers of Turks came as guest workers and stayed. Generally, non-European immigrants are not welcomed. (See Letter 130.)
- **Hong Kong:** An ethnically Chinese population with a large white minority.
- **India:** An enormous multi-ethnic country (with a multireligious, multilingual, and multiracial population). The Indian states are divided by linguistic lines. Most Indians are bilingual or multilingual. (See Letter 129.)
- **Indonesia:** The majority of ethnic Indonesians are Muslims, but there is a comparatively wealthy and influential ethnic Chinese minority and a small indigenous population.
- **Italy:** Italians have strong regional loyalties. There has been a recent influx of immigrants from Balkan states. (See Letter 130.)
- **Japan:** The population has been and remains homogenous. This can lead to an ignorance about and suspicion of foreigners. South Korean immigrants to Japan have not been fully accepted. (See Letter 126.)
- **Mexico:** Over 80 percent of the population has some mixture of Spanish and indigenous blood. There is a lot of emigration to the neighboring U.S. (See Letters 125 and 130.)
- **Netherlands:** A multi-ethnic country (there was a Dutch colony in Indonesia, and people from Morocco and Turkey came to work in the 1970s). It is estimated that by 2010, 15 percent of the population will be of non-Dutch origin. (See Letter 130.)
- **Norway:** See Japan. (See Letter 130.)
- **Poland:** The vast majority of Poland's people, over 90 percent, are of Polish origin. The remainder are of German, Ukrainian, or Belorussian descent. (See Letter 126.)
- **Russia:** An enormous multinational state made up of people from many nations. Each "nation" is really an ethnic group, distinguished by racial, linguistic, and religious differences. There are some inter-ethnic tensions. (See Letter 128.)
- **Saudi Arabia:** This is a strictly religious (Muslim) culture. The large and wealthy Saudi elite is supported by mainly imported labor from Europe, the U.S., and Asia. (See Letter 129.)
- **South Africa:** "The rainbow nation," it is multi-ethnic with citizens of European (British and Dutch-German, i.e., Boer), African (Zulu

and Xhosa), and Asian ancestry. Even though political power is in the hands of the black majority, economic power is mostly in white hands. Affirmative action programs mean more non-whites are entering management.

- **South Korea:** See Japan.
- **Spain:** There is a strong regional awareness that has given rise to a vociferous (and violent) Basque separatist movement. (See Letter 130.)
- **Sweden:** The population has been homogenous until relatively recently. Now, 1.5 million people out of the total population of 9 million are immigrants or have at least one parent who was an immigrant. The influx of political and economic refugees has led to some tension. (See Letters 127 and 130.)
- **Switzerland:** Large numbers of guest workers have moved to Switzerland from poorer countries. It has proved very hard for them to be granted Swiss citizenship.
- **Taiwan:** Taiwanese are mostly ethnically Chinese, with a small (2 percent) indigenous population.
- **Thailand:** The country has been an Asian crossroads and is used to absorbing immigrants from other Asian nations. It has a relatively prosperous ethnic Chinese minority that has been well integrated into the Thai culture.
- **Turkey:** The country's largest minority are the Kurds. The use of the Kurdish language is discouraged but it is no longer forbidden. There is a widespread Turkish suspicion of its Kurdish minority. (See Letter 129.)
- **UK:** Made up of four countries: England, Wales, Scotland, and Northern Ireland, each of which has varying degrees of autonomy. It has been multi-ethnic for over fifty years, with immigrants coming from former colonies in the Indian subcontinent, Africa, and the West Indies. Ethnic tensions arise from time to time. (See Letters 125, 129, and 130.)
- **US:** The original "melting pot," the U.S. has a multi-ethnic population with large and well-established African American and Asian American minorities. The continuing numbers of Spanish-speaking immigrants from Latin America make the Hispanic

population the biggest minority. Ethnic tensions arise from time to time. (See Letters 125, 127, and 130.)

- **Venezuela:** Venezuela has a higher percentage of people with African descent than any other South American nation. Between 65 and 90 percent of Venezuelans are *pardo*, a combination of Indian, African, and European descent. (See Letter 130.)

CHAPTER 7

Our Roles and Relationships

The last chapter discussed some of the characteristics that make us who we are—gender, age, ethnicity—and at the way attitudes about these characteristics mold our individuality. But being human means we have to find a place for ourselves in the wider world. As social creatures, unless we belong to the tiny minority who doesn't have to work for a living, there comes a time when we have to conform to societal pressures, usually energetically reinforced by the parental variety, and get a job. When that happens, "who we are" meets "what we do."

Of course, it makes sense for everyone if these two very different parts of our lives, the "being" and the "doing," are in harmony with each other, for most of us believe that people perform better if they enjoy their work. However, for many millions today the idea of having a choice of jobs, and of picking one that suits them, is a hardly conceivable luxury.

When it comes to picking and choosing, the large global corporations have the edge. Their success depends on getting people with the correct personal, educational, and professional profiles to work for them. How do they find the right person for the job? In some countries and areas, like the U.S., the U.K., and Scandinavia, large corporations are likely to perform psychological tests to find the best people, especially for management roles. But in other countries, like France and Germany, the right academic qualifications (and in the case of France the right university) are given top priority. In all these cultures, "who you are" is all about your skills, intellectual and otherwise, and when such an organization selects you, it is because it wants you to use these skills on its behalf.

That's not to say that in these countries social or family networks are irrelevant—membership in such networks plays a greater or lesser role in workplaces all over the world. In the cultures of Latin America, Africa, Southern Europe, the Middle East, and most of Asia, belonging to the right family may be the best indication of future success in an organization, and although this is given the rather ugly name *nepotism* by more egalitarian societies, it is a system that tries to integrate the social roles of an individual (son, wife, cousin, friend) with his or her work roles. This makes sense in practical terms, because it shortens the long "getting-to-know-you" process that is essential for a business relationship built on trust. The reasoning goes that if you went to school with your colleague's cousin, and your parents and his are distant relatives, you can trust him to honor your agreement more than, say, a lawyer with a prestigious law degree from Harvard or Oxford. In these relationship-based cultures your role as employee is not simply to provide your company with of a set of skills; it is to be an irreplaceable part of a unique social network that co-exists along with and as part of the organization you work for.

Of course, social networks also exist within companies in more task-oriented cultures, even though relationships (especially in such change-friendly cultures as the U.S., Canada, and Northern Europe) may be short-lived as companies reorganize, people move on, or employees get promoted. The changes associated with promotion can be particularly tricky for some people. I've spoken to a number of middle- and lower-ranking managers in European and North American companies who say that as soon as they were promoted to a managerial role they lost their friends at work—not that their friends left the organization, but these new managers became excluded from the group they had previously belonged to.

A blurring of social and work roles is common in, among other places, traditional rural societies. In the 1950s, the old-age pension was introduced in Sweden, and the old farmers who received it eagerly awaited the arrival of the mail carrier who delivered it, and as a mark of their appreciation would offer him a glass of vodka. This was fine as long as he did his rounds on his bike, but his downfall came when the postal service gave him a little van, which was much more difficult to get back on the road once it had wandered off. The problem ("problem" in the eyes of the postal service, that is) was that the islanders didn't distinguish between the mail carrier's work role and that of generous friend. They rewarded him in the same way they would if a long-lost cousin had arrived with the surprise payment of a family inheritance.

This kind of story is not so common now in industrialized Western cultures, where the line between "who we are" and "what we do" has become more and more clearly defined as organizations have become "businesslike." But wherever we come from, it is at our workplaces where the two strands of our lives, the public and the private, meet. It's important for all of us that the meeting is a happy one.

◆ MORAL

Do not trust your first impressions of people from other cultures. Public and private roles affect how people act, and if you are unaware of what their roles entail, you may come to faulty conclusions.

Leaders and Managers

Why has the word *leader* become more popular than *manager?* I was discussing this with an accountant on the verge of retirement, and he remarked rather sourly that it was simply a matter of fashion, adding that the only people he knew more susceptible to fashion than teenagers were executive managers. However, detecting more than a note of cynicism in his reply, I turned to my dictionary where I discovered that a leader is "a person who rules, guides, or inspires others," whereas a manager is "a person who directs or manages an organization." You have to admit it: Most of us would like to guide and inspire others. However, *directing* is what police officers do after traffic accidents, and "managing an organization," though impressive, also sounds boring. Frankly, a *manager* isn't half as sexy as a *leader.*

The change in terminology reflects a shift in organizational structure in many multinational corporations. In the 1990s there was a movement in the U.S., Scandinavia, and to a certain extent in the U.K. toward flatter more decentralized organizations. As employees were split into small teams, the priority was that the team's objectives were met, not whether it said "manager" on your business card. Staffs were told that a preoccupation with status was old-fashioned, and that working on short-term projects where everyone was a team player would enable them to work more efficiently. *Hierarchical* became a term of abuse for an organization, and hierarchies were seen as a threat to all the creativity that a more democratic organization would unleash. These smaller units had leaders rather than managers, and their role was to serve the team and to make it possible for it to achieve its goals. Suddenly, there were no project managers, only project leaders.

But in the rest of the world, companies saw hierarchical organizations as having advantages when it came to speed of decision-making, continuity, and clear chains of command and communications. And the egalitarian Danes soon realized that the word *manager* on their business cards was still an important door opener when they went abroad, not least to France, Mexico, or Japan. Indeed, once there they would be asked detailed questions about how many subordinates they had, which made the poor Danes blush with embarrassment. To their egalitarian, democratic way of thinking, they had coworkers, and the word *subordinates*, implying that in some way some people were "above" others, shocked them.

In many cultures it is possible to judge the authority a person wields by the number of people "under" him or her, and not appreciating this fact can lead to problems. Asked at a meeting how many subordinates he had, an Icelandic manager in a group of French and Spanish managers answered truthfully that he didn't have any, and was promptly ignored by the rest of the group. However, when decisions had to be made, he was the only one who had the authority to make independent decisions. I also know of a case in Norway of a top manager working with business development who didn't have any subordinates and was forced to "steal" employees from a department in order to get his French colleagues to listen to him. The "kidnapped" employees didn't move location and their duties remained the same, but the department number on their business cards changed.

Of course, you cannot expect consensus about what makes a good leader or a good manager. In the U.S., for example, business leaders should be charismatic, high-profile go-getters. In some South American countries, in more traditional companies, managers may be where they are by virtue of belonging to the right family, and their management style is often autocratic. However, if the role of the patriarchal manager brings with it unquestioned power and authority, it also brings with it a personal responsibility to employees that gives their well-being, and the well-being of their families, a higher priority than, say, the next year's budget estimates being delivered on schedule.

I once asked a group of employees of different nationalities to prioritize a list of qualities they valued in their mangers. "The ability to motivate" and "the ability to delegate" appeared near the top of most lists, but the choice of one Polish participant surprised me. He was an engine designer, one of those opinionated, awkward, creative people that companies are forced to employ because they are brilliant, even though getting on with other people (sometimes even acknowledging other people exist) is often not their strong suit. Anyway, he had selected at the top of his list "a sense of humor."

When I asked him about this, he told me that in a group like his a manager who could make everyone laugh diffused hostility, made people feel better, and most importantly, began to forge a team out of a group of individuals. I thought his reasoning quite persuasive, but the German and Belgian members of the group were rather shocked by it. As they put it, "It's not the boss's job to be a comedian." If managers did inspire their teams to laugh, it indicated that they weren't taking their jobs seriously enough!

This just goes to show that there may be a place for humor in business, but the decision where and when to employ it is no laughing matter.

LETTERS 131–133

What qualifications should a manager have? Definitions differ depending on where you come from.

Language skills   Letter *131*

FROM THE U.S. ABOUT A **GLOBAL ORGANIZATION**

I'm looking for managerial positions in large global companies and have applied to one that requires managers to be willing to move abroad (which I am) and to be able to speak a foreign language fluently (which I cannot). I know the corporate language is English, and I also know that it takes years to learn to speak a foreign language fluently. Why aren't proven leadership skills and technical knowledge enough?

It's not the actual level of your French, Spanish, or Japanese that the company is most interested in. It's simply that by learning another language you learn another way to think. You will find, for example, words for which there isn't an equivalent in English, and visa-versa. By learning a foreign language you actually get access to another perspective on the world, as well as the opportunity to develop your relationships with your business partners in an entirely new way. (No matter how good a salesman you are, being forced to take an interpreter with you for a meal with a client is going to hamper the development of a close and trusting relationship.) Those are two prime reasons why companies find people with foreign language skills valuable. Of course, a willingness to spend the time learning a language also demonstrates a respect for and a wish to understand other cultures, which is a must for any manager moving abroad.

I might add, as someone to whom foreign language learning has *not* come easily, that the process is very humbling. You make a fool of yourself, you have to trust people not to laugh at you, and in the beginning you communicate like a very dim-witted three-year-old (at best). For all these reasons, learning a language as an adult is very instructive, especially for future managers, who may be a bit short in the humility and patience department. If you really want a job with this firm, start by enrolling in a foreign language course and then apply. The company might be impressed by your determination and give you a chance.

Family influence

FROM THE U.S. ABOUT **CHINA**

We need to appoint some more departmental managers in China,
but before we have even written the advertisement we have been
inundated with inquiries from family members of our existing group
of managers. Their applications show many of them to be well quali-
fied, and naturally we would avoid a lot of time and trouble if we did
hire folks this way, but being a close relative of a manager is surely
not a good reason that a person should in turn be made manager.

Using one's family connections to win advancement worries U.S. Americans. It seems to go against their values of self-sufficiency, of "going it alone" and standing on one's own two feet. To be a "self-made man" (or woman) is a mark of pride in the U.S., and is one of the reasons why Abraham Lincoln and Oprah Winfrey, though admittedly for very different reasons, have a special place in people's hearts. Family connections provide a time-honored way of doing things in China and the rest of Asia, Latin America, Africa, and the Middle East, where an individual's first loyalty is to the family, not to him- or herself. If you could tap into this system of well-established networks it could certainly help your business.

Obviously, it would be unfair and unethical to look only at family "qualifications" when you fill your new managerial position. You will have to look at experience and educational and personal qualifications too. But there are advantages to appointing people from the same family. When a number of family members work for one company, they have everything to gain if the company succeeds and all to lose if it fails. This can be a motivating factor in getting the best out of your management team. And coming from the same background will speed up the communications and decision-making processes, which can be time-consuming in a company where managers have different aims, expectations, and ways of doing things.

On the other hand, appointing family members would be a step away from diversity, which most large corporations nowadays regard as an asset, and toward homogeneity. You will also have to decide whether family ties in certain circumstances will prove stronger than company loyalty, and whether a very united management team would be too hard for you to steer, especially if your headquarters is located half a world away.

Not a graduate!   Letter *133*

FROM SWEDEN ABOUT **FRANCE**

A few weeks ago our plant in France requested help in solving a technical problem. We sent one of our best workshop technicians, but the management at first refused to work with him when they discovered (after careful questioning) that he hadn't gone to college, was dyslexic, and wasn't on our management team. However, we insisted they cooperate with him, and he solved the problem within twelve hours. What was the reasoning behind their attitude?

The French management's strong reaction stems from the fact that most French firms operate on very hierarchical lines, and there is a sharp line between managers and subordinates—sharper than in almost any other European country, and more similar to the status-based distinctions common in Latin America. French managers are simply not used to treating non-managers as equals. There the unquestioned status of the boss is one of the foundation stones of the national business culture, and to challenge it is to challenge the whole system.

To compound the problem, in France, as in Belgium and Germany, it is one of the manager's roles to supply specific technical competence as well as company knowledge and leadership skills. It is this expert knowledge, acquired during many years of study, that gives managers the power, status, and authority associated with their roles. Knowledge and problem-solving skills are associated with high levels of education, rather than experience or learning "on the job," which is more the case in Sweden. The emphasis on intellectual as opposed to practical skills is illustrated in the story of a high-level meeting between a U.S. American and a French civil servant. On being presented with a workable solution to a problem by the American, the Frenchman is supposed to have responded, "We can see that it works in practice. But will it work in theory?" So to find that the theoretical approach failed while the "hands-on" approach worked must have really ruffled some French feathers.

Although similarly respectful of a solid academic background (many managers have Ph.D.s in engineering), German organizations are less concerned than the French with issues of hierarchy and status, and German managers would probably have taken the pragmatic view that finding a workable solution was more important than maintaining prestige. Swedes are different again, as they pay little attention to academic qualifications in themselves—it's the individual's performance that counts. This attitude obviously annoyed these particular French managers, who felt they would lose face if a relatively unqualified (in their eyes) employee were to succeed where they had failed. Obviously that is just what happened, and one can only hope that they survived the shock.

LETTERS 134–135

Along with the management role comes increased status, which in turn affects how other people regard you.

Lets himself down
Letter *134*

FROM SPAIN ABOUT **DENMARK**

> *I recently visited our head office in Denmark and was shocked to see that the CEO came to work every day in a beat-up old Nissan. Is this really the image he wants the firm to have? I just hope he takes a few more pains when he comes to Spain, or his workforce will lose respect for him.*

In Denmark and in other Scandinavian countries, this egalitarian style is more likely to *earn* him respect from his employees than damage his reputation. The British too have a soft spot for eccentrics, people who don't follow the rules.

A CEO driving a "banger" is a leader making an anti-materialist statement, and if it's symptomatic of the whole company and part of the firm's identity, you'll just have to get used to it. In Scandinavia, where too much time or money spent on appearances is regarded with suspicion, it may be excellent business to adopt a frugal, down-to-earth image, where top managers travel economy class and don't wear ties to work (although they may wear Saville Row suits and have BMWs at home). Of course, when your CEO goes to visit his international subsidiaries, he is going to have to adapt to another set of expectations, the first being that he *look* and act like a CEO.

Yes boss, no boss   Letter *135*

FROM AUSTRALIA ABOUT **THAILAND**

I have worked as a manager for ten years in my home country of Australia and now have been transferred to a factory in Thailand. At home I had a good relationship with the employees. We were all on first name terms and could share a joke together, which made going to work a lot of fun. Here, while people are friendly, they don't seem to trust me. I have been here for about six months and have never once had a conversation that goes beyond the "Yes, boss," "No, boss" level.

You must accept that because of cultural differences, relations will be formal, at least to start with. Thais, along with their Malaysian neighbors and the people of Indonesia and Latin America, are used to a strict hierarchy at work, and you will be treated with a great deal of respect simply because of your position. This may make you uncomfortable, because you are from a culture that doesn't make a big thing about status. Your decisions won't be questioned, not because they are necessarily the right ones, but because it's the manager's job to make them. In the short term you have no alternative but to accept these attitudes, and though you may find working within a hierarchical structure uncomfortable, you need to accept that hierarchies give each individual a role and a degree of security that many employees welcome.

LETTERS 136–138

What role managers should play is a question sometimes asked by the rank and file. Not all managers can provide a satisfactory answer.

Checking up on me   Letter *136*

FROM NORWAY ABOUT **BELGIUM**

> *I'm working in Belgium on a project, but I find the way they treat employees here really demeaning. On Monday I get my orders for the week, and every Friday I have to show the manager exactly what I've done. If I haven't achieved what he thinks I should have, he starts questioning me. The assumption seems to be that I will do as little work as possible, and this means that I never use my own initiative, I feel unmotivated, and I don't work as hard as I did at home.*

Not all Belgian managers are like the one you describe, of course, but certainly most Belgian and French managers see one of their most important roles as ensuring they have a high degree of control over what their subordinates are doing. In Scandinavia and the U.K., on the other hand, most managers see the most important aspects of their roles as coordinating the work of people in their departments and providing the right kind of support to enable employees to do a good job. There's obviously a clash of expectations here, but don't take your boss's lack of trust in you personally. It's a small comfort, but I'm sure he treats all his subordinates the same way.

Tell us what to do   Letter *137*

FROM AUSTRALIA ABOUT **BRAZIL**

> *I have been working as divisional manager here in Brazil for two years now, but my Brazilian workforce still surprises me. Last month,*

*for example, I was asked as a matter of priority what menu I would
like for the staff picnic, and last week as I entered the building at least
three people came rushing up to tell me a dead snake had been found
on the path outside. Why do they feel they have to consult me on
everything?*

Because you are the manager! In cultures that have clearly defined
hierarchies, like those of Latin America, Turkey, and the Middle East, managers have a paternalistic role. They have the power to hire and fire (not
like Australia or many of the countries of Western Europe, where legislation makes it is very difficult to get rid of an employee) and also to grant
favors, so employees are going to make sure that they do not displease
their bosses. If employees have not been used to making their own decisions, and authority in the company is highly centralized, it's not surprising that people feel they have to check with you about everything. If you
want to change things, you will have to plan for the long term. Be consis-
tent in delegating responsibility and encourage employees to trust their
own judgment. But bear in mind that it's difficult to change corporate culture if it is at odds with national culture.

No clear structure   Letter *138*

FROM BELGIUM ABOUT **SWEDEN**

*When dealing with Sweden, I have great difficulty in figuring out
exactly who has responsibility for what. No one seems to know! They
do not seem to have a clear management structure, and I can't
understand how they ever get things done.*

This is a comment I hear frequently from people who have just
started to do business with Sweden. What foreigners often don't understand is the emphasis placed on teamwork and consensus in companies
in some European countries including the Netherlands and the Scandinavian nations. The decision-making process in Sweden often involves a
number of individuals: the manager of the department, or in the case of
matrix organizations, the function, the "specialist" who knows the most

about the issue in question, and the others in the department who will be affected by the decision. It is not assumed here that the manager alone is always the best person to decide an issue, and the power to make decisions is often assumed by those working most closely with the specific issue or project. This consensus-seeking process may be time consuming, but it usually means that decisions are implemented relatively smoothly.

From the other angle, it's interesting to hear Swedes who work with other countries comment on how strange it is to contact a manager, who may know nothing about the area, for a decision about something that affects their work.

IN A NUTSHELL: *Leaders and Managers*

GLOBAL BUSINESS STANDARD

Most people the world over want a manager who is trustworthy, encouraging, and positive, communicates well, and is administratively competent. He or she should also be able to inspire others by providing a vision of what can be achieved. (If you work for a manager like this, you've won the jackpot!)

GLOBAL WARNING

Managers are individuals, and it would be unusual to find one who conformed to all the "standard" business norms of his or her particular culture.

- **Argentina:** It helps to belong to the "right" family or to have the "right" connections. Managers have the least authoritarian management style of South America. (See Letters 132, 133, 135, and 137.)

- **Australia:** Little attention is paid to your background, more to what you achieve. Managers are not automatically treated with respect as in many other cultures. (See Letters 135 and 137.)
- **Austria:** Consensus is not of central importance. Managers make decisions and can be autocratic if need be.
- **Belgium:** Academic qualifications are very highly valued. French-speaking managers are more likely to have an authoritarian style than the Flemish. Managers are unlikely to delegate, and they are not enthusiastic team players. (See Letters 133, 136, and 138.)
- **Brazil:** A comparatively authoritarian management style is the norm. It helps to belong to the "right" family or have the "right" connections. (See Letters 132, 133, 135, and 137.)
- **Canada:** There are differences between the English- and French-speaking managers' styles. French-speaking managers are more authoritative and directive.
- **China:** Managers will accept that sometimes things are "outside their control." They tend to think more long term and take a more "holistic" approach than Western counterparts. In state-owned companies, managers are responsible for child care, education, health care, and so on. It is important to have the right connections (*guanxi*). (See Letter 132.)
- **Denmark:** There is little emphasis on status and the appearance of status. Managers are valued for, and value, practical skills. Managers are prepared to work as part of a team, with subordinates, to address problems. (See Letters 134, 136, and 138.)
- **Finland:** Managers are not as consensus-oriented as their Scandinavian neighbors. They are prepared to make their own decisions and to issue direct instructions. (See Letters 134, 136, and 138.)
- **France:** Academic qualifications (especially from the "right" university) are more highly valued than experience or practical skills. Being of the right social background may be important. Managers are unlikely to delegate, and they are not enthusiastic team players. They feel it is important to be able to answer all subordinates' questions. (See Letters 133 and 136.)

- **Germany:** Academic qualifications are highly valued. Many managers have doctorates. They feel it is important to be able to answer all their subordinates' questions. They will make expectations of employees quite clear. Managers are often rather blunt. (See Letter 133.)
- **Hong Kong:** It helps to belong to the "right" family or have the "right" connections. (See Letter 132.)
- **India:** Many young foreign-educated people with progressive management styles return home to work, but traditionally authority of the manager is never questioned, and any kind of challenge is almost unknown. It helps to belong to the "right" family or have the "right" connections. (See Letter 132.)
- **Indonesia:** The manager's authority is never questioned. It helps to belong to the "right" family or have the "right" connections. Keeping the boss happy is a priority for most employees, but he in turn should help his employees. There is little managerial accountability or delegation. (See Letters 132 and 135.)
- **Italy:** Managers are expected to act and look the part, and may be unwilling to delegate. The manager may cultivate a "macho" image as a strong man of action. It is part of the manager's role to answer all subordinates' questions.
- **Japan:** Managers spend more time listening than issuing orders. Humility and thorough knowledge of the company are regarded as important management qualities. Academic qualifications (especially from the "right" university) are highly valued. (See Letter 132.)
- **Mexico:** Open disagreement with a manager or between managers is almost unknown, but there may be an element of distrust between the managed and manager. Managers have an authoritarian/paternalistic management style. Managers may cultivate a "macho" image. It helps to belong to the "right" family or have the "right" connections. (See Letters 132, 133, 135, and 137.)
- **Netherlands:** Managers will often seek consensus. Status is downplayed. Managers are some of Europe's best linguists. They are prepared to work with subordinates on an equal basis to answer questions. (See Letter 138.)

- **Norway:** See Denmark. Very egalitarian management style. (See Letters 134, 136, and 138.)
- **Poland:** Managers tend to be divided into two distinct groups: older managers who learned skills under communists, with authoritarian/ paternalistic management style, and foreign-educated younger managers.
- **Russia:** See Poland.
- **Saudi Arabia:** Family connections are all-important. Saudi Arabian managers may refuse to do work they regard as beneath their status. Management is reactive and crisis-oriented. (See Letters 132 and 137.)
- **South Africa:** A "macho" attitude toward women managers is not helped by a powerful "old boys' network." Managers may be of British, Dutch (Boer), or African origin. (See Letter 132.)
- **South Korea:** Managers are quicker to make decisions than their Japanese or Chinese neighbors, and opportunism is rewarded. Subordinates follow managers' decisions without question. (See Letter 132.)
- **Spain:** Managers work best when the hierarchical status of individuals is clear. Promotion is very often associated with length of service. Only senior managers make decisions, and consensus is not sought. (See Letter 134.)
- **Sweden:** See Denmark. Managers will often seek consensus and are often criticized by foreigners for being indecisive. (See Letters 133, 134, 136, and 138.)
- **Switzerland:** Managers are usually reluctant to take risks and prefer to follow the "tried and true." The German and French Swiss have a tendency to use universal rules to solve problems, while the Italian Swiss usually prefer to become personally involved in each situation.
- **Taiwan:** See Hong Kong. (See Letter 132.)
- **Thailand:** Open disagreement with or between managers is almost unknown. Subordinates are expected to respect superiors, and never to criticize. New generation of young Western-educated graduates may practice new behavior patterns. (See Letters 132 and 135.)

- **Turkey:** There are strict hierarchical divisions between managers and non-managers. The manager's word is law. (See Letter 137.)
- **UK:** Managers are often generalists and may have qualifications not directly related to the job they do. A non-confrontational style is preferred, and good communication skills are very important. (See Letters 131, 134, and 136.)
- **US:** Personal charisma and being seen as a "doer" are highly regarded in a top manager. Most are prepared to work with subordinates to answer questions. They don't feel they have to know everything themselves. However, what they say goes. (See Letter 131.)
- **Venezuela:** See Mexico. (See Letters 132, 133, 135, and 137.)

Working in Organizations

Imagine for a moment that you work for a smallish, moderately successful company of about thirty employees, with its workshop and office in a major city. It makes wooden shelving units and kitchen furniture, and started out as a family firm fifteen years ago. Four members of the founding family currently work there in different capacities. It has a good local reputation for producing quality products and most of its employees are happy to work there. In which country do you think this company is located?

Almost any answer you give will fit the bill, for companies like these can be found in just about any country. So if organizations are of about the same size, need the same sort of expertise, make the same product, but are located in different parts of the world, will there be any differences in how they organize the work of their employees? Of course there will. Even when the end purpose is the same—in this case to make and sell wooden furniture—the way the organization is structured, the way jobs are carried out, and the roles of the individuals who work in the organization will all be different, because the ways we manage and conduct business are deeply influenced by our cultural values and the behavior that goes with them.

In Culture A, the managing director of the furniture business is seldom in the office before 10:00 in the morning, and is often away for a couple of hours at lunchtime meeting suppliers and customers. He has two secretaries who attempt to structure his day, answer his correspondence, and whose duties also include making him coffee and buying presents for family birthdays. His employees must go through them if they want to speak to him. The boss knows all his employees personally and will often allow them days off to deal with family emergencies.

Despite that, he keeps a close eye on how they work and makes sure that the supervisor keeps the workers busy, so they don't just stand around chatting. The only person who always seems to know exactly what to do is the one employed to sweep up the wood shavings—and it's an important job, because the health and safety officials enforce strict rules about the handling of flammable waste. Luckily, one of the family members is married to a relative of the inspector, so they get prior notice of when inspections are going to take place. In an emergency, and out of personal loyalty to the boss, the workforce would come in during a day off to help complete a rush job, but it is seldom that deadlines are regarded as so pressing.

Where are you likely to find an organization like this? The example best illustrates a smaller Latin American organization (although in many respects the description could also fit similarly sized companies in Asia, Africa, the Middle East, and Southern Europe). Of course not all companies of this size and from this area will follow this pattern, but most will.

In Culture B, the boss and a couple of family members are currently working sixty-hour weeks in the company. They figure it is worth sacrificing time with family and friends now if it means they can win and deliver more orders. The manager doesn't have a secretary, as his priority is to keep costs down. Instead he handles communication with the help of an e-business tool and lots of e-mails. When he goes into the workshop, the employees all call him by his first name and are not afraid to ask him questions or to make suggestions about how to improve their work practices. The boss usually listens to their ideas, and if they are good, he will make sure they are implemented.

In the workshop the employees practice job rotation and everyone is responsible for disposing of his or her own wood waste. Employees are presented with their targets at the beginning of the week and it is their own responsibility to achieve them. The workforce is expected to work weekends if a rush order comes in, and the manager accepts as inevitable the fact that people will move on if they can find a more highly paid job.

Like the Culture A manager, the boss has to take health and safety regulations seriously, and even though his wife is a cousin of the inspector, the company was fined a few years ago for a breach of regulations. If any major decisions are to be made that are likely to result in a written agreement with a customer or supplier, the first thing the manager does is call in the legal adviser—that's the way they do things here.

Where are you likely to find an organization like this? The answer would be the U.S., although there is much that Scandinavian countries would identify with, like the lack of interest in status and willingness to listen to workers if they can come up with ideas for improvements.

To sum up, culture is the soil out of which an organization grows. Sow the same beans in different soils and the resulting bean plants will look different. The company might not be aware of the way it is affected by the culture it exists in, but the culture is in fact a prerequisite for its very existence and greatly influences the way it develops. It is not surprising that difficulties arise when companies expand across national borders and leaders transplant their nationally influenced company cultures into foreign environments. Getting a company to work well when moved to a new country is not a simple process, and if the difficulties are ignored or underestimated they can lead to the failure of the enterprise.

LETTERS 139–140

The way a business is organized is affected by the culture where it is located, and both corporate and national cultures affect how individuals work.

A cog in the machine   Letter *139*

FROM AUSTRALIA ABOUT **SPAIN**

I am a project leader who has been transferred to my company's Spanish business partners for a year. In Australia I was used to making decisions together with the members of my team and working

hard to meet set targets. Here I feel like everyone's kid brother.
Everyone has been here for many years, and although they are very
kind, I have a set role and fixed responsibilities, and I'm expected to
confine myself to them. No one seems interested in my ideas or
opinions, and there's no sense of urgency about anything.

It sounds as if you have not only swapped one country for another,
but that you have also swapped organization cultures. Even when working
within the same corporation and the same business area, people in different countries find it natural to work in different ways. You have moved
from a task-oriented company used to working in teams, and would probably have found the transition to a U.S. or U.K. company relatively easy, as
this way of working is well established in these countries. However, you
have moved to what sounds like a more traditional organization common in Western and Southern Europe, where there are fixed hierarchies
and set roles. If you are going to benefit from your time there try to look at
the advantages of this system. Staff turnover is low, people take a long-
term view of their firm's future, as they invest many years of their lives
there, and it sounds as if the working atmosphere is good, with relatively
low stress levels. See what you can learn over the coming year that you can
use to improve ways of working back home. No organization has all the
right answers.

Work-life balance   Letter *140*

FROM BRAZIL ABOUT THE U.S.

I came to work for a company here about a year ago, and will shortly
be returning home for the sake of my health. The way the business is
organized depends on people spending long hours working overtime,
and there aren't enough full-time workers employed. Like many
others in my unit, I have been working fifty-hour weeks and taking
work home on the weekends. I now feel that I cannot manage any
longer.

It sounds like you are wise to leave. However hard most Brazilians or other Latin Americans work, they seldom forget that there is more to life than the office or manufacturing plant, and that time spent with family and friends is time well spent. They share this attitude with Africans and Southern Europeans, but not with most U.S. Americans. This "live to work" attitude was compounded in the 1980s when many U.S. companies were downsized and entire tiers of management and administrative support staff were eliminated. Suddenly people had to produce their own graphics for presentations and managers were forced to work out their own budgets. Not only that, these changes were followed by the replacement of work processes by project-driven targets, which in turn required enormous efforts by staff and extremely long hours at the workplace.

Of course, overwork is not solely a U.S. problem (as the Japanese, the South Koreans, and the British can verify), but the changes in the workplace over the last twenty years, coupled with the American emphasis on the value of hard work for its own sake, is a combination that threatens both physical and mental well-being. You may have a more balanced and healthier attitude to the work-life balance in Brazil.

LETTERS 141–143

Corporate headquarters is often the place where major decisions are made. An enormous amount depends on just where the office is located.

Control freaks?   Letter *141*

FROM FRANCE ABOUT THE **U.S.**

We are part of an IT company taken over by a big American multinational a year ago, and since then have been bombarded with information about its "corporate standards." There is a "driving

*policy," would you believe, telling us among other things to use our
seat belts and not to drink and drive (already French national laws).
To top it all, we learned on the company's intranet site that it also had
a "beard policy" with guidelines about shape and length. When will
headquarters realize that it is dealing with individuals with minds of
their own rather than robots programmed to obey every rule?*

You don't say in which area you work. A beard policy probably has
its roots in some sort of industrial safety guidelines, but what that has
to do with IT escapes me. It sounds as if the people at corporate headquarters are doing a good job of alienating many of their non-U.S.
employees even though the motives are certainly good. Most U.S. Americans believe it is right that the same rules apply to everyone without exception, and if a corporate rule needs to be applied in Paris, Texas, in the
interests of equality it should also be applied in Paris, France. In this U.S.
Americans are not alone, and in Germany, Austria, and Switzerland rules
and regulations both inside and outside the workplace are enforced across
the board.

However, it does seem to be unnecessary to make a great point of
enforcing corporate regulations when there already exist identical
national laws. The reason can be that the company is trying to protect
itself from lawsuits from employees involved in accidents while driving
company cars, but I agree that this exercise of corporate power is going
to cause antagonism in a country like France, where individuals pride
themselves on being unique individuals first and corporate employees
second.

As these are corporate standards and they come from HQ, objections
to policy coming from one person will stand little chance of being heard.
However, if you can find colleagues, and in particular senior French executives, who share your irritation, you could approach HQ together. And
you could (tactfully) point to the example of what happened to Disneyland Paris in the 1990s when the Disney organization was taken to French
court contesting the company's strict dress code. The Europeans believed
the dress code violated French labor law, and as a result the organization
restructured its requirements.

Why won't they do as we say?   Letter *142*

FROM THE U.S. ABOUT **INDONESIA**

We have recently taken over an Indonesian company and have introduced the same standard reporting procedures that we have introduced in our other subsidiaries. However, we are having problems there in getting employees to follow them.

Traditionally, U.S.-based headquarters have exercised very tight control over the financial side of their business, and this has served as a way of checking the performances of both subsidiaries and individuals. However, you may find that your Indonesian management team is used to thinking in broader terms, prioritizing the building of relationships and the long-term aims of the company over short-term easily quantifiable goals. Perhaps they don't understand the importance of these procedures in the total scheme of things and may feel they have to invest a lot of work in an activity that gives them nothing in return (a favorite complaint of rank-and-file employees about HQ, wherever they are in the world).

Your Indonesian employees will not express their dislike of the new measures openly, for like Chinese, Japanese, Thais, and the citizens of the Latin American countries, they would regard it as unthinkable to come right out and say that a certain management request was unsuitable or unworkable. They would regard this as unspeakably rude, as well as risking open conflict that would result in a loss of face for everyone. Instead, you will find that the work is simply shelved, or directives "lost," and you will be expected to draw your own conclusions from this. To avoid this, make the effort to talk to your employees directly, explain why the work has to be done, and ask them if they need any support from you to do it. Remember that in some cultures it is difficult for individuals to tell a superior that they think they have made the wrong decision or that there are problems in implementing some measures, and it's up to managers to use their communication skills to find out where the problems lie.

No help from HQ

FROM GERMANY ABOUT JAPAN

We have been taken over by a Japanese company and much of the top management at the new headquarters is now Japanese. The problem is that we now get no directions from them—they show no interest in us. What I want to know is when they intend to tell us what to do.

One explanation is that you are expecting German-type leadership while your Japanese HQ is expecting you to behave like Japanese managers. If yours was previously a solely German company, you are probably used to a clear chain of command from HQ downward and a clear and unambiguous communication style. So while you are waiting for clear directives, the new Japanese HQ is probably waiting for suggestions and ideas from you who have experience "in the field." Japanese executive management is not likely to involve itself in giving direct orders, and Japanese middle managers are supposed to be able to interpret what to Germans might be the rather vague visions of their leaders. Your new Japanese bosses may well be expecting you to do the same, so scrutinize again any information you have already received and try to read between the lines. This sort of process, the attempt to look beyond the words to the thinking behind, is not one that comes naturally to Germans, Australians, Israelis, or U.S. Americans come to that, who are used to taking words at face value.

Another explanation is that they expect "business as usual" from you for the moment, realizing that they know little about the conditions operating in Germany but that you do. They will be observing and learning about the way you work before making any decisions about changes. For the Japanese it is more important to make a correct decision than a speedy one. However, you should let your opinions be known to your superiors and try to get explicit feedback from your Japanese bosses about what they expect from you.

This situation shows the danger that can follow if a company allows itself to be divided along national lines, with one group of employees having one set of expectations and a second quite another. The Japanese company would be well advised to get some German input at the corporate level before the divide deepens.

LETTER 144

What is a team? Is it people working together with the short-term aim of solving a problem, or a longer-term grouping whose aim is to support its members? And how can you get them to work together successfully?

Teamwork doesn't come naturally   Letter *144*

FROM SWEDEN ABOUT **FRANCE**

I've recently been in France trying to set up a team to deal with customer problems and complaints, but the problems I am encountering give me the impression that working together as a team is not something that comes naturally there.

You are right. You just need to look at the differences in your two educational systems to see where the differences start. In Sweden you are trained to work in teams at an early school age, and teachers ensure that everyone in a group is listened to with respect. The educational system in France, Belgium, the U.K., and the U.S., among others, is more competitive, and individual academic success is the goal of the student. Those values we receive during our schooling will naturally have an effect upon how we think when we start to work.

Teamwork is an accepted way for Swedes to get things done, and most companies work on the premise that the total capacity of a work team is greater than the sum of the capacities of its individual members. In the workplace it implies a "flat" organization where the managers are also team players, not simply bosses.

However, these principles that are so familiar to Swedes may be unfamiliar to other cultures, and French organizations have traditionally been more formal, centralized, and hierarchical in structure, and the position of manager has meant the individual has become the unquestioned leader of the group. Added to that is the French pride in their own individuality; they value the fact that they are unique individuals, and if told they "stand out from the crowd" (or the team) they are likely to regard that as a compliment rather than a criticism. As one rather desperate English manager remarked to me sourly, "Getting the French to work in a team is like herding cats."

If you are going to encourage the growth of a Swedish-type team, you will have to get the group's manager behind you and see that he or she starts to delegate responsibility to his or her coworkers, and spends more energy listening to their suggestions about how to improve performance.

IN A NUTSHELL: *Working in Organizations*

GLOBAL WARNINGS

Companies from the same national culture may still have very different corporate, regional, or professional cultures that affect how their employees work.

Global corporations cannot afford to be ethnocentric. Policies made in HQs that work in the "home culture" of the corporation may well be unpopular or impossible to implement in others.

- **Argentina:** People like to have a clear work-related structure. They rely on rules and procedures. This is balanced by informal ways of getting around the rules. (See Letters 140 and 142.)
- **Australia:** Rules have to be understood and supported by employees. They will not be obeyed automatically. (See Letters 139 and 143.)
- **Austria:** Personal ambition and achievement are important driving forces within an organization. Organizations are hierarchical and change is not welcomed for its own sake. (See Letter 141.)

- **Belgium:** There is a dislike of uncertainty and risk-taking. This is balanced by informal ways of getting round the rules. There is a preference for a clear hierarchical structure. (See Letter 144.)
- **Brazil:** Hierarchical organizational structure is the norm. *Jeitinho*—the little way round the rules—is a common way of cutting through regulations and procedures. (See Letters 140 and 142.)
- **Canada:** They are less competitive than in the U.S. In French-speaking Canada there is more emphasis on rules and more hierarchical organizations. English-speaking organizations are less formal and hierarchical.
- **China:** Traditionally hierarchical structure is the norm. There are two main types of organizations—state-owned and private sectors—but even private companies are not focused solely on profit. Tasks are not usually tightly defined. (See Letter 142.)
- **Denmark:** Flatter egalitarian organizations are the norm. People are happy working in teams and without many strict rules.
- **Finland:** See Denmark.
- **France:** Clear hierarchical and centralized structures are common. Working in teams may be tricky. High level of discomfort with uncertainty. This is balanced by informal ways of getting around the rules (*Le Système D*). (See Letters 139, 141, and 144.)
- **Germany:** Technical specialists have much influence on organizations. Less centralized structures than the French. Procedures and rules are taken seriously. Personal ambition and achievement are an important driving force within organizations. (See Letters 141 and 143.)
- **Hong Kong:** People are happy working without many strict rules. Tasks are not usually tightly defined. There is a hierarchical system where power and decision-making are concentrated at the top.
- **India:** People are happy working without many strict rules. Traditionally there is a very centralized management system. There are signs in some more modern organizations of less hierarchy and more risk-taking, trust, and initiative.
- **Indonesia:** Extended family (patriarchy) is the backbone of most business institutions, and administrative behavior and business

structures are hierarchical. Decisions are handed down from the top. (See Letter 142.)

- **Italy:** Personal ambition and achievement are important driving forces within the organization. There is a hierarchical system where power and decision-making are concentrated at the top. (See Letters 139 and 140.)
- **Japan:** Organizations are hierarchical, but with a two-way communication flow (up-down and down-up). Cooperativeness within the group is balanced by competitiveness outside it. People like to work within a tightly regulated system. There is a very low level of employee turnover. (See Letters 140, 142, and 143.)
- **Mexico:** Personal ambition and achievement are an important driving force within the organization. The business structure is patriarchal and hierarchical. (See Letters 140 and 142.)
- **Netherlands:** Flat hierarchies are the norm. Teamwork and consensus seeking are preferred ways to work.
- **Norway:** See Netherlands.
- **Poland:** Traditionally, Poland has a very centralized and authoritarian management system combined with an assertive workforce. The comparatively new private sector is flourishing.
- **Russia:** An oligarchy is emerging. There is a handful of extremely rich business leaders with almost absolute power within their spheres of influence (e.g., oil and gas). Traditionally organizations are very centralized. People prefer to work within tightly regulated systems, which is balanced by informal ways of getting around the rules.
- **Saudi Arabia:** Extended family (patriarchy) is the backbone of most business institutions, and administrative behavior and business structures are hierarchical.
- **South Africa:** Decisions are made at the top of the hierarchy, but blue-collar unions are a force to be reckoned with. (See Letter 140.)
- **South Korea:** People prefer to work within a tightly regulated system. There is a very low level of employee turnover. Tradition of family ownership means companies have a paternalistic structure. Hierarchical and centralized organizations are common. (See Letter 140.)

- **Spain:** See Argentina. Working in teams may be tricky as everyone waits for a superior to take control. (See Letters 139 and 140.)
- **Sweden:** See Netherlands. Matrix organization is accepted. Specialists are given a lot of autonomy. People are happy working without many rules. Consensus is the accepted way to make decisions. (See Letter 144.)
- **Switzerland:** See Austria. (See Letter 141.)
- **Taiwan:** See Hong Kong.
- **Thailand:** The tradition of family ownership means authority takes a paternalistic form. Hierarchical and centralized structures are common. (See Letter 142.)
- **Turkey:** People prefer to work within a tightly regulated system, so there are lots of written rules and regulations. These are balanced by informal ways of getting around them. (See Letters 139 and 140.)
- **UK:** People prefer to work without many rules and written regulations. Instead, individual cases are considered on merit. Personal ambition and achievement are important driving forces within organizations. (See Letters 139, 140, and 144.)
- **US:** Of the world's richest corporations, U.S. corporations make up 41 percent of the total. U.S. organizational style is internationally influential. Hierarchies are clear and decision-making processes clearly defined. There is a reliance on written rules and procedures. Matrix organizations are common. (See Letters 139, 140, 141, 142, 143, and 144.)
- **Venezuela:** See Austria. (See Letters 140 and 142.)

Personal Relationships in Business

A recent survey done in Scandinavia on what young people were looking for in a job found that one of their top priorities was working with pleasant colleagues. This didn't surprise me—indeed, I'd be surprised if it wasn't a priority on most people's lists, wherever they come from. That's because we are more than a bundle of skills, a brain, and a pair of hands; we are also a complex and unique mixture of feelings, prejudices, and passions. Of course, most of us don't choose to reveal the most personal sides of our natures at work, but we do want to feel that as we carry out our jobs, our peers see us for who we are, that they accept and respect us, and even (we hope) like us.

Our cultural background shapes our ideas and expectations of what makes for a good relationship with a colleague (and indeed, what being a good colleague means). For example, do you think it is important to maintain an appropriate level of formality and professional distance in relationships with colleagues? If you are French or Japanese you may, but not if you are a U.S. American, Australian, or Israeli, for you are more likely to prefer "matey" informal relationships. Or another question: How much open conflict will a good relationship stand? In France it should stand a lot, because people are used to vigorous, even aggressive, debate, whereas in Japan, Thailand, and the Philippines, where harmony is highly valued, a person openly expressing an opinion that was likely to upset people would be regarded as a troublemaker rather than a loyal colleague.

And how about revealing what you are feeling at work? I know an intercultural consultant who asked groups of Finnish and Italian businesspeople which four emotions they thought were acceptable to show in the workplace. The Finns took ages to find three and then gave up, while the Italians didn't understand the question. (You mean there are some emotions that you would *hide?* Why would you want to do that?)

There is also the question of after-work socializing, whether that means eating and drinking together or playing softball or golf. If you don't participate in South Korea or Japan, for example, you may be regarded as "standoffish" and unfriendly, as well as shirking the obligation to build your network of contacts. In Scandinavia it's difficult to get people to give up their evenings to entertain foreign visitors—their private life is more important to them. The problem is that if you break the unwritten rules governing relationships in a specific culture, you may be seen as revealing a negative side of your personality rather than simply following a different set of norms. That's one of the reasons why it can be so difficult to build relationships with people from other cultures.

Smooth relationships among people from the same company are of course desirable, but the way company employees relate to people from other organizations (especially if they are customers) can be vital to the success of a business. In Latin-American, Southern European, Arab, and most Asian countries, personal relationships are seen as being the foundation of business, and agreements are based on relationships of trust built up over many years rather than papers drawn up by a lawyer. It may be understood that service or prices vary depending on how good the relationship between the salesperson and customer is. That's why the first chapters of this book dealt with the subjects of gift giving and eating and drinking together, because if things go right from these earliest stages the chances are that a longer-term and deeper relationship will have a chance to develop.

But these sorts of close interpersonal relationships, so desirable in Asia and Latin America, are sometimes regarded with suspicion by corporations in cultures like the U.S., for instance, which make a clear distinction between the individual and the job he or she does. It is an asset to be "well-liked," as Willy Loman, the archetypal salesman in Arthur Miller's *Death of a Salesman* puts it, but it's not enough to guarantee you success. Indeed, there are large successful U.S. corporations whose policy is to change the account manager every two or three years so that the relationship between employee and customer does not become too "personal" or cozy, for the concern is that employees might put the interests of their customers above that of their own company. I would be interested to see if this way of doing things would be happily or profitably adopted by managers working in countries like China, India, and in the Middle East, where long-standing and deep-rooted personal relationships are a prerequisite to doing business. In a situation like this, hard-headed business strategists are faced with a dilemma: To achieve a pragmatic goal (to do business), managers may actually be required to spend time getting to know and taking an interest in people they neither work with nor are related to. Squaring that particular circle could keep them occupied for a while.

LETTER 145

How people get on together plays a vital part in how well their company performs.

Business backslide   Letter *145*

FROM NORWAY ABOUT **SAUDI ARABIA**

> *Our company has had an excellent relationship with a Saudi Arabian customer for many years, but since the retirement of the last sales manager we haven't received any orders. The new sales manager is really worried and is planning to go down there to see what's happened. What do you think has gone wrong?*

It sounds as it the change from one manager to another could have been better handled. Your previous manager was obviously older and may have had personal contacts in Saudi Arabia for many years. In many countries, especially outside the U.S., Canadian, and Western European cultures, personal relationships are the most reliable way of doing business, and business is done largely between individuals rather than between companies. If you do business with a trusted business contact, you have an unspoken guarantee that he or she will take a personal interest in your business and take care of any problems that may arise.

When your previous sales manager retired he should have introduced his replacement personally to his Saudi Arabian customers, but as that obviously hasn't happened I suggest he write a letter of introduction that the new manager can take on his first visit. Alternatively, he could ask the former manager to take a half hour away from the golf course or garden and phone his Saudi contacts for a chat and to explain the new situation. Otherwise your new manager is going to have to start from scratch to build personal relationships, and that can take time.

LETTERS 1 4 6 – 1 4 7

Certain patterns of behavior are encouraged or expected in different cultures. However, when practiced abroad they can result in disapproval.

Too dependent   Letter *146*

FROM THE U.S. ABOUT **MEXICO**

I was in Mexico a couple of years ago and worked quite closely with a Mexican colleague, who was very helpful. Now he is working here in New York on a six-month placement, but we are not working on the same project. He seems to be having some problems getting authorization for some of our systems, but I have a target to meet and if I spend time helping him I'm going to end up behind schedule myself. He also expects us to lunch together most days, but I usually just have a sandwich at my desk, and he wants to make arrangements for after work when I have other things to do. He needs to learn to stand on his own two feet.

The poor guy. He must be having a hard time adjusting to the pace of work at your company. I know that stress is the killer of empathy and you obviously have a lot to do, and if you are working toward a bonus or a promotion you are not going to take kindly to acting as mentor to a new employee. However, forget your schedule for a minute and try to remember the inevitable adjustments you had to make to working in Mexico. Your friend eased this adjustment period for you, and you have a duty to do the same for him. In Mexico, and indeed in most Latin American cultures, long-term personal relationships are more important, both inside and outside the work environment, than they are in the U.S. in general, and New York in particular. And if you don't return his kindness you are going to confirm the preconception that U.S. Americans are opportunists who are only interested in using short-term personal relationships for their own ends. So introduce him to your network, and if necessary have a quiet word with his manager to see if you can ease any authorization issues. Don't let your belief that people should stand on their own feet stop you from offering a helping hand to a friend in need.

The role of personality   Letter 147

FROM THE U.S. ABOUT **THAILAND**

My department has to send a representative to Thailand to see if we can do business there and I have to decide who should represent us. We have one guy (U.S. American like the rest of us) who's had very good results in Europe. He's a real extrovert with a great sense of humor, but he's a bit temperamental and I wonder how the Thais will react to him.

It might be risky to send him. The Thais, like the Japanese and Indonesians, are a people who prize self-control and quiet rather than raised voices. You say your guy is temperamental, which means he runs the risk of losing his temper on occasions, which is bad news in a country that regards such lack of control as at best childish and at worst the sign of immaturity, selfishness, and stupidity. If he lost face by behaving badly (in Thai eyes, at any rate), then the reputation of your company would also suffer and it would be difficult to establish good relations later. You want someone who will understand the Thai wish for a harmonious and mutually respectful relationship, and who has the patience to work at achieving it.

Generally speaking, you cannot ask people to adopt a very different behavior pattern when they move to a new culture. To do so can compromise their sense of identity, and they will feel uncomfortable if they cannot "be themselves." On the other hand, you can ask them to adapt to the new culture and modify their behavior as best they can. If you have any doubts that this man will be able to do this, don't send him.

LETTERS 148–151

Anger and irritation are often the result of cross-cultural contacts where people have misunderstood each other totally.

False friendliness   Letter *148*

FROM POLAND ABOUT THE **U.S.**

I have recently started working for an American hotel chain and have taken a training course on how to deal with customers. Two things that really irritate me are, first, that we have to have a permanent smile on our faces, and second, that we have to finish any conversation in English with "Have a nice day." This sort of false friendliness is just not me, and I feel hypocritical and insincere when I'm forced to behave like this.

You didn't say where you would be working—in the U.S. or Poland—but if you are to work in the U.S., your customers will be surprised if they don't receive, in their terms, "friendly" treatment, including a smile and a greeting and farewell. If you are working with Polish customers, I agree that they might find a broad smile of greeting a bit surprising ("What are you so happy about?"). I have also heard your reaction to the "Have a nice day" greeting from many Europeans—that it's phony and that they are only out to sell you something, and why disguise that fact with warm wishes for your future happiness? Personally, if I'm a customer I expect courteous treatment and have no objections to a friendly greeting. I'd much rather have that than the cold contempt of some "customer service" personnel in Germany, France, Russia, and Eastern Europe who seem to find customers a nuisance. U.S. Americans are not especially deferential to, nor formal with, customers, and their forms of greetings reflect an egalitarian and friendly attitude toward people. You're not compromising your personal integrity if you do the same.

The useful thing about the expression "Have a nice day" is that it covers so many situations. It's not used much in Britain, where they tend to be more specific and will choose between, "Good morning/afternoon," "See you again, I hope," "Have a good trip," "Bye for now," or even the common or garden-variety "Good-bye," depending on the situation.

Don't want to upset them   Letter *149*

FROM BELGIUM ABOUT **JAPAN**

We have a number of Japanese managers we feel are underperform-
ing. We would like to discuss the situation with them, not to
apportion blame but to help them improve performance. However, we
have heard that one has to be very careful how one proceeds here.

Confronting anyone, however tactfully, with their failure is always
tricky, especially in cultures where "face" is important, like Japan, China,
and South Korea. It may be better to handle this indirectly, perhaps through
a Japanese third party. Before doing this, you should ensure that the problem in fact does lie with the individuals concerned, that the course of action
they implemented was not decided by a group, or that they thought they
were implementing management decisions. Otherwise your criticism will
be resented as being unfair. You mention that there are several managers
you are worried about. Perhaps you should have a meeting with all of them
first to see whether they have a common problem, but when telling them
about the meeting avoid the use of the word *problem*. Say instead you would
like them to come up with ways of improving performance. If you do identify some managers who in your opinion are making repeated mistakes,
ensure that any feedback is delivered with tact and sympathy, is given on a
one-to-one basis, and is kept completely confidential.

Why a lawyer?   Letter *150*

FROM SOUTH AFRICA ABOUT THE **U.S.**

We have been in touch with an American company off and on for a
couple of years with the aim of our possibly acting as their agents here
in South Africa. We were very surprised when their sales director had
a company lawyer with him on his first visit. This seems to us like
"putting the cart before the horse." We don't even have an agreement
in principle yet. This displays the lack of even a basic degree of trust
or goodwill, and in my opinion is not a good sign for the success of
any future business.

Lawyers are an important part of the American business scene. There is probably a greater need for their services in cultures like the U.S. that put a high value on individual initiative and "going it alone" than in cultures like South Africa, Japan, or Finland, for example, where business is based on relationships of trust, probably going back a number of years. There are cultures where a handshake is enough to guarantee an agreement, but in the U.S. this is not the case, and lawyers are often involved from the very earliest stages of an agreement (like the drawing up of prenuptial contracts, which have become a big business in the U.S.). It's not that they don't trust you or your company in particular—that's just their way of doing business.

Don't judge us   Letter *151*

FROM ITALY ABOUT **SWEDEN**

We have just heard from our Swedish headquarters that we are all going to be subjected to a performance appraisal. In our department we are all very worried and some of my colleagues are rather angry. This seems to mean that people who don't understand the nature of our work are going to judge whether our performance is satisfactory.

First of all, performance appraisals are usually carried out by your immediate manager, who probably has a good idea of your work. Secondly, don't take this process as any sort of suggestion that you aren't performing well. Most companies in the U.S. and many multinationals now regard the performance appraisal process as routine. It is seen by management as an opportunity to give employees feedback on how they are doing, so they can learn and improve. This feedback is meant to be constructive and, as well as looking at what you already do well, will concentrate on what can be improved. Its purpose is not simply to find fault, and it should not be regarded as a call to the "principal's office" because you have done something wrong! Indeed, the best companies use appraisal interviews to give employees an opportunity to comment on how their jobs can be improved, how they see their own careers developing, and how their superiors are performing (although I can imagine this last point may be difficult for Italian mangers to accept, as they are not used to being questioned or criticized—however constructively—by subordinates).

LETTER 152

Building an international team can be fraught with difficulty, but if you get the communication right from the start, relations between team members will benefit.

Before you start   Letter *152*

FROM TURKEY ABOUT **WORKING GLOBALLY**

I work for a large multinational organization and have recently been appointed project leader for a global team. I know from past experience how important it is that relationships start off on the right foot, and I wonder if you have any advice on how to achieve this.

The golden rule is to meet face to face as often as your organization can afford it. Obviously it is very expensive and time-consuming to arrange meetings all over the globe, but you can't get around the fact that such meetings reduce the possibilities of misunderstandings and contribute hugely to good interpersonal relationships. One reason is that when you speak to a person in a conference room as opposed to, say, communicating via e-mail, you receive the whole message, and not only the part that is made up of words. That means you can pick up the tone of voice and hear the suggestive pause before a certain word, as well as see the nonverbal clues of facial expression and body language that can tell you so much. And naturally, the better you understand each other the better your relationships are going to be.

Face-to-face meetings are particularly important for participants who do not have the same native language as the majority of the group, who are used to expressing themselves indirectly, or who place a high value on *how* the message is put across, as well as the concrete information it conveys. For different reasons, most of the people from Asia and Latin America fall into this group. They tend to be more interested in the individual behind the message than the more pragmatic Aussies or U.S. Americans who concentrate on the content of the message itself. For this reason, when people do meet face to face it is very important to give them the opportunity to socialize before or after meetings.

The best alternative to a physical meeting is a videoconference, although that inhibits the kind of social interchange that is a natural part of face-to-face meetings. If you are going to set these up, make sure they don't inconvenience the same people every time (having to turn up repeatedly at the office at 8:00 P.M. or 6 A.M. because that is a good time for the people at HQ, which is in a different time zone, is going to put a damper on the warmest interpersonal relationships).

IN A NUTSHELL: *Personal Relationships in Business*

- **Argentina:** See Brazil. There is a certain distrust of authority figures. (See Letters 146 and 152.)
- **Australia:** It is important to be regarded as friendly (not "snooty") and have social skills, but ultimately you are judged by job performance. (See Letter 152.)
- **Austria:** Business and personal feelings are kept strictly separate. Business relations are usually quite pragmatic, although loyalty and long-term relationships are valued.
- **Belgium:** Personal and business relationships are kept strictly separate. Relatively formal business relationships are the norm. Being overly friendly or personal is regarded negatively. Interpersonal conflict is not regarded with as much fear as in many other cultures. (See Letters 145 and 149.)
- **Brazil:** *Personalismo* is very important—the personal element. Ties of emotional warmth are sought. Preference is often given to family and friends. (See Letters 146 and 152.)
- **Canada:** It is important to be regarded as a pleasant person and have social skills, but ultimately you are judged by job performance. (See Letter 145.)

- **China:** Loyalty is a Confucian virtue. Tight social networks (family and work teams) are held together by this quality. Business is facilitated by *guanxi* (connections). They place community concerns above individual ones. (See Letters 149 and 152.)
- **Denmark:** Most business does not require a personal element. Feelings are kept out of business. Business relations are usually quite pragmatic. (See Letter 145.)
- **Finland:** See Denmark. (See Letters 145 and 150.)
- **France:** See Belgium. (See Letter 148.)
- **Germany:** Business and personal feelings are kept strictly separate. Business relations are usually quite pragmatic, although loyalty and long-term relationships are valued. (See Letters 145 and 148.)
- **Hong Kong:** See China. (See Letters 149 and 152.)
- **India:** Family firms with traditional loyalties to family, caste, and friends are common. Young highly educated employees in multinationals may be more dispassionate. (See Letters 151 and 152.)
- **Indonesia:** An individual's status in an organization determines how fellow employees and business contacts relate to him or her. Employees place family and community concerns above individual and business concerns. (See Letters 147 and 152.)
- **Italy:** Rivalry can affect relationships between different regions of the country. *Clientelismo*, exchanging favors with friends or business connections, is important. Business relationships are based on loyalty and trust. (See Letter 151.)
- **Japan:** Life-long employment by the same company encourages ties of loyalty to coworkers. (However, life-long positions are rapidly disappearing.) The value placed on harmony means interpersonal conflict is rare. People place community concerns above individual ones. (See Letters 147, 149, 150, and 152.)
- **Mexico:** See Brazil. (See Letters 146 and 152.)
- **Netherlands:** See Denmark. (See Letter 145.)
- **Norway:** See Denmark. Relationships are usually informal and friendly. (See Letter 145.)
- **Poland:** Poles can be assertive and individualistic, and are not afraid of debate. This will not interfere with the formation or continuation of a good relationship. (See Letter 148.)

- **Russia:** Russians are reluctant to deal with anyone they have not met personally. Building a relationship is vital before business takes place, and it can be a long process. (See Letter 148.)
- **Saudi Arabia:** Business is done with an individual (who may happen to belong to another organization) rather than with the organization itself. Interpersonal relationships are more important than intercompany business. (See Letter 145.)
- **South Africa:** In the white community, belonging to the "old boys' network" is an advantage. (See Letter 150.)
- **South Korea:** An individual's status in an organization will determine how fellow employees and business contacts relate to him or her. Written agreements and contracts are not taken as seriously as in the U.S. (See Letters 149 and 152.)
- **Spain:** Social class affects business relationships. Status is linked more to the individual's position in the hierarchy and less to performance.
- **Sweden:** See Denmark. (See Letters 145 and 151.)
- **Switzerland:** See Austria.
- **Taiwan:** See China. (See Letter 152.)
- **Thailand:** Respect is accorded to age, experience, and wisdom. Loyalty is to individuals rather than institutions. (See Letters 147 and 152.)
- **Turkey:** See Saudi Arabia.
- **UK:** See Canada. (See Letters 145 and 148.)
- **US:** Business relationships may be cordial, but they are often short-term. Business and personal feelings are kept strictly apart. Legal agreements are more important than individual relationships and loyalties. (See Letters 145, 146, 147, 148, 150, 151, and 152.)
- **Venezuela:** See Brazil. (See Letters 146 and 152.)

CHAPTER 8

Work in a Wider Perspective

The problem with using our brains is that thinking requires a lot of energy, and in many ways it's easier to act first and think second. However, as we leave our teens and have to deal with some of the more uncomfortable consequences of acting on impulse, most of us learn that decisions based solely on instant gratification are seldom wise ones and realize that a period of reflection before we act can be a good idea. Faced with some of life's important decisions we may be forced to examine our *priorities,* our *ethical standards,* and/or the *assumptions* we learned as we grew up about what is "normal" or "abnormal" behavior. In all three key areas our native culture has a significant influence on our answers, for it provides the cornerstones on which we base our thinking.

These three key points naturally have a place in our working lives too. *The first one,* how we judge what is more or less important, is something we do all the time.

The book *Funky Business: Talent Makes Capital Dance* by Jonas Ridderstråle and Kjell Nordström claims that as social institutions in the West are dying—families are getting smaller or splitting up; the state is less able to provide health care, education, and social benefits for its citizens; religion is seen as irrelevant—companies will have to provide their employees with the sense of belonging and the security that they previously found in their lives outside work. In this way jobs will become even more important in life, and presumably occupy even more time and energy. Some cultures already give a very high priority to work. In Japan, long hours in the office, and equally long hours socializing with coworkers and customers, mean that businessmen have little time with their families. Although there are signs that things are changing, vacations are often still taken with fellow employees, and loyalty to the company means that people rarely change employer by choice. In the U.S., on the other hand, there is a lot of mobility in the job market, but people are just as determined to "better themselves" through hard work. There, too, people work long hours and claim that they work sixty hours a week for the sake of their families.

Yet there are cultures, like those of Southern Europe, the Middle East, and Latin America, where people think that expressions like "time is money" and "work before pleasure" show that someone's priorities are wrong, and that the best way to be a good family member is to spend time with your relatives. Everyone knows that work is only part of the picture.

The second key point is about ethics—whether a course of action is right or wrong. Any job for any company can involve the individual in ethical dilemmas. I know a teacher who came, like me, from England to Scandinavia to teach English. He was sent to a middle-sized town in the center of Sweden, but after finding out where he was expected to teach, he broke his contract and returned home. He was a Quaker, and his biggest client would have been the local armaments factory. His decision was based on an ethical stance and a matter of individual conscience.

But what about corporate ethics—what are they based on? For example, what about the U.S. pharmaceutical company that tried (unsuccessfully) to patent turmeric, a locally grown spice, in India? In India most people know that if turmeric-based formulations are applied to wounds they will heal faster, and most Indian people would regard it as unnatural and indeed unethical to lay claim to knowledge that had been passed down from generation to generation, for they come from a culture where it is regarded as natural to share "cultural property" with other members of the community.

But I'm sure that the CEO and directors of that particular American company would have been pained to have their attempt at patenting described as "unethical." But if you belong to a culture, either national or corporate, that prioritizes the individual over the collective and that does not accept the idea of a common intellectual heritage; if something does not have a legal owner, it's up for grabs.

The third point, about what constitutes "natural" behavior, is not one we ask ourselves until faced with a situation that challenges our assumptions of normality—and we are more likely to face such situations when dealing with another culture.

Companies and corporations can have conflicting ideas about what is "natural." So if the boss of a German company, for example, asks if it is possible for a Mexican supplier to deliver 5,000 widgets to his warehouse on December 2 and the supplier says "Yes," on December 1 the German manager will ensure there is enough empty shelf space available for tomorrow's delivery, for he comes from a culture where people are very proud of the fact that they say what they mean.

The Mexican manager, however, may be surprised to receive a phone call on December 3 asking why the widgets aren't there. Yes he had said it was *possible* for him to deliver, and indeed it was, but only if he made all his other long-standing customers wait, and of course he couldn't do that. And by the way, hadn't the German seen the TV reports about the hurricanes in the area, which meant that staff had had problems coming to work? The Mexican executive is shocked and angry when the German threatens legal action for breach of contract. That is no way to build a long-term relationship.

This stalemate is the result of each party making different assumptions about what is a normal, acceptable way to behave. And of course it doesn't occur to either of them that they need to explain or justify their actions to the other party, because everyone knows what "normal, acceptable" behavior means. I'm afraid neither of them had read the rather depressing but wise words of Nancy Adler in *International Dimensions of Organizational Behavior*: "Assume difference until similarity is proven." Those words should be written in gold above the doors of corporate headquarters around the world. It would save everyone a lot of trouble.

◆ **MORAL**

What we regard as right, as important, and as natural in one country may be regarded as the opposite in another.

Priorities

It's been a long time since I read the story of "The Sleeping Beauty," but I remember it started with the good fairies each giving the baby princess a gift. I wonder if you told this story to people of different cultures which they would choose as the most precious qualities for a baby girl. Should she be beautiful, dutiful, rich, fertile, intelligent, happy, charming, strong, honest, or chaste? Our answers would naturally be influenced by our gender, age, and education, but also very much by the cultures we came from.

In the West, chastity, for example, is not particularly high on most people's lists of priorities, but for parents in Saudi Arabia or Somalia it might well be "top of the pops," as sex outside marriage is not only a disgrace to the family but may also be punishable by death. The word *dutiful* has a similarly exotic ring to it if you happen to come from the West. It implies that there are links of duty and responsibility between individuals—parent and child, for example, or siblings, or manager and employee. To be undutiful means ignoring your obligations to others and putting yourself first, and it would be regarded most unfavorably in cultures such as the Chinese or Indian. Indeed, many people from these cultures would regard being rich (the number one choice, I suspect, of many U.S. and British families) as pretty pointless if they couldn't use their wealth to help family members or, even more fundamentally, produce children themselves.

But it's not only in life's big issues that we reveal our priorities. John Cleese, the comedy writer and actor, is supposed to have said that an Englishman would rather have a reputation as being a poor lover than as having no sense of humor. I have to agree. For the English, living well has not entailed what it has in other cultures, where people have set a great store by the cultivation and enjoyment of the senses. We have never really understood why other nationalities have laid great value on such relatively unimportant aspects of life as food, sex, the pursuit of happiness, or warm bathrooms. For us the real priorities in life, depending on age, social class, and gender, are

- watching soccer and cricket matches,
- going to the pub with mates,
- having a nice back garden,
- and getting a hot beverage (tea or instant coffee) on demand.

Not only individuals are influenced by national cultures, of course. Companies also reflect the culture of the country where they have their roots. Indeed, in different countries there are different ideas about why companies exist at all. In the U.S., the belief is that they exist to provide profit for the shareholders, so the "bottom line" is of the utmost importance. In Japan, the aim is to achieve increased market share, so they give top priority to finding out what customers want and giving it to them. In the old Soviet bloc their purpose was to provide jobs, and in certain European countries with a strong social democratic tradition, local and national government still sees this as a company's prime function. In these countries, like Germany and Sweden, it is a priority to safeguard employees' rights (to information, consultation, etc.) because only then can the company expect to have a committed and responsible workforce.

As there are differences in such fundamental questions as what a company is for, it is not surprising that employees from different cultures prioritize different ways of behaving. Managers from the U.S., for example, prioritize action above all else, even if the action is not guaranteed to solve the problem. Any action is better than none. The Chinese and Japanese, with a very different view of time and the power of fate, may prefer to allow things to take their course rather than expend a lot of useless energy trying to achieve the impossible. The French prioritize a logical, well-thought-out solution to a problem, while the Swedes will always prefer to wait for a consensus before acting. With such different priorities, doing business with people from other national or corporate cultures requires flexibility.

LETTERS 153–155

What's more important—your company, your colleagues, your family, or yourself?

Who to sack? Letter *153*

FROM GERMANY ABOUT THE **U.K.**

In the last recession, the British headquarters of my company got rid of a high percentage of its older middle managers in order to cut costs. This means that now there is no one there with any experience of how the business works, and no knowledge of whom we in the German subsidiary are. We cannot understand how they could be so disloyal to people who have invested large parts of their lives in the company as to make such a shortsighted and essentially unproductive decision. Here in Germany we can see our younger managers are looking for jobs in other companies because they understand what the future might hold for them as they get older.

To be fair, who to get rid of in the bad times is never an easy decision to make. But there are differences in how different countries act in times of economic downturns. One study shows that faced with a call for financial cuts, the British will prioritize spectacular short-term gains and tend to get rid of older, more expensive staff to keep the shareholders happy, while Germans take into account the difficulty older employees have finding work and are more prepared to get rid of younger employees, even if they are cheaper.

Unions also play an important role in France and Sweden when it comes to the question of who is to go during periods of downsizing. In these countries, people usually lose their jobs on a "last in, first out" basis, which protects older workers but leaves companies with an aging workforce. This can have undesirable consequences in certain high-tech industries that rely on new skills coming into the company. Britain, on the other hand, can get away with its strategy of getting rid of older and more expensive workers first because the position of the labor unions is quite weak (Mrs. Thatcher "handbagged" them and they have not recovered yet), but with anti-ageism legislation in the pipeline in the EU this might be about to change in Britain too.

Family first	Letter *154*

FROM AUSTRIA ABOUT **TURKEY**

Our company currently employs a female manager in her thirties who works in her home country of Turkey. She has all the qualifications and qualities our company is looking for and she has been a major success in Turkey. We are hoping to transfer her to our Pakistan office because we believe she can repeat her success there. She is single, and in Turkey she lives with her parents. The problem is that she is refusing to move because she says it is not "seemly" for her to live on her own. This is a lady who has lived for three years in the U.S. when studying (albeit with her uncle's family) and who can hold her own in negotiations with anyone we know. She is certainly no shrinking violet. We are not sure if this is a ploy to win an increase in salary or if this is a serious objection.

I'm sure this is a genuine problem for your employee. In India, and in predominantly Muslim cultures such as Turkey, Indonesia, and Saudi Arabia, even comparatively liberal families may draw the line at a single daughter living on her own, whatever her age, character, and position at work. The reasons are not hard to find. Families take the reputations of their unmarried daughters very seriously, and a single woman living on her own would inevitably be the subject of gossip. Not only that, her parents are probably concerned about her physical as well as her moral safety in a culture where male relatives, rather than the police, are the first people a woman may turn to for protection against crime. Also, coming from a culture where the extended family is the norm, and free time is spent with other family members and seldom on one's own, a choice to live alone is going to be regarded as unnatural. What can spell privacy in one culture can mean loneliness in another.

Your employee has shown great commonsense in refusing your proposal. She understands, probably better than you, the problems she would face living alone in another Muslim country. Her decision also tells you something that executives need to hear regularly and often—that there are more important things in life than work. Paradoxically, the fact that your employee listens first to her family, and only secondly to you, makes her more useful to the company. She is more in tune with her culture, and the culture of your customers, than you are—which is probably why she has been so successful at her job so far. Try to hang on to her.

Better job   Letter *155*

FROM MEXICO ABOUT THE **U.S.**

I joined the large American company I currently work for after school, and since then they have provided me with training and opportunities to develop myself. Naturally I am very grateful to them. Now a Mexican company has offered me a very good job and they want me to start immediately, but my employers have said that if I leave right now this is going to cause them a lot of trouble. I know this is correct and do not want to repay their faith in me with disloyalty.

Your concerns do you credit, but you are going to have to be hard-nosed about this. American firms do frequently give their employees chances to learn and develop, but their motives are not altruistic. They do it to attract high-quality recruits and to provide themselves with a skilled workforce. Should the market change and the need for certain skilled groups diminish, they will lay off groups of workers without hesitation. In U.S. business culture, the work roles that people occupy are much more important than the individual. The rules of the marketplace take precedence over feelings. You may have had firsthand experience of smaller Mexican companies where ties of personal loyalty between owners and employees are very strong. The same traditions of loyalty between employer and employee exist in Japan and Germany too, but most larger international companies will probably play by U.S. rules.

Your employers will understand your motives for leaving, even if they don't admit it, and after a few years of experience in another company you will be even more attractive to them. You may even find yourself back working for them in the future!

LETTERS 156–157

Bad feelings can result if you feel others disregard your own priorities.

Written or spoken?   Letter *156*

FROM AUSTRALIA ABOUT **TURKEY**

We are trying to get an agreement with a Turkish supplier but are having problems getting a contract drawn up, let alone signed. Although they seem anxious to do business with us, they do not seem to think that it is important to set down their requirements, or agree to ours, in print.

The Turkish culture prioritizes what is said rather than what's written, which means that Turks prefer doing business with people they already know and trust, and working with loose verbal agreements avoids the whole question of contracts, deadlines, and penalty clauses. Written agreements are all about rules, and Turks, like their Greek neighbors, are not especially keen to conform to rules that might soon become irrelevant in a fast-moving business environment. Flexibility and creativity are regarded as more important qualities in a businessperson than the ability to draw up detailed plans for future action. Even if you do get your agreement written and signed, it would be difficult to enforce in a court of law because such cases tend to be very time-consuming. You will find the same attitudes about written contracts in Japan, South Korea, and Indonesia, where they are regarded as a reference point or guidelines rather than a set of points carved in stone. So your best bet is to prioritize a good relationship with the top man of the Turkish firm and to try to get his personal promise to honor your agreement.

Good product comes first   Letter *157*

FROM THE U.K. ABOUT **GERMANY**

> *We are trying desperately to get our German engineers to work to our specifications, but they have lots of objections. They want to use more durable materials to extend the life of the product, but if we followed all their suggestions we would almost double the price. They do not seem to have the faintest interest in the financial consequences of their actions, and take no notice of the British managers who are telling them that the bottom line is important.*

German manufacturing companies, like the Swiss, Austrian, Swedish, and Finnish, take great pride in the quality of their products, and traditionally they prioritize safety, reliability, and the highest possible quality. In the past they have believed that if you produce a good product customers will buy it regardless of price. Graduate engineers in Germany are widely respected and have a prominent role in the management of many firms, whereas finance and accounting personnel, a group that usually commands a lot of influence in U.K. companies, are less influential. See if you can find a British manager with a strong engineering background as well as a good grasp of finance to win over his or her German counterparts.

IN A NUTSHELL: *Priorities*

GLOBAL WARNING

The following are simple but, I hope, useful generalizations. There are naturally enormous differences in the priorities of companies and individuals within the same culture.

- **Argentina:** Who you are is more important than what you achieve. It is important to enjoy life. Good interpersonal relationships are very important. (See Letter 156.)
- **Australia:** What you achieve is more important that who you are. (See Letter 156.)
- **Austria:** It is important to behave formally and with dignity. Status, job title, and prestige are extremely important. (See Letters 153, 154, and 157.)
- **Belgium:** Financial rewards are not so important (as the tax system takes a lot) but status, job title, and prestige are important. (See Letter 153.)
- **Brazil:** Work is not an end in itself—it's a necessity. See Argentina.
- **Canada:** See Australia. Work comes before pleasure.
- **China:** The extended family has great influence on the lives of its members. The individual's main responsibility is to the family.
- **Denmark:** Being open and honest (other cultures may regard this as bluntness) is a priority.
- **Finland:** It is important to judge people by what they do, not by what they say. Work comes before pleasure. (See Letters 153 and 157.)
- **France:** It is important for individuals to be well educated, articulate, and confident (rather than simply rich). Who you are is more important than what you achieve. Protecting someone else's feelings is not a priority. (See Letter 153.)
- **Germany:** Long-term thinking takes priority over short-term, hence research and development is a priority. The welfare of employees and quality of products are also very important. (See Letters 153, 155, and 157.)
- **Hong Kong:** See China.
- **India:** Extended family has a great influence on the lives of its members. Compared with Japanese or U.S. Americans, Indians identify less with their company. (See Letter 154.)
- **Indonesia:** It's important for the majority to be good Muslims and family members. Success at work is less important. Saving peoples' face is crucial, as is avoiding open conflict. Who you are is more important than what you achieve. (See Letters 154 and 156.)

- **Italy:** Who you are is more important than what you achieve. (See Letter 153.)
- **Japan:** Saving face is crucial, as is avoiding open conflict. Extremely high degrees of loyalty to the company are the norm. Most individuals hope to stay with the same company their entire working lives. Loyalty to group or team is often more important than individual achievement. Socializing outside workplace is vital in building relationships. (See Letters 155 and 156.)
- **Mexico:** Saving face is crucial, as is avoiding open conflict. Individual ties of loyalty have high priority. Who you are is more important than what you achieve. (See Letter 155.)
- **Netherlands:** See Denmark. (See Letter 153.)
- **Norway:** Very high taxes mean employees value free time above increased salaries. Being open and honest is a priority.
- **Poland:** Having a network of personal contacts is important. Displaying formal (old-fashioned) good manners is important in facilitating business relationships. (See Letter 153.)
- **Russia:** A Russian priority is to prepare for the worst. Good working relationships and a comfortable environment can be as, or more, important than a high salary.
- **Saudi Arabia:** It is important to be a good Muslim and extended family member. Who you are is more important than what you achieve. (See Letter 154.)
- **South Africa:** Businesspeople try to build consensus and like to see all sides of a question. Fair play is a priority.
- **South Korea:** See Mexico. It is important to know an individual's position in order to know how to relate to him or her. Socializing outside workplace is vital in building relationships. (See Letter 156.)
- **Spain:** Personal relationships may be just as important as the facts when making a decision. Who you are is more important than what you achieve. Individual ties of loyalty have high priority. (See Letter 153.)
- **Sweden:** Long-term thinking takes priority. There is much reliance on teamwork and developing consensus. Very high taxes mean

employees value free time above increased salaries. (See Letters 153 and 157.)

- **Switzerland:** It is important to be perceived as responsible, respectable, and honest. Maintaining control over your emotions is also important. (See Letter 157.)
- **Taiwan:** See China.
- **Thailand:** Saving face is crucial, as is avoiding open conflict. Good relationships with colleagues are more important than personal achievement.
- **Turkey:** Individual ties of loyalty have high priority, especially to family members. Avoiding open conflict is very important. (See Letters 154 and 156.)
- **UK:** Short-term profits and satisfying the shareholders are most important for companies. Good interpersonal and communication skills are vital for individuals to succeed in their careers. (See Letters 153 and 157.)
- **US:** Time is money, and the bottom line is all-important. Corporations can be generous givers to charitable organizations, but the interest of the corporation comes before loyalty to or the interests of individuals. What you achieve is more important than who you are. (See Letter 155.)
- **Venezuela:** See Brazil.

Ethics

Two of Europe's best-known interculturalists, Fons Trompenaars and Charles Hampden-Turner, have conducted research among businesspeople from a host of international companies for many years to pinpoint differences in the behavior and values of employees from different cultures. The research has involved asking the participants a battery of questions and processing the answers to get objective, quantifiable results. The results of the study are impressive, but I have to confess that what I remember most from the study is not so much the answers as one of the questions they put to the participants. I still ponder it from time to time and wonder how I would have answered if they had asked me.

The question goes something like this. "You were traveling as a passenger in a close friend's car. Your friend hit a pedestrian while driving at 35 miles per hour in an area where the maximum allowed speed was 20. You are the only witness, and you know that if you lie under oath you can save your friend from serious consequences. Should your friend expect you to lie to protect him from prosecution?"

The results were used to show different attitudes toward rules and laws, and toward relationships. But of course the situation also revealed different views as to what constituted right and wrong behavior. In many places (like the Scandinavian countries, the U.S., Canada, Australia, and the U.K.), the vast majority of participants thought it was right to obey the rule of law regardless. For others (South Korea, Russia, Venezuela, China, and India), it was seen as the right thing to do to protect a friend, and the fact that you had to tell a lie to do so was not so important—the end justified the means.

We are faced with ethical dilemmas all the time, both at home and at work, though in most cases the situation is not so dramatic, nor the consequences so momentous, as the case quoted above. But making even minor decisions based on what's right and wrong challenges us at a very deep level, because it forces us to look at the ethical standards we learned in childhood from our culture in general and our family in particular. I realized this a few years ago when I was shopping for potatoes at home in Sweden. It was a year when the quality of potatoes was particularly bad, and in my local supermarket a sign above the container said, "In the interest of fairness use the scoop provided." People had obviously been hand-picking the good ones and leaving the rest. The Swedish staff obviously believed strongly in fairness. I believed that too, but I also believed that the free market was, on the whole, a good thing, and did not see why I should buy produce I could clearly see was bad. However, I couldn't solve that particular ethical dilemma—so I bought pasta instead.

In some cases ethical standards may be the consequence of religious laws. It is for religious as well as ethical reasons that practicing Muslims neither borrow nor lend money with interest. This means that special Islamic banks have been set up to ensure that both their customers' religious and business requirements are met. But religion is far from being the only influence on business ethics. Values, the core beliefs that guide or motivate attitudes or actions, may be quite different in cultures that share the same religion but will nevertheless have a key role in shaping attitudes about right and wrong.

You cannot run a business without considering what is right and fair, whatever your position within a company and whatever your nationality. Ethics and business go together. That's why it can cause a national scandal when a CEO (whether in the U.S., the U.K., or anywhere else) is awarded a fat bonus by his colleagues on the board when the company is doing so badly it has to lay people off.

At the other end of the spectrum, anti-capitalist protests at the G7 and G8 trade summit meetings have been about ethical considerations. Protesters at these meetings of the world's richest nations believe strongly that the actions of global corporations, whether moving their production facilities around the world to find the cheapest source of labor, or outsourcing production as a convenient way of avoiding responsibility for pay or working conditions, amount to the strong exploiting the weak. And interestingly, what seems to unite this protest movement is not the nationalities of the protesters, but their age. It is ironic that the global corporations that have created a generation of young consumers who wear the same clothes, eat at the same hamburger restaurants, listen to the same music, and wear the same sneakers, whether in Moscow or Miami, will find these same internationally minded young people throwing bricks at them and condemning their business practices as unethical.

This is something global corporations are taking seriously, and has resulted in companies cultivating "ethical" profiles, working to become environmentally friendly, or giving donations to organizations like Greenpeace or Amnesty International. Even ethics is big business now.

LETTERS 158–159

When personal loyalty clashes with our loyalty to a system of values, we are likely to feel very uncomfortable.

Is this fair?　　　　　　　　　　　　　　　　　　Letter *158*

FROM THE U.K. ABOUT **SOUTH KOREA**

*I work for a company that has a subsidiary in Korea, so I go there
quite frequently on business. I have a good relationship with a highly
esteemed Korean manager who has worked for us for many years.
We now need to find a local firm to supply a component, and this
manager has strongly recommended his brother's company. I am
rather wary about this and feel that this manager has put me in an
awkward position. I don't want to lay myself open to accusations of
favoritism or even corruption. Anyway, I am going to put the job out
to bid, but feel that by doing so I am risking creating ill feeling within
my own company.*

In South Korea loyalty to one's family is a duty, and your manager
would be failing in his duty if he did not try to help his brother win the
order. On the other hand, he appears to be a loyal member of your company too, and may genuinely feel that his brother's company is likely to be
your best supplier. Certainly personal relationships can facilitate business
wherever in the world you find yourself, and in Eastern Asia knowledge of
someone's background and family is seen as providing a form of guarantee of their personal commitment to your business. Naturally you should
listen to what other companies have to offer, but be prepared to spend
time in discussions with the company your manager recommended. It
would be silly to exclude the best contender because of an exaggerated
sense of fairness, and certainly most Indians, East Asians, and Latin Americans would find such a decision totally incomprehensible.

Outright dishonesty　　　　　　　　　　　　　Letter *159*

FROM THE U.K. ABOUT **TURKEY**

*I have Turkish parents but was brought up and educated in the U.K.
Now after college I am living and working in Turkey in a small
company owned by a cousin. My relatives are extremely kind and
supportive and the business is flourishing. However, I noticed that*

when we send out invoices to certain customers they are regularly wrong and the "error" is always in our favor. I've raised this with my uncle, but he just laughs and shrugs. This practice is not only unethical, but by trying to cheat his customers he risks losing them in the long run.

You sound rather shocked, but your uncle's customers, though angry, probably wouldn't be surprised. Although most Turks have an extremely strict code of honor when it comes to doing business within the family or with people they know well, when there is no pre-existing personal relationship with people, there is no duty to show the same consideration. Your uncle would probably say that it was up to his customers to check their invoices more thoroughly, otherwise they have only themselves to blame. Coming from the U.K. you may find it hard to accept a system where you have one set of standards for people you know and another for strangers, but this is common in many other cultures, including Latin American and Asian countries, where there is one code of conduct for friends and family, who are members of the in-group, and an entirely different one for strangers or acquaintances, the out-group.

LETTERS 160–161

If our beliefs about what is right and wrong are challenged by those from another culture we are likely to feel threatened, for it is according to these standards that we live our lives.

Is this bribery?   Letter *160*

FROM AUSTRALIA ABOUT **INDONESIA**

My company is trying to get planning permission to open a small factory in Indonesia. We have been told that quite a modest payment to a local official will speed up the process considerably, but we really do not like this sort of thing and feel that it's the start of a slippery slope.

When you say "this kind of thing" I guess you are thinking in terms of bribery. There is an international organization called Transparency International (www.transparency.org) that claims to show which countries are most likely to offer bribes, and Australia (followed by Sweden, Switzerland, Austria, and Canada) is the country where this behavior is least accepted. This explains why you are so uncomfortable with the suggestion. Perhaps there is a lot of time and trouble involved in getting planning permission, in which case the official deserves payment. When local salaries are very low, as they are in Indonesia, this is an accepted way for employees to make ends meet, and it is certainly not regarded as immoral. It is hardly surprising that those countries at the bottom of the Corruption Perceptions Index, which relates to perceptions of the degree of corruption of individual countries, are dirt poor. (As a matter of interest they are, in descending order, Angola, Madagascar, Paraguay, Nigeria, and Bangladesh.) It is easy for those of us with comparatively good salaries to claim the moral high ground here, but we should perhaps consider how we would act if our families lived in poverty, and we were in this official's shoes.

If after doing a little research you decide that there is some time-consuming administration involved and you will make the payment, make sure it goes through your company account (perhaps as "consultancy fees") so that you don't lay yourself open to charges of bribery at a later stage. But in the long term you will have to decide how you will come to terms with locally accepted ways of doing business, because if you are going to open a factory in Indonesia you will run across this sort of thing all the time.

Blood suckers   Letter *161*

FROM RUSSIA ABOUT A U.S.-OWNED MULTINATIONAL

I work for a foreign-owned hotel chain in Russia, and even though we have plenty of guests and are making a lot of money, there is constant pressure on us to cut costs and focus only on "the bottom line." This means that the employees at the bottom of the pile, like the cleaners, are making much less than those at the top, even though they work just as hard. Our employers are exploiting us by giving the money we have earned to rich people on the other side of the world.

Russia, and indeed the whole of Eastern Europe, has been subjected to a crash course in capitalism in the last few years, and it hasn't been an easy lesson. Few people would say that capitalism is "fair," for it favors those who are clever and well-educated, are fit and healthy, have the right connections, are ambitious, and prepared to work very hard. But it's those people who were the most successful under the communists too. And there are, of course, greedy and unscrupulous capitalists, just as there were greedy and unscrupulous communists. However, from what you have said it does not sound as if your employers are exploiting you. You do not say how well you are paid in comparison with other Russians workers, but usually people are glad to work for foreign companies because they earn more than by working for local firms.

In keeping costs down so that it can pay its shareholders a good return on their investment, the company is merely following one of the founding principles of capitalism that says that nobody is going to lend you money to set up or expand your business unless they are going to earn a profit from doing so. Similarly, by paying people with qualifications and leadership skills more than those without, your employers are following the law of supply and demand that says you pay more for what there is less of, and there are usually more unskilled workers than skilled around. There is a huge amount of injustice and unfairness associated with the capitalist system that you, coming to it as an outsider with a non-capitalist background, find hard to accept. I can only say, consider the alternatives.

LETTER 162

How employees are treated and treat each other is a reflection of both national and corporate culture.

Is this ethical? Letter *162*

FROM POLAND ABOUT THE U.S.

The American company I work for here in Poland has set up a confidential telephone line that we are supposed to use to report our colleagues if we find out that they have been doing something the company wouldn't like. They describe this as a way of protecting the company's ethical standards, but to me it's extremely unethical to get people to spy on their colleagues. It reminds me of our communist past.

I have to admit that this is a difficult issue. The reason your U.S. bosses have introduced this measure is to make sure that the sort of criminality and corrupt practices that can drain the resources of corporations and whole countries alike do not get a grip on your company. You just have to look at the example of the way organized crime in Russia is discouraging foreign investment to see what management is up against. Americans believe strongly that everyone should follow the same rules and that nobody is above the law, and they certainly believe that by giving employees the chance to report wrong-doing anonymously they are protecting the "whistle-blower" from reprisals. I agree that these measures have to be handled with great sensitivity. To work together efficiently in organizations employees have to be able to trust each other. Let's hope that this measure does not encourage employees to be suspicious of each other instead.

IN A NUTSHELL: *Ethics*

GLOBAL WARNING

The same behavior can be regarded in very different lights depending on which culture you come from. A lot depends on the word you use:

- Bribery *or* consultancy services
- Nepotism or cronyism *or* networking
- Commission *or* kickback

In the list below, T.I.C.P.I. refers to the 2003 Transparency International Corruption Perception Index, and T.I.B.P.I. is the 2002 Transparency International Bribe Payers' Index. For more information about these, go to www.transparency.org.

- **Argentina:** The duty to help a friend is much more important than the duty to keep to the law or obey rules. Of the 33 countries in this book, Argentina is perceived as being the third most corrupt on the T.I.C.P.I. (See Letter 158.)
- **Australia:** According to the T.I.B.P.I., Australia is the country least likely to offer bribes. It is also perceived as being one of the least corrupt countries in the world on the T.I.C.P.I. They believe everyone should be subject to the same rules. (See Letter 160.)
- **Austria:** There is a natural trust in and compliance with rules and regulations in society and business. (See Letter 160.)
- **Belgium:** Loyalty to an individual's linguistic and ethnic group may override observance of rules sometimes.
- **Brazil:** Rules are for your enemies. The duty to help a friend is much more important than the duty to keep to the law or obey rules. (See Letter 158.)
- **Canada:** Everyone is subject to the same rules. Canada is perceived as being among the most honest on the T.I.C.P.I. (See Letter 160.)
- **China:** Family and friends are entitled to help and favors. Rules can be bent and exceptions made depending on the circumstances. China is one of the countries most likely to offer bribes according to the T.I.B.P.I. (See Letter 158.)
- **Denmark:** Denmark is perceived as being the (joint) third least corrupt country in the T.I.C.P.I.
- **Finland:** Finns believe everyone is subject to the same rules. Finland is perceived as being the least corrupt country in the T.I.C.P.I.
- **France:** Companies have many rules and regulations, but people accept that there are ways to get around them. There is always room for an exception or a special case.
- **Germany:** There is a natural trust in and compliance with rules and regulations, large and small, in society and business.
- **Hong Kong:** Family and friends are entitled to help and favors. (See China.) (See Letter 158.)

- **India:** Family and friends are entitled to help and favors. Rules can be bent and exceptions made depending on the circumstances. Of the 33 countries in this book, it is one of those regarded as most corrupt on the T.I.C.P.I. (See Letters 158 and 159.)
- **Indonesia:** Indonesia is perceived as being one of the most corrupt countries in the world according to the T.I.C.P.I. (See Letters 158 and 160.)
- **Italy:** Family and friends are entitled to help and favors. Italy is perceived as being the most corrupt country in Western Europe according to the T.I.C.P.I.
- **Japan:** The Japanese use gift giving to build relationships, but despite rules governing gift giving, sometimes it is hard to tell where gifts and favors become bribery and corruption. (See Letter 158.)
- **Mexico:** Family and friends are entitled to help and favors. Rules can be bent and exceptions made depending on the circumstances. (See Letter 158.)
- **Netherlands:** The Netherlands is perceived as being among the most honest on the T.I.C.P.I.
- **Norway:** The belief is that everyone is subject to the same rules, and Norwegians do not accept bribery as a way of doing business.
- **Poland:** Family and friends are entitled to help and favors, but the rest of the world may be treated with suspicion. (See Letters 161 and 162.)
- **Russia:** See Poland. Rules can be bent and exceptions made depending on the circumstances. It is perceived as being one of the more corrupt countries of the 33 in this book in the T.I.C.P.I. It's also one of those most likely to offer bribes according to the T.I.B.P.I. (See Letter 161.)
- **Saudi Arabia:** Ethical standards are based on interpretations of Islamic law. Family and friends are entitled to help and favors.
- **South Africa:** Family and friends are entitled to help and favors. Crime rates are rising and corruption rates with them.
- **South Korea:** See Mexico. One of the countries most likely to offer bribes according to the T.I.P.B.I. (See Letter 158.)
- **Spain:** Family and friends are entitled to help and favors.

- **Sweden:** See Switzerland. Sweden is also one of the least corrupt in the T.I.C.P.I. (See Letter 160.)
- **Switzerland:** Everyone is subject to the same rules. This is one of the countries least likely to offer bribes according to the T.I.B.P.I. (See Letter 160.)
- **Taiwan:** See China. (See Letter 158.)
- **Thailand:** See Spain. (See Letter 158.)
- **Turkey:** There is a general distrust of administration and bureaucracy. See Poland. (See Letter 159.)
- **UK:** They believe everyone is subject to the same rules. Offering bribes is strongly disapproved of. (See Letters 159 and 160.)
- **US:** U.S. Americans believe everyone is subject to the same rules. (See Letters 161 and 162.)
- **Venezuela:** See Mexico. It is perceived as being one of the more corrupt countries in the T.I.C.P.I. (See Letter 158.)

Assumptions

I'm always fascinated by those famous black-and-white illustrations that at first appear to be one thing, then change as if by magic into something else. The young woman with the big hat looking away from you suddenly metamorphoses into the portrait of a wrinkled old crone, or the white vase on a black background that in a split second disappears and is replaced by two faces in profile. Of course the pictures themselves don't change, it's just your perception of them that does. A minority of people who look at these pictures cannot manage the shift of perception. They remain stuck in one dimension, incapable of understanding what is revealed to the other observers.

It's the same with things we have always taken for granted—"normal" ways of behaving, the "natural" way of perceiving. We are used to looking at them from a certain perspective, and may have done so all our lives, when suddenly in a flash we get a glimpse of another dimension and realize that, contrary to our previous assumptions, there is another way of interpreting the familiar.

Examining our assumptions is not something we are used to doing. Assumptions are, by definition, those beliefs we do not question, and I know many intelligent and educated people of different nationalities (and admittedly a bit on the smug side) who have never questioned the fact that their part of the world is basically God's own country, and that although there are regrettably a few exceptions to the rule, their fellow citizens are basically nicer, wiser, and more trustworthy than those of any other country you could mention.

This attitude was certainly widespread in England in the nineteenth century when Cecil Rhodes, the Englishman who opened up much of Southern Africa to European "development" (and who founded the Rhodes scholarships), could say without the slightest doubt, "Ask any man what nationality he would prefer to be, and ninety-nine out of a hundred will tell you that they would prefer to be Englishmen." Strange as it may seem, people like Rhodes have not followed the example of the dinosaur or dodo and joined the ranks of extinct species. Indeed, many men and women with an ingrained belief in the innate superiority of their own nation or culture are appointed to responsible positions abroad where, not surprisingly, they fail miserably.

This book is all about assumptions and our reactions to other ways of thinking, behaving, or simply being. The reaction may be surprise when we find out that money isn't some people's main indicator of success, or it can be a quick surge of embarrassment or disorientation when we meet the colleague we have spoken to so often on the phone and feel we know so well and realize she doesn't share our skin color. We may feel bewildered when we realize that some languages don't have a word for (or concept of) privacy, or shocked when we find people behaving in a way that seems to contradict what we had always assumed were universal male (or female) patterns of behavior. Worst of all, we may feel real, blood-pressure raising fury at perceived insults by people who don't know us and don't appreciate our culture or our roles in it. It's very rare for anyone with international contacts *not* to feel at least one of these emotions when dealing with people from a different culture, because foreigners unconsciously challenge many of the things we had up to then assumed were "normal" or "natural."

I know of a German manager who was known among his employees for his brusque and chilly manner (in a country where "brusque" and "chilly" managers are not a rarity). He always kept his employees at arm's length, was blunt to the point of rudeness, and didn't show even the most rudimentary personal interest in or courtesy to the people he worked with.

His company was taken over by an American multinational, quite a hard-nosed organization, but it didn't put a lot of store by job titles or formal manners and preferred to downplay its hierarchical side. He spent a couple of months studying the bright and breezy communicative style of the U.S. American executive managers in corporate communications and e-mails, and after the Christmas holiday his staff was astounded to receive a message from him which, instead of the usual itemization of things they had done wrong in the previous year, was a sentimental and rambling letter describing his grandchildren's reactions to their Christmas presents and their questions about what the New Year would bring.

He had always assumed that managers behaved toward and communicated with their staff in one particular way, but after contact with another culture he learned that this was not always the case, and in deference to his new foreign bosses had decided to adopt their style. Unfortunately his abrupt change of tone was not an unqualified success, provoking giggles in his subordinates rather than warm feelings of camaraderie.

A lot of what you have read in this book describes occasions where what we take for granted is challenged during some form of intercultural contact. There are times when we suddenly realize that our assumptions, unquestioned at home, are regarded as strange and inexplicable abroad. That is the moment when the focus changes—when the picture of the young girl becomes the old lady, or the picture of the vase melts into two faces. That is the moment too when we are given the chance to see things from a new perspective, to think in a new way. These moments are worth waiting for, and those chances are well worth taking, for they help us make sense of our fast-changing world.

LETTERS 163–164

It's not only the big things that surprise us in another culture. Our assumptions may be challenged by little things too.

Trust them   Letter *163*

FROM SWEDEN ABOUT **ARGENTINA**

> *I am in Argentina on a six-month trainee placement, and one*
> *particular thing here irritates me a lot. At home the supply cabinet is*
> *unlocked and staff are allowed to take what they need. Here I have to*
> *go to the appropriate person who will decide if I can have a new pencil*
> *or box of paperclips. Apart from being petty and time-consuming, the*
> *assumption seems to be that people here are just waiting for the*
> *chance to steal stuff, but I have always believed that if you trust*
> *people they will respond.*

People aren't fundamentally more honest in Sweden. I know of a
car plant there where all the components necessary to make a car were
smuggled out over a period of a few weeks and carefully assembled to
make a brand-new vehicle. I guess it's so expensive to employ people in
comparatively wealthy countries like Sweden that it would be cheaper to
write off losses than to employ someone to supervise supplies.

But there are other reasons why the supply cabinet is so tightly super-
vised. Workplaces aren't separate from the society in which they are
located, and the locked cupboard reflects the fact that Argentina is a more
hierarchical and authoritarian society than the one you are used to. Individual workers are not usually given much power or responsibility, and
people are subject to a system of controls, often in the form of rules and
regulations, that is designed to curb what is regarded as the natural dishonesty or laziness of employees. The consequence of this tight system of
controls is of course that people devise ingenious ways to get around
them, and will make determined attempts to get away with as much as
they possibly can. The assumption is that the company is in some way
the enemy, to be thwarted whenever and wherever possible. The Spanish
even have a phrase for it, *Obedezco, pero no cumplo*, which means "I obey
but do not comply."

So your boss is probably wise to lock up the paperclips, as in the current cultural climate, if the contents of the cupboard were left unlocked

they would disappear in the twinkling of an eye. It sounds as if your workplace is typical in at least one respect of most offices in Spain and Southern Europe, the Middle East, India, and Latin America: it is difficult for one company to change practices widely accepted in a culture as a whole.

Lack of respect   Letter *164*

FROM FRANCE ABOUT **SWEDEN**

We've been taken over by a Swedish company, and they are now trying to ban wine in our cafeterias. They say they have that rule in their factories in other countries and so it should be the same here. I cannot understand their reasoning. Why should there be the same rule for all when it is clear that the French have different traditions? Swedes may not be able to handle wine, but that is no reason to ban it here where we have learned to treat it in a civilized way.

The importance of wine in French life has been underestimated by several global corporations. The U.S.-based Disney Corporation had a policy of not serving alcohol in its parks in California, Florida, and Tokyo, and extended it to France. This caused astonishment and rebellion in France, where a glass of wine for lunch is a given. After much consideration, in 1993 the Disney changed its policy and allowed wine and beer in its Paris theme park. Similarly, IBM does not allow alcohol in its company dining rooms—except in IBM France.

Certainly the Swedish and French cultures could not have more different traditions when it comes to alcohol. Until 1954, alcohol was rationed in Sweden, and until 2000 you couldn't buy a bottle of wine anywhere there over the weekend, whereas in France, as in Italy and Spain, the production and appreciation of wine has been an expression of its culture for a thousand years. The problem arises not only because there are many Swedes who believe that alcohol consumption is fundamentally a bad thing, but also because Swedes assume that the same rules should apply to all. It is an expression of their belief in equality and fairness, but this can appear to be heavy-handed and lacking in flexibility to people from other cultures. France has traditionally not considered consistency a virtue, but regarded flexibility as a more useful quality. They also believe that for every rule there is an exception. However, there is certainly proof that control of machinery (including cars) is impaired after drinking alcohol, so I can certainly understand them banning it in a factory, where accidents can happen so easily.

LETTERS 165–166

Our underlying assumptions affect how we react to each other— and because of this we sometimes shock our counterparts from other cultures.

Not in the mood   Letter *165*

FROM THE U.K. ABOUT **VENEZUELA**

I've been working here in Venezuela for several months and am amazed by the response I get from some of my coworkers occasionally when I ask them to do something. They may not say it directly, but the essence is, "I don't feel like doing that today. I'm not in the mood." How can they assume that I will take an answer like that seriously? On the other hand, there are periods when they do work very hard—it's just not possible to predict when—and it's driving me mad.

People from cultures with a very strong work ethic combined with a relatively fixed view of how to organize time, like the U.K., the Netherlands, Switzerland, and Austria, will find this very hard to understand. But for a Venezuelan it is important to "go with the flow," because if you are not in the right frame of mind to do something, you are bound to make a mess of it. It's much better, they reason, to wait until the time is right and you're full of enthusiasm and energy, and then you will be able to accomplish things in half the time with a minimum of effort. Venezuelans are very skilled at "reading" each other to see what mood they are in, and will time their requests to ensure that the other person is in the right frame of mind to act before asking them to do something. It's not laziness, or *skiving* as you might call it in the U.K., which causes them to dig their heels in, it is simply an awareness of their own feelings. This means that you will need to develop a sensitivity to how your coworkers are feeling if you are going to get the best out of them.

Management by walking about   Letter *166*

FROM BRAZIL ABOUT THE **U.S.**

We have a new manager from the U.S. who does not seem to enjoy working in his office. He spends the whole time wandering around the corridors spying and eavesdropping. It's making us all nervous and we're wondering when he has the time to do any work himself.

Poor man. I doubt very much that he has ambitions to emulate James Bond, and I would guess that his motive in wandering around is not to check up on you, because he probably trusts you to work on your own. Instead, he is trying to be approachable, and to break down the kinds of social barriers that often exist in Latin American companies between managers and employees. These hierarchical divisions, which can be a barrier to communication, are taken more seriously in Latin America than they are in the U.S., Canada, Australia, and the Northern European countries. These barriers are also seen as undesirable because they prevent the manager from getting a complete picture of the company in which he works as they isolate him from the majority of the workforce. It's this complete picture of the workings of your office I believe your manager is looking for in his wanderings. Unfortunately, no one has told him that employees in Latin America generally prefer that their bosses keep their distance and get on with what they are paid for rather than being "one of the guys."

LETTERS 167–169

An assumption that yours is the only "natural" way to work implies that people who don't share your culture's norms are being stubborn or difficult.

Compromise = weakness?   Letter *167*

FROM THE U.S. ABOUT **RUSSIA**

> *This is our third visit to Russia and our team is currently involved in a trading deal with a local partner. However, these negotiations are dragging on and on and we are not getting anywhere. They simply do not seem willing to make any compromises, and they try to justify this by giving us a lot of philosophical and ideological reasons for why they are not going to budge.*

Compromise is certainly central in a democracy, but democracy is something the Russians haven't had much experience with. It's the same for the Poles. Poland joined the European Union in 2004, and other European negotiators were surprised in their preliminary negotiations by the difficulties they met in discussions with the Poles. The "give and take" and routine compromises that accompany the decision-making process in other democracies was largely unfamiliar to them.

In the U.S., compromise is considered desirable and is assumed to be an inevitable part of doing business, but this does not form part of the Russian heritage. In fact, in Russian the word *kompromiss* has negative overtones and is considered a sign of weakness. The reasoning goes that if you have a correct and morally justified position you stick to it (a belief that kept the communist state up and running for over seventy years,) but that makes doing business pretty difficult. Things are changing, though, and a new breed of younger businesspeople is emerging, but they are regarded with suspicion by many of the population who see, among other things, their willingness to compromise as yet another sign of lack of solidarity and moral fiber.

However, it is possible to negotiate with the Russians if you are prepared to display patience; for Russians, in common with East Asian business people in general, are prepared to wait in order to gain concessions from partners who are in a hurry. "Time is money" is not a Russian saying, and the quick agreement (usually based on mutual compromises), which is part of the American way of doing business, is alien there.

As a final point, if you are dealing with middle-ranking employees rather than the top man himself, they may not have the authority to negotiate terms autonomously. This might be another reason for their lack of flexibility.

No news is good news   Letter *168*

FROM THE U.S. ABOUT **GERMANY**

I've been working here in Germany for over a year but cannot get used to the complete lack of positive feedback on my performance. I have worked hard and, if I say so myself, have made a positive contribution to the department's improved performance. However, nobody has ever given me the slightest indication that they think I have worked well. But if I make the smallest mistake in filling in an order form, or misspell someone's name, I hear about it loud and clear.

Don't take this personally. If you look around your department, I suspect nobody receives positive feedback. It's the German way. It is assumed that you will do your best without being told, and that you won't need the boss to tell you what you already know. Too many compliments would make a German employee, or a Scandinavian one for that matter, suspicious that the boss was being insincere. Germans tend to see the "hamburger" approach as patronizing, where criticism (the meat) is surrounded by empty praise (the bun). The same applies in France, where both positive and negative feedback may be regarded as an unwelcome commentary on who you are rather than on your job performance. There's no question about comments not being taken personally. For the French, and indeed for Southern Europeans and most Latin Americans, you can't get more personal than when someone tells you how they think you do your job.

As a U.S. manager you find this difficult to accept because you have been taught to believe that an important part of doing your job is to give feedback to subordinates, and to focus on their positive contributions to encourage them to do their best in all areas of their work. This isn't the case in Germany, and while you are working there you will have to adjust your expectations, because it doesn't sound as if your boss is likely to break the mold.

Where's their initiative?   Letter *169*

FROM THE U.S. ABOUT **MEXICO**

I work for a medium-sized production company in the U.S. and am in Mexico to try to raise productivity at our subsidiary. What amazes me is the lack of initiative of the workers. If, for example, they see that we are going to run out of a certain component, they never say anything until production has come to a halt. And I continually come across employees sitting around doing nothing because they are waiting for instructions from the boss, when the job is in front of them and waiting to be finished!

You answered your own question in your last sentence. They were waiting for the boss's instructions. In Latin America, Spain, Africa, Indonesia, the Middle East, and India, where companies are usually organized in a clearly defined hierarchy and people are very aware of who is responsible for what, senior managers are the people expected (and paid) to make decisions, and management as a whole ensures that these decisions are executed. In particular, people at the lower levels of the organization often expect an authoritarian type of management accompanied by clear and specific instructions, and would worry they would get into trouble if they stepped outside these parameters and started to use their own initiative. The standard of education and training of employees at this level of the organization is often not very high, and they are used to bosses checking on their performance. If you want to change this way of working you are going to have to communicate clearly to your employees that you respect their judgment, make it clear *what* you expect them to do, and arrange training so they know *how* to do it. You should also accept that if people are to be encouraged to use their initiative, they will also be granted the power to make mistakes. You should make clear that they will not be blamed if they fail, and give them plenty of praise when they succeed.

IN A NUTSHELL: *Assumptions*

GLOBAL WARNING

When working across borders there will be times when we suddenly realize that our assumptions, unquestioned at home, are regarded as strange and inexplicable abroad.

Here are a few examples of what different countries take for granted:

- **Argentina:** Lack of trust in fellow workers results in tight systems of controls. Hierarchical divisions, which can be a barrier to communication, are taken for granted. (See Letters 163, 166, 168, and 169.)
- **Australia:** Strictly observed social barriers between bosses and employees are regarded as unnatural and undesirable. (See Letter 166.)
- **Austria:** A strong work ethic is combined with a relatively fixed view of how to organize time. (See Letter 165.)
- **Brazil:** Lack of trust in fellow workers results in tight systems of controls. Hierarchical divisions, which can be a barrier to communication, are taken for granted. (See Letters 163, 166, 168, and 169.)
- **Canada:** Strictly observed social barriers between bosses and employees are regarded as unnatural and undesirable. (See Letter 166.)
- **China:** Patience is seen as an important virtue and a contributor to long-term success. (See Letter 167.)
- **Denmark:** Strictly observed social barriers between bosses and employees are regarded as unnatural and undesirable. (See Letters 166 and 168.)

- **Finland:** Giving and receiving feedback does not come easily, and is not regarded as a priority. (See Letters 166 and 168.)
- **France:** Feedback may be regarded as an unwelcome commentary on who you are rather than on your job performance. (See Letters 164 and 168.)
- **Germany:** Giving positive feedback is not a priority. You can assume you have done a good job unless told the contrary. (See Letter 168.)
- **Hong Kong:** Patience is seen as an important virtue and a contributor to long-term success, though the pace of business here is high. (See Letter 167.)
- **India:** Lack of trust in fellow workers results in tight systems of controls. People at the lower levels of the organization often expect an authoritarian type of management (See Letters 163 and 169.)
- **Indonesia:** People at the lower levels of the organization often expect an authoritarian type of management. (See Letter 169.)
- **Italy:** Lack of trust in fellow workers results in tight systems of controls. (See Letters 163, 164, and 168.)
- **Japan:** Patience is seen as an important virtue and a contributor to long-term success. (See Letter 167.)
- **Mexico:** Lack of trust in fellow workers results in tight systems of controls. Hierarchical divisions, which can be a barrier to communication, are taken for granted. (See Letters 163, 166, 168, and 169.)
- **Netherlands:** A strong work ethic is combined with a relatively fixed view of how to organize time. (See Letter 165.)
- **Norway:** There is a relatively high degree of trust in the honesty and integrity of the average worker. Strictly observed social barriers between bosses and employees are regarded as unnatural and undesirable. (See Letters 166 and 168.)
- **Poland:** Compromise is considered a sign of weakness. (See Letter 167.)
- **Russia:** The word *kompromiss* has negative overtones and is considered a sign of weakness. (See Letter 167.)
- **Saudi Arabia:** Lack of trust in fellow workers results in tight systems of controls. People at the lower levels of the organization

often expect an authoritarian type of management. (See Letters 163 and 169.)

- **South Africa:** People at the lower levels of the organization often expect an authoritarian type of management. (See Letter 169.)
- **South Korea:** Patience is seen as an important virtue and a contributor to long-term success. (See Letter 167.)
- **Spain:** An authoritarian type of management operating through clear and specific instructions is commonly expected. (See Letters 164, 168, and 169.)
- **Sweden:** There is a relatively high degree of trust in the honesty and integrity of the average worker. Strictly observed social barriers between bosses and employees are regarded as unnatural and undesirable. (See Letters 163, 164, 166, 168, and 169.)
- **Switzerland:** A strong work ethic is combined with a relatively fixed view of how to organize time. (See Letter 165.)
- **Taiwan:** Patience is seen as an important virtue and a contributor to long-term success, though the pace of business here is high. (See Letter 167.)
- **Thailand:** Patience is seen as an important virtue and a contributor to long-term success. (See Letter 167.)
- **Turkey:** Feedback may be regarded as an unwelcome commentary on who you are rather than on your job performance. (See Letters 163 and 169.)
- **UK:** A strong work ethic is combined with a relatively fixed view of how to organize time. Compromise is considered desirable and assumed to be an inevitable part of doing business. (See Letter 165.)
- **US:** A strong work ethic is combined with a relatively fixed view of how to organize time. Compromise is considered desirable and assumed to be an inevitable part of doing business. (See Letters 166, 167, and 168.)
- **Venezuela:** Lack of trust in fellow workers results in tight systems of controls. Hierarchical divisions, which can be a barrier to communication, are taken for granted. (See Letters 163, 165, 166, 168, and 169.)

Bibliography

Series

I referred to books about individual countries from the following two series:

Passport to the World
World Trade Press
1505 Fifth Avenue
San Rafael, CA 94901 USA
415-454-9934

Culture Shock
Graphic Arts Center Publishing
P.O. Box 10306
Portland, OR 97210 USA
503-226-2402

Books

Adler, Nancy J. 1991. *International Dimensions of Organizational Behavior*. Boston: PWS-Kent.

Adler, Nancy J. 1994. *Competitive Frontiers*. Oxford: Blackwell Business.

Axtell, Roger E. 1993. *Do's and Taboos around the World*. White Plains, NY: Wiley.

Bradburn, Roger. 2001. *Understanding Business Ethics*. London, NY: Continuum.

Brennan, Lynne, and David Block. 1991. *The Complete Book of Business Etiquette*. London: Piatkus.

Broome, Benjamin J. 1996. *Exploring the Greek Mosaic*. Yarmouth, ME: Intercultural Press.

De Botton, Alain. 2000. *The Consolations of Philosophy*. London: Penguin.

Economist. 2003. *Pocket World of Figures*. London: Profile Books.

Forslund, Catharina. 1998. *Oskrivna Regler.* Stockholm: Industrilit-
    teratur.

Furnham, Adrian, and Stephen Bochner. 1989. *Culture Shock: Psycho-
    logical Reactions to Unfamiliar Environments.* London: Routledge.

Gundling, Ernest. 2003. *Working GlobeSmart.* Palo Alto, CA: Davies-
    Black Publishing.

Hall, Edward T., and Mildred Reed Hall. 1987. *Hidden Differences:
    Doing Business with the Japanese.* New York: Doubleday.

Hampden-Turner, Charles. 1994. *Charting the Corporate Mind: From
    Dilemma to Strategy.* Oxford: Basil Blackwell.

Hampden-Turner, Charles, and Fons Tromperaars. 2000. *Building
    Cross-Cultural Competence.* Chichester, England: Wiley.

Hickson, David J., and Derek S. Pugh. 1995. *Management Worldwide:
    Distinctive Styles amid Globalization.* London: Penguin.

Hofstede, Geert. 1980. *Culture's Consequences: Comparing Values,
    Behaviors, Institutions and Organizations Across Nations.* Beverly
    Hills, CA: Sage.

Hofstede, Geert. 1991. *Cultures and Organizations: Software of the
    Mind.* New York: McGraw Hill.

Klein, Naomi. 2001. *No Logo.* London: Flamingo.

Kohls, L. Robert, and John M. Knight. 1994. *Developing Intercultural
    Awareness.* Yarmouth, ME: Intercultural Press.

Kras, Eva S. 1995. *Management in Two Cultures.* Yarmouth, ME:
    Intercultural Press.

Lewis, Richard D. *1996. When Cultures Collide.* London: Nicholas
    Brealey Publishing.

Lipp, Doug. 2003. *The Changing Face of Today's Customer.* Atlanta,
    GA: Longstreet Press.

Marx, Elisabeth. 1999. *Breaking Through Culture Shock.* London:
    Nicholas Brealey Publishing.

Mattock, John. 1996. *Russia: The Essential Guide.* London: Kogan Page.

Mehrabian, Albert. 1972. *Nonverbal Communication.*Chicago, Illiois.
    Aldine Atherton.

Mole, John. 1995. *Mind Your Manners.* London: Nicholas Brealey
    Publishing.

Monbiot, George. 2003. *The Age of Consent.* London: Flamingo.

Morgan, Gareth. 1997. *Images of Organization.* Thousand Oaks, CA:
    Sage Publications.

Morrison, Toni, Wayne A. Conaway, and George A. Borden. 1994. *Kiss, Bow, or Shake Hands*. Holbrook, MA: Adams Media Corp.

Mårtensson, Rita. 1998. *Affärsrelationer i Europa*. Lund, Sweden: Studentlitteratur.

Nordström, Kjell, and Jonas Ridderstråle. 2000. *Funky Business*. Financial Times Prentice Hall.

Olsson, Ingela. 1999. *Kulturmöten och Kulturkrockar*. Södertälje, Sweden. Astra Läkemedel.

Richmond, Yale. 1992. *From Nyet to Da*. Yarmouth, ME: Intercultural Press.

Richmond, Yale. 2003. *From Da to Yes*. 2d ed. Yarmouth, ME: Intercultural Press.

Ricks, David A. 1993. *Blunders in International Business*. Cambridge, MA: Blackwell Business.

Schneider, S. C., and Jean-Louis Barsoux. 1997. *Managing Across Cultures*. NJ: Prentice Hall.

Sharma, Karin. 1996. *Alla dessa Kulturer*. Stockholm: Industrilitteratur.

Stephenson, Skye. 2003. *Spanish-Speaking South Americans*. Yarmouth, ME: Intercultural Press.

Storti, Craig. 1999. *Figuring Foreigners Out*. Yarmouth, ME: Intercultural Press.

Storti, Craig. 2001. *The Art of Crossing Cultures*. Yarmouth, ME: Intercultural Press

Tannen, Deborah. 1995. *Talking from 9 to 5: Women and Men at Work*. London: Virago.

Trompenaars, Fons. 1993. *Riding the Waves of Culture*. London: Nicholas Brealey Publishing.

Trompenaars, Fons, and Charles Hampden-Turner. 2000. *21 Leaders for the 21st Century*. New York: McGraw-Hill.

Walker, Danielle, and Thomas Walker. 2003. *Doing Business Internationally*. New York: McGraw Hill.

Wattley Ames, Helen. *Spain is Different*. 1992. 2d ed. Yarmouth, ME: Intercultural Press.

Weber, Max. 1976. *The Protestant Ethic and the Spirit of Capitalism*. London: George Allen and Unwin.

Young, Gavin. 1995. *From Sea to Shining Sea*. London: Penguin.

Zachary, G. Pascal. 2000. *The Global Me*. London: Nicholas Brealey Publishing.

Journal Articles

Agerberg, Miki. 2001. "Psykisk våldtäkt på jobbet." *Ny Teknik, 17,* August.

Segalla, Michael, Gabriele Jacobs-Belschak, and Christiane Müller. 2001. "Cultural influences on employee termination decisions: Firing the good, average or the old?" *European Management Journal, 19,* February.

Internet Sources

The Delta Intercultural Academy: *www.dialogin.com*

This is great source of information, in the form of articles, research, information about fellow professionals, etc., for all those involved in intercultural business and management communication.

GlobeSmart: *www.globesmart.net/secure/default.asp*

GlobeSmart provides in-depth information on how to conduct business in more than thirty countries around the world.

Intercultural Insights: *www.egroups.com/group/interculturalinsights*

This is a members-only discussion group for students and professionals involved in the field of intercultural relations. Sometimes it's infuriating, occasionally bad-tempered, but always interesting.

Transparency International: *www.transparency.org/index.html*

This organization campaigns for the eradication of corruption internationally. To this end it publishes the results of two surveys every year. At the time of writing, these were the latest available versions:

- Transparency International Bribe Payers Index 2002
- Transparency International Corruption Perceptions Index 2003